THE SHADOW OF A GREAT ROCK

The Shadow of a Great Rock

A LITERARY APPRECIATION OF THE KING JAMES BIBLE

Harold Bloom

Yale

UNIVERSITY PRESS

New Haven and London

Published with assistance from the foundation established in memory of
Philip Hamilton McMillan of the Class of 1894, Yale College.

"Boaz Asleep," from *Selected Poems of Victor Hugo: A Bilingual Edition,*
trans. E. H. and A. M. Blackmore (Chicago: University of
Chicago Press, 2001). Copyright © 2001 by The University of Chicago.

"The Dark Night," from *The Poems of St. John of the Cross,*
trans. John Frederick Nims, 3rd ed. (Chicago: University of Chicago Press,
1989). Copyright © 1959, 1968, 1979 by John Frederick Nims.

"Peter Quince at the Clavier," from *The Collected Poems of Wallace Stevens,*
by Wallace Stevens. Copyright © 1954 by Wallace Stevens and renewed
1982 by Holly Stevens. Used by permission of Alfred A. Knopf,
a division of Random House, Inc., and Faber and Faber Ltd.

Yale University Press books may be purchased in quantity for
educational, business, or promotional use. For information, please e-mail
sales.press@yale.edu (U.S. office) or sales@yaleup.co.uk (U.K. office).

Designed by Sonia Shannon.
Set in Stempel Schneidler type by Duke & Company, Devon, Pennsylvania.
Printed in the United States of America.

Library of Congress Cataloging-in-Publication Data
Bloom, Harold.
The Shadow of a Great Rock : a literary appreciation of the King James Bible /
Harold Bloom.
p. cm.
Includes index.
ISBN 978-0-300-16683-5 (alk. paper)
1. Bible. English—Versions—Authorized. I. Title.
BS186.B56 2011
220.5′203—dc22   2011003148

A catalogue record for this book is available from the British Library.

This paper meets the requirements of ANSI/NISO Z39.48–1992
(Permanence of Paper).

10   9   8   7   6   5   4   3   2   1

To Leslie Brisman

And a man shall be as an hiding place from
the wind, and a covert from the tempest; as
rivers of water in a dry place, as the shadow
of a great rock in a weary land.

—*Isaiah 32:2*

Contents

THE APOCRYPHA

THE GREEK NEW TESTAMENT

Introduction
The Bible as Literature

THE TWO CENTRAL MASTERWORKS of English literature emerged together in the years 1604–11: the Authorized Version, or King James Bible (KJB), and the plays of Shakespeare's major phase, from *Measure for Measure* and *Othello* through *King Lear, Macbeth,* and *Antony and Cleopatra* on to *The Winter's Tale* and *The Tempest.* The King James Bible was completed in 1611, the same year that *The Tempest* was performed, the last drama Shakespeare composed by himself. (King James I had commissioned his Authorized Version in 1604, the year of *Othello*.) Four centuries later the sublime summit of literature in English still is shared by Shakespeare and the King James Bible. Shakespeare died in 1616; seven years later the First Folio appeared. From then until now, Shakespeare has become for many a single work, even as the King James Bible has been a single, comprehensive text for its common readers.

No one except scattered Bardolators like myself believes that Shakespeare is the Word of God, though there are millions who believe, in some sense, the King James Bible to be divine. I was raised to trust in Tanakh, the Hebrew Bible, but I find it impossible to trust Yahweh, and except on a purely aesthetic basis cannot learn to love Tanakh more than Yahweh. Shakespeare seems preferable to the Bible since he does not moralize, yet aesthetically the English Bible and Shakespeare divide the homage of the best readers of the language.

Shakespeare was influenced by the Geneva Bible, one of the KJB's direct ancestors, but rather in the way he responded to Ovid or to Chaucer. It is an oddity of literary history that the Geneva Bible was Milton's preference also, but he was accustomed to reading the Scriptures in Hebrew and Greek, though certain elements in his style and diction perhaps can be traced to the KJB.

With the 1660 Stuart Restoration, the KJB finally displaced the Geneva and achieved an ascendancy that continued until the late twentieth century and remains dominant in the United States today. Cormac McCarthy's one great novel, *Blood Meridian,* may be a last stand of the KJB's literary influence. Even when echoing Melville and Faulkner, McCarthy tracks passages heightened by allusions to the KJB.

And yet the King James Bible is itself a composite work, weaving together an allusive web out of previous translations: not only that of the greatest English translator, William Tyndale, but those of Miles Coverdale and the group that produced the Geneva—William Whittingham, William Cole, Thomas Sampson, Christopher Goodman, and the Hebraist Anthony Gilby—were absorbed and transmuted by the more than fifty King James translators, of whom the chairmen (or "directors") of six companies or committees were Lancelot Andrewes, Edward Lively, John Harding, John Duport, Thomas Raxis, and William Barlow. Among the others I would single out the eloquent Puritan Miles Smith, whose beautiful preface to the KJB is unfortunately omitted from nearly every current edition I have seen.

The inexplicable wonder is that a rather undistinguished group of writers (except for Lancelot Andrewes and Miles Smith) brought forth a magnificence almost to rival Shakespeare's. Without Tyndale as fountainhead, it could not have been done, but Tyndale's powerfully rugged prose is very unlike the orchestration of the sentences of the KJB. The language of the Authorized Version is even more metaphorical than that of its precursors, though this can be puzzling because its diction is so economical. Shakespeare's vocabulary remains extraordinary in the history of imaginative literature: more than twenty-one thousand words, eighteen hundred of which he coined. Racine, grandest of French tragic dramatists, confines himself to just two thousand. The KJB keeps to eight thousand, a figure that surprises me because I would have guessed many more.

The richness of Shakespeare's language gives very different effects from that of the KJB. At once opulent and elliptical, Shakespeare's cognitive music is unique in literature. You cannot speak of Shakespeare's styles as "integral": they are friends of departure. Nor will the incomparable poet-dramatist deign to any mere consistency in his many voices and voicings. At his strongest he individualizes minor characters like Barnardine in *Measure for Measure* and the fig-seller in *Antony and Cleopatra*.

The translators of the English Bible, from Tyndale to Andrewes, were not dramatists, though Tyndale came closest. They do not *voice* their characters: Jacob and David do not *sound* different to us. That is a loss from the Hebrew. Beneath the hum of the redactors I hear in the Tanakh an original voice that both links and distinguishes Jacob and David. A great ironist (perhaps even two) precedes and plays against the pious tonalities of the redactors. Yahweh, in his relation to Jacob and to David, is a personality and not an "anthropomorphic" entity. They are theomorphic, but since the god is an outrageous fellow, well then so are they. That is why they matter, humanly and aesthetically, across the millennia.

Spiritual concern, a different matter, necessarily governs most devoted readers of the KJB. My subtitle, "A Literary Appreciation," defines my own stance and purpose in this brief book. By "appreciation" I mean what the aesthetic critic proper, the sublime Walter Pater, intended in his superb volume *Appreciations* (1889). To appreciate is to be fully aware of quality. Perception is of the essence: the Latin for "to appreciate" is the source, and the finer edge of appreciation is to apprehend a value that will only increase over time. Period pieces in furniture or costume are one thing, but in literature quite another. It has to fascinate me that the KJB is the one compendium of great writing that millions in our post-literate era continue to encounter, though whether it is often *read* is uncertain.

A literary appreciation of the KJB must risk blasphemy because truly what is most powerful in the unread Scriptures is blasphemous at its core: the god who is an astonishing, outrageous personality upon whom theologies have been imposed. All too often he is bad news: his passions are violent, excessive, ill-tempered, unfathomable, and horribly dangerous. If in some of his aspects he evokes awe, in others he engenders fright. Yahweh has taken care that we do not even know the meaning of his name, and we cannot know his nature because it is not nature.

And yet it is his book, though his presence ebbs in the Hebrew Original Testament and is supplanted by Jesus in the Greek Belated Testament. Twenty years ago I recall arousing resentment and protest when I wrote of the Western worship of an incommensurate literary character, Yahweh, and his transmutations, Allah and the Trinity's God the Father.

My observations, though amiable enough, would have seemed capital offenses to all the sixteenth- and seventeenth-century translators of the English Bible. But this is a literary critic's book, and it comes near the end of six decades of writing commentaries upon Western works of the metaphorical imagination. I keep the

Hebrew and Greek texts in mind throughout my discussions in this book, if only to meditate upon the many places where the English version surpasses the original, and those where it comes short. Tyndale's New Testament is so vast an aesthetic improvement upon the Greek text that I am perpetually delighted. The Tanakh, a far stronger original, comes even in honors with Tyndale, Coverdale, Geneva, and the KJB committees. Sometimes even Coverdale, who had little or no Hebrew, invented graces and glories beyond the ancestral text, but more frequently he crashes. Tyndale, Geneva, and the KJB company rarely fail utterly, yet when they miss, it can be (and has been) lamentable. The ongoing translations of the Hebrew Bible by Robert Alter and the marvelous notes in Herbert Marks's Norton edition of the English Bible are exemplary antidotes.

I extend these opening observations by contemplating that lame but useful phrase "the Bible as literature." Plainly we would wince at "the *Iliad* as literature" and even at "Plato as literature." Yet that is because Homer and Plato are safely secular for us, while the Bible even now has an aura for many, even when they are not fundamentalists. To the ancients, Homer was the prime textbook, bestowing an education worldly yet bordering on the spiritual. Plato disputed Homeric authority in the name of his own teaching and its exclusive assertion of truth.

Desperately secular, I reread the Bible in many of the ways I turn again to Shakespeare or to Walt Whitman yet remain uneasily aware that Yahweh's numinosity disturbs me as Lear's and Walt's do not. Still, Yahweh—whatever else he is—is in the first place a literary character and has to be interpreted as such. So is the Jesus of Mark's Gospel, the most ambiguous of the contrarian versions that inhabit the Greek Testament.

Our literary sense of the Bible emerged from Romanticism and now seems inescapable, however haunted by nostalgias. Carlyle and Emerson, Ruskin and Pater, D. H. Lawrence and Wallace Stevens all echo the King James Version's cadences but do so as skeptics. It remains true that their biblical sonorities, unlike their Shakespearean allusions, are in the service of transcendental long-ings. Anyone reading Lawrence at his most powerful, as in the opening chapter of *The Rainbow,* will wonder at his extraordinary reliance upon Genesis. Walt Whitman, whose influence on Law-rence eventually displaced that of the King James Bible, himself had the ambition to write a new Bible for Americans, and could not have started it if his Quaker boyhood had not provided both the experience of reading biblical texts aloud and hearing testi-monies of the kind favored by followers of the radical Quaker circuit-rider Elias Hicks.

In this book I intend a literary appreciation, but there is a large question as to what precisely is the proof-text. The Hebrew Bible goes back to the thirteenth century before the Common Era and is followed by the Greek New Testament, more or less completed in the second century C.E. The English Bible culminates in 1611. No one can appreciate a version without some regard to the original. When I am carried to a dramatic ecstasy by the War Song of Deborah and Barak, precisely what is the poem I respond to in KJB, Judges 5? Is it the fierce original in the Hebrew Bible or the dignified, high-pitched paean to Yahweh's victory wrought by the English translations? Where do the poetic honors belong?

The Hebrew is difficult and the text doubtful, yet one learns an aesthetic lesson in apprehending it. It fascinates me that the two earliest and greatest victory odes in Hebrew are ascribed to the women who lead their chanting, Miriam the sister of Moses in the Song at the Red Sea in Exodus 15 and Deborah the prophet-ess in Judges 5. One would not expect the authorities who made the canon to admit a woman into the company of those who composed the Teaching or the Law, but some may have guessed (in private) that one component of the voice we now call J was a woman's.

Reading Dante in translation is rarely a good experience. Even the best recent versions are not as effective as the John Sinclair prose rendering in giving you an Englished Dante. T. S. Eliot, after decades of depreciating Shelley, went on to quote a passage from *The Triumph of Life,* Shelley's last, unfinished poem, and remarked that it was better than he could do. If we take that as Shelley's *Inferno,* we also have his translation of Matilda gathering flowers from the *Purgatorio,* again the best rendering in the language. Shelley wisely avoided the *Paradiso,* and I know of nothing in English I could recommend there.

The Bible haunts Shelley, who loathed Christianity but carries the rhythms and metaphors of the KJB into his ecstatic visions of a redeemed human world and a transmembered nature. It may no longer be possible for any poet in English to convey transcendental yearnings without the diction and cadences of the Bible as refracted into the idiom of the King James translators.

William Blake, in his own mode, which rivals Rabelais's, read the Bible in the light of his rebellion against Yahweh, whom he characterized as an "old Nobodaddy" or Urizen, the marker of horizons to all human aspiration. And yet in his more than Gnostic reading, the Bible was the "Great Code of Art," and not Yahweh's imposition of order.

For Blake this was not an inconsistency: he read the Bible by a light so inward that he could assume he found therein his own imaginings. As a radical post-Protestant he fulfilled the fears of those who had kept the Bible so long out of English. Eliot, who became a twentieth-century throwback to sixteenth-century Anglican orthodoxy, maintained a consistent rejection of the Inner Light and chastised Blake before going on to denounce Thomas

Hardy and D. H. Lawrence as heretics dazzled by their inward illuminations.

Almost a century later, Eliot possesses a kind of nostalgic charm in his rebellion against his New England Puritan lineage. The biblical allusions in his poetry rarely reflect an idiosyncratic reading; they are even more Augustinian than Dante's. Eliot's devotion to Lancelot Andrewes had more to do with sermons than the KJB, yet this fealty may have evoked in *The Waste Land* that allusive strand of lamentation so curiously Hebraic in the anti-Semitic obsessive who later composed "The Idea of a Christian Society."

The literary influence of the KJB was surprisingly contested by C. S. Lewis, who said he could not detect its cadences even in Bunyan or Ruskin, where they are palpable enough. Polemically, Lewis wanted to suggest that it was pernicious to read Scripture for an aesthetic reward. He has his truest disciples in American fundamentalists, who have made his *Mere Christianity* a sacred text, and who possess the KJB as an unread fetish.

Literary ought to be among the most comprehensive of terms. A literary appreciation of the KJB need not exclude the spirit (in any sense) and does not depend upon trusting in the Sinai Covenant or believing that the Resurrection took place. "Revelation" ought not to be confined to biblical contexts. *King Lear* is one of the most unsettling of revelations, as is *Macbeth*. Read closely, the enigmas of *Hamlet* can be regarded as nihilistic revelations outsoaring the negations of Dostoyevsky's Svidrigailov and Stavrogin.

In vainly disputing Homer as the educator of Greece, Plato implicitly saw Socrates as a savior yet found no place for his mentor in the harshness of the *Laws*. These days our shock is provoked by those who govern though their interpretations of the Qur'an. Israel has its nightmares with literalist appliers of Torah and Talmud. The secularization of Christian countries is complete in Western

Europe and Latin America and Canada, yet remains ambiguous in the United States.

Reading the Bible as a monument of literary culture akin to Shakespeare frees the text not only of the lacquer of dogma but also of much social history that has crippled apprehensions of its permanent value to those who have been and still are denied justice and equity. If it has been usurped endlessly by oppressors, nevertheless it was and is an ultimate resource for heroic endurance and resistance by the insulted and injured. The Hebrew prophets from Amos and Micah on through James the brother of Jesus constitute an authoritative proclamation of the pragmatic works of goodness required of societies and individuals. "Turn now!" is the prophetic *davar*: word, act, thing, and truth held together by an immanent urgency.

Plato or Isaiah? Athens or Jerusalem? We no longer can afford to choose in this darkening time when the light of the Book—be it Shakespeare or the Bible, Homer or Plato—flickers and threatens to go out in the glare of visual media. In this literary appreciation of the KJB, I set aside all questions of truth or of how to live, what to do. Shakespeare and Homer, or at least their works, do not desire to help us solve our problems. Manifestly Plato and the Bible (not all of it, though) share a moral urgency I find alien to Homer and Shakespeare, but I have tried to set that aside here.

My parenthetical qualification above reflects a conviction that readers too often regard the Bible as an integral monolith. Quite aside from the utterly irreconcilable differences between the Hebrew Scriptures and the Greek New Testament, the Hebrew canon itself includes such sublime outriders as the book of Job, Ecclesiastes, and the Song of Songs. Whatever revisionists and allegorists have done to these is blown away by the winds of time. Canonical by chance, they break the canon and redefine ancient Hebrew literature for us.

The Yahwist

The Hebrew text of Genesis, Exodus, and Numbers is more a palimpsest than a mosaic; and centuries of scholarly fiction have failed to render a persuasive account as to how it works, since it *has* worked and goes on performing. Fashions rise and ebb in Bible scholarship, and I scarcely know why I should prefer one scholarly trope to another as an aid in how I read. The nineteenth-century hypothesis of its authorial origins still more or less persuades me since my reader's experience confirms it.

There is a southern writer, the Yahwist or J, who may well have composed at the court of David and Solomon. A northern revisionist, E (possibly more than one), who called the god by the plural Elohim, wrote about 150 years later. The northern Kingdom of Israel collapsed in 722 B.C.E. and an editor in the southern Kingdom of Judah may have combined the J and E strands. During the Babylonian Exile, after the fall of Jerusalem, the Redactor, a scholar of genius, rewove the web, keeping Deuteronomy in the fabric, and integrating a later Priestly (P) document. Under the Persians, this complex text returned to Jerusalem with some (though not all) of the exile community.

This account is now unfashionable, but I rub my eyes at the currently modish vista, in which the great Redactor in Babylon worked not with continuous texts but with fragments or building blocks, putting them together in a pattern that somehow reconciled secular and priestly materials. Against this I observe that nothing *is* reconciled: the composite text is self-contradictory and sometimes sublimely weird. Dr. Samuel Johnson, my lifelong guide in literary criticism, remarked that the true critic worked to "improve opinion into knowledge." By that high standard the current scholars of the Bible are untrue. They inherit a wilderness and transform it into a desert.

I prefer to simplify by urging the reader to distinguish between two voices, one that tells its stories with an irony so large and pervasive that literalists simply fail to hear it. That, ultimately is the voice of the Yahwist: aristocratic, skeptical, humorous, deflationary of masculine pretenses, believing nothing and rejecting nothing, and particularly aware of the reality of personalities, Yahweh's most of all; the other voice is pious, fearful, cultic, ornately slow, pretentious, distrustful of women, impatient as to the vagaries of personality.

One of the universe's greatest writers—the Yahwist—is confined in the Redactor's text rather in the way that Hamlet is entrapped in his textual Elsinore, a revenge tragedy he disdains, a part he scorns to play. Shakespeare, between the prince and the play, takes neither side, and yet Hamlet rebels against Shakespeare and tries to write his own play. Who wins this agon is unclear; Shakespeare himself may have been uncertain. Division between incredibly vital protagonists and their godlike creator, Shakespeare, is not confined to *The Tragedy of Hamlet.* I weary at hosts of scholars who tell me that Hal/Henry IV prevails over the invincible Falstaff, when Shakespeare's own contemporary audiences decided otherwise. The Yahwist's great creature is Yahweh, who contains Falstaff's vitalism, Hamlet's ontological denials, Iago's destructiveness, and Lear's jealous furies and shattering madness. The Bible matters most because the Yahwist imagined a totally uncanny god, human-all-too-human and exuberant beyond all bindings.

The Aesthetic Agon of the KJB and Tanakh

The aesthetic experience of rereading the "Old Testament" of the KJB is altogether different from that of returning to the Hebrew text. There is a baroque glory in the KJB and a marvelously expressionistic concision in Tanakh: the contrast is nearly total. The KJB has some affinities with the prose of Sir Thomas Browne and of Robert Burton's *Anatomy of Melancholy;* I cannot think of an Anglo-American analogue to Tanakh. American writers from Walt Whitman and Melville through Hemingway and Faulkner on to Cormac McCarthy echo the cadences of the KJB, but not even the Kafkan Philip Roth suggests the terse, coiled energies of biblical Hebrew.

The largest aesthetic paradox of the KJB is its gorgeous exfoliation of the Hebrew original. Evidently the KJB men knew just enough Hebrew to catch the words but not the original music. Their relative ignorance transmuted into splendor because they shared a sense of literary decorum that all subsequent translators seem to lack. Miles Coverdale, bare both of Hebrew and of Greek, set a pattern that Miles Smith perfected. It is another of the many paradoxes of the KJB that its elaborate prose harmonies essentially were inaugurated by Coverdale's intuitive journey into the poems and prophecies his master Tyndale did not live to translate. We have Tyndale's Jonah and a medley of prophetic passages, eleven from Isaiah, in the *Epistle Taken out of the Old Testament.* How wonderful it would be to have Job, Ecclesiastes, and Jeremiah from the hand of Tyndale, though probably that would have prevented Coverdale's astonishing flair for style and rhythm from manifesting itself. This flair was unsteady, yet at its best it gave us something of the sonority we associate with KJB.

Tyndale, Coverdale, and the Geneva translators (including their best Hebraist, Gilby) all possessed the gift of literary authority. Their revisionist, Miles Smith, explicitly displays his sense of style in the 1611 preface, "The Translators to the Reader," and implicitly stands forth by his editorial responsibility for the ways in which the KJB men handle their inheritance from previous English Bibles. Again paradox intervenes: from Tyndale through

KJB the quest is to get closer to the literal sense of the Hebrew, while the consequence is to increase a cognitive music farther and farther away in regard to the Hebrew Bible's relative freedom from metaphors. Since all metaphor is a kind of mistake anyway, even the plain errors of the KJB sometimes add to the resultant splendor.

Can there be a precise estimate of aesthetic loss when the KJB is contrasted with the Hebrew? Gerald Hammond, whose ear is the most acute among scholars of the KJB, rightly says that "it suffers from the featurelessness which compromise will sometimes create: in reading it there is not the sense of the individual voice of a Tyndale or Coverdale." Tyndale never sounds stilted or merely formulaic, but alas the KJB sometimes does. So elliptical is the Hebrew that frequently you must tease the meanings out, but that is Shakespeare's rhetorical art also.

Again, Hammond praises the KJB's extraordinary command of Hebrew syntax in translating the Prophets and the poetic books, where they surpass Coverdale and make a return to Tyndale. Here, Hammond believes, the formulaic element allowed the KJB men to achieve a syntax of "neatness" in rendering very difficult effects of the Hebrew. Yet some loss can be felt as well. Biblical Hebrew probably was never a vernacular, even in the time of the Yahwist. Few writers in any national tradition are so sophisticated as the Yahwist, whose punning wordplay and incessant irony must have been directed to an elite, whether at Solomon's court or elsewhere in Jerusalem. But then much of Tanakh seems directed to an elite: Ecclesiastes, Job, Song of Songs, the chants of Isaiah, Jeremiah, Ezekiel. As poems in poetic prose these are all complex, difficult, piercing literary masterworks. They exemplify a breaking of conventional forms, and often they experiment with unruly syntax. Those who canonized them may have realized that they were "choosing forms of worship from poetic tales" (William Blake's sly charge).

If most of Tanakh is written in a Hebrew far removed from the vernacular, that is true also of the KJB, as of Coverdale and the Geneva Bible before it. Tyndale's mastery of plain style is better preserved in the KJB's New Testament than in the Old. We do not know whether the earliest writers preserved in Tanakh can be said to have remade or invented Hebrew. Luther's Bible translation in effect created a new German. Tyndale's New Testament even more strongly affected all subsequent expression in the English language.

The 1611 Preface

Miles Smith, who pragmatically might be called the editor-in-chief of the KJB, wrote an eloquent preface to the first edition. Only seldom reprinted, it is one of the most poignant unread essays in the language. Arguing for the necessity of Bible translation, from the Alexandrian Septuagint (Hebrew into Greek) to the labors of the KJB men, Smith emphasizes that *their* purpose was not to make a new translation, "but to make a good one better, or out of many good ones, one principal good one."

Between the lines of the preface is Smith's awareness that for Christian Europe, the Bible had always been a translated work. This is emphasized by Robert Carroll and Stephen Prickett in their introduction to the admirable Oxford World's Classics edition of the KJB (1997), which I have preferred as my fundamental text throughout this appreciation.

No translation of the Qur'an is accepted by Muslims anywhere as the words of Allah, dictated by him through Gabriel to Muhammad, who supposedly was illiterate. Arabic always will remain the sacred language of Islam, even when highly literate Muslims primarily speak and write Urdu or Farsi, the prime tongues, respectively, of Pakistan and Iran. Jews have a more puzzling relation to the Hebrew of the Bible, which may not have been the original language of the wandering people. They could have spoken the common Aramaic of the ancient Near East, and have absorbed Hebrew only through their conquest of Canaan.

There is no scholarly agreement on this, but Abraham (if he existed) came out of Haran, where Aramaic was spoken. It is possible that biblical Hebrew may never have been a vernacular. If the Yahwist was a writer at the Davidic or Solomonic court, she or he may have been composing for a highly sophisticated elite, one even quasi-secular. The redactors in Babylonian exile could well have spoken Aramaic even as they labored to piece together a national literature from texts already five centuries or more old.

The New Testament is frequently an awkward body of work in the original, since its authors thought in Aramaic while writing in demotic Greek. Nearly everything memorable in the English New Testament is the achievement of the matchless (except by Chaucer and Shakespeare) William Tyndale and not of the early Christian authors. I have been reading the Greek New Testament incessantly since taking a course on it as a Cornell undergraduate more than sixty years ago, and have just reread it side by side with Tyndale's New Testament. No honest critic able to read the koine original could resist the conclusion that Tyndale throughout transcends his proof-text to a sublime degree. Since the KJB New Testament is well over 85 percent Tyndale, his pioneer transformation of the text into an eloquent plain style remains beyond praise.

Reading the KJB therefore constitutes a curious double experience: there is (for the fully prepared reader) an aesthetic agon between the Hebrew and English Bibles, but no contest at all in regard to the New Testament. I myself vacillate between Tanakh and the KJB when I read for the experience of sublimity or pathos. In English, Chaucer, Shakespeare, and Milton are the only worthy agonists for aesthetic supremacy, setting aside all questions of faith, trust, and the spirit, since this book overtly is strictly a *literary* appreciation.

What the KJB Contributed to the English Bible

Is there a design to the KJB's revisions of its principal precursors, Tyndale, Coverdale, and the Geneva men? If there is a pattern, no one has uncovered it, and I am uncertain that it exists. Tyndale is a greater writer than all the translators who have come after him, while Coverdale's Psalms and the Geneva Bible's Prophets are consistently inspired work. One thinks of Coverdale's "the valley of the shadow of death" (Psalm 23) and Geneva's rendering of Isaiah 40:31:

> But they that wait upon the Lord, shall renew their strength:
> they shall lift up their wings as the eagles: they shall run,
> and not be weary, and they shall walk and not faint.

Nevertheless there is a cognitive music that is distinctly the KJB's own, particularly invoked in closures. Perhaps the most familiar of all biblical poems is the Twenty-third Psalm, KJB version:

> 1 The LORD *is* my shepherd; I shall not want.
> 2 He maketh me to lie down in green pastures: he leadeth me beside the still waters.
> 3 He restoreth my soul: he leadeth me in the paths of righteousness for his name's sake.
> 4 Yea, though I walk through the valley of the shadow of death, I will fear no evil: for thou *art* with me; thy rod and thy staff they comfort me.
> 5 Thou preparest a table before me in the presence of mine enemies: thou anointest my head with oil; my cup runneth over.

6 Surely goodness and mercy shall follow me all the days of my life: and I will dwell in the house of the Lord for ever.

Geneva had "he maketh me to rest in green pastures"; "to lie down" is far better. The KJB went beyond Geneva's "and I shall remain a long season in the house of the lord" and made it "for ever."

The KJB's committees did not always match Coverdale's inner ear, but frequently their baroque inventiveness surpassed the Geneva men, as here in Song of Solomon 8:6:

Set me as a seal on thine heart, and as a signet upon thine arm: for love *is* strong as death: jealousy is cruel as the grave: the coals thereof *are* fiery coals, and a vehement flame.

[Geneva]

Set me as a seal upon thine heart, as a seal upon thine arm: for love *is* strong as death, jealousy *is* cruel as the grave: the coals thereof *are* coals of fire, *which hath* a most vehement flame.

[KJB]

The Hebrew, rather more sharply, calls love as fierce or intense as death or dying. The Elizabethan "jealousy" is closer to "zealous" in its meaning. In the Hebrew, the poet chants that passion is "as strong as Sheol," while the "coals of fire" are "darts of fire." Here the KJB perhaps falls short of the original.

A test for great poetry and prose is an aura of *inevitability* in the phrasing. The KJB does participate with singular power in this testing in Job 38:7:

When the stars of the morning praised *me* together, and all the children of God rejoiced.

[Geneva]

When the morning stars sang together, and all the sonnes
of God shouted for joy.

[KJB]

There the KJB triumphs exuberantly. The book of Job, the height
of ancient Hebrew poetry, is also the aesthetic summit of the
Hebrew Bible. One of Yahweh's rhetorical splendors is his paean
to the warhorse's courage:

> 19 Hast thou given the horse strength? hast thou clothed
> his neck with thunder?
> 20 Canst thou make him afraid as a grasshopper? the
> glory of his nostrils *is* terrible.
> 21 He paweth in the valley, and rejoiceth in *his* strength:
> he goeth on to meet the armed men.
> 22 He mocketh at fear, and is not afrightened; neither
> turneth he back from the sword.
> 23 The quiver rattleth against him, the glittering spear
> and the shield.
> 24 He swalloweth the ground with fierceness and rage:
> neither believed he that *it is* the sound of the trumpet.
> 25 He saith among the trumpets, Ha, ha; and he smell-
> eth the battle far off, the thunder of the captains, and the
> shouting.

[Job 39:19–25]

Though the Geneva is close to this, it does not build so inevitably
to anything as strong as "the thunder of the captains, and the
shouting." Rather than go on to multiply a myriad of instances, I
think it better to state a rough principle. The impulse that guides
a strong poet to end a work with a touch of finality was shared
by the KJB revisionists.

The best study of the KJB in the context of its major precursors

(Tyndale, Coverdale, Geneva Bible) is Gerald Hammond's *The Making of the English Bible* (1982). No one else has shown so persuasively the struggle of the Renaissance English translators to "reshape English so that it could adopt itself to Hebraic idiom." Hammond is both an authority on seventeenth-century English literature and a formidable Hebraist, alert to every nuance or vagary in the word choices of Tyndale, Coverdale, and the Geneva group.

Tyndale, the authentic genius of English Bible translation, invented a new prose vernacular in his quest for a "literal" rendering of Hebrew into English. Hammond rightly commends Tyndale for his closeness to Hebrew syntax and his astonishing skill at narrative, which results from his extraordinary directness. Has anyone surpassed Tyndale in mastery of prose rhythm until Shakespeare's Falstaff? Hammond, citing Tyndale's influence (through the KJB) upon Bunyan and Defoe, plausibly places the Protestant martyr at the origin of the English novel.

Coverdale, who revered Tyndale, began as his assistant. Though devoid of both Hebrew and Greek, Coverdale had a remarkable ear, and his lyrical style still survives in many of the KJB's Psalms. Hammond credits Coverdale with setting the style, both lyrical and gnomic, for much of the poetic and prophetic books of the KJB.

The Geneva Bible prevailed for a hundred years, blocking out the KJB for its first fifty years or so. It was Shakespeare's, Spenser's, and Milton's Bible. I myself am not at all certain that aesthetic preference should be given to the KJB over the Geneva Bible, from which in any case it is frequently indistinguishable, since the KJB simply reproduces it. Alas, James I fiercely resented the Geneva Bible's marginal notes, which help readers in grasping the difficulties of the Hebrew. They disappear in the KJB, to its impoverishment.

Hammond commends the Geneva Bible for its useful division

of every text into numbered verses, an immense aid in apprehending Hebrew verse, though sometimes a narrative loss. The absorption of the Geneva Bible's prophetic books into the KJB testifies to its splendor in correcting yet appreciating Coverdale's cadences.

Hammond eloquently stresses the integrity and consistency of the style of the Renaissance English Bible. The movement from Tyndale's plain speaking through Coverdale and Geneva to the KJB, with its golden diction and baroque rolling periods can seem surprising, but in a sense Tyndale's followers unpacked what is implicit in their great forerunner. Shakespeare, master of all styles, finds materia poetica in the Geneva Bible, but only as he does in Ovid. Whatever he believed, we cannot know nor does it matter, since *King Lear* transcends faith and skepticism alike.

Should the Bible Be Read as Literature?

Matthew Arnold (1822–1888) has enthralled modern literary critics from the mandarin Lionel Trilling on to my formidable contemporary Christopher Ricks. I am a dissenter, since Arnold's poetry seems weak to me when compared to others in his era: Tennyson, Browning, Gerard Manley Hopkins, and the Pre-Raphaelites Dante Gabriel Rossetti, A. C. Swinburne, William Morris, Christina Rossetti, and George Meredith. Arnold's literary criticism illuminates little for me. I vastly prefer John Ruskin and Walter Pater, George Saintsbury and John Churton Collins, Swinburne and Oscar Wilde, who all aid my appreciation of imaginative literature, while Arnold rarely does.

Yet Arnold, more than Ruskin or Pater, inaugurated the mode I am following in composing a literary appreciation of the KJB. The very phrase, "the Bible as literature," is Arnold's invention. From *Literature and Dogma* (1873) on, Arnold made a transition to religious criticism, which emerges fully in *God and the Bible*

(1875). Second Isaiah became Arnold's exemplary educational text (particularly as he reworked it) and was the basis for his *Isaiah of Jerusalem* (1883), a work that makes me uncomfortable. It is not that Arnold's passion for the literary power of the KJB overwhelms his judgment, but Second Isaiah is itself as much an anthology of prophecies as are First and Third Isaiah, and Arnold just did not know enough.

A century after Arnold, the Canadian critic Northrop Frye reduced the Bible to a great typological code that endowed words with power. I myself prefer to appreciate the Bible, whether Tanakh or KJB, "as literature," since my experience as a reader is that rhetoric and not typology generates literary power. Yet the problem of spiritual codes abides in our response to the Bible. The history of literature may provoke disagreements, but how gentle these are compared to the clamors of religious history! Arguments about Shakespeare are not always amiable, yet disputes concerning the Bible have been murderous.

As I keep noting throughout this study, Tanakh and the KJB are for me rival aesthetic eminences, whereas the Greek New Testament as a literary work is weaker than Tyndale's version, which persists strongly in the Geneva Bible and the KJB.

Neo-Christians like C. S. Lewis and T. S. Eliot argued against reading the Bible as though you were reading Shakespeare. Religious belief is hardly in itself a mode of literary criticism. Frank Kermode, an authentic critic, once chided me for making literary criticism into a religion, which may be true enough, but that seems to me what the Gnostic tendency always has been throughout history.

I was and remain a dissenter in regard to Erich Auerbach's secularization of the Christian trope *figura,* in which literary texts fulfill one another. Sometimes I fret when rereading the KJB because its inaccuracies stem as much from spiritual ideology as from inadequate grasp of Hebrew. But I think such a reaction is a mistake. The KJB is an English Protestant polemic against contemporary Catholic and ancient Jew alike. Accept that, and its errors are themselves fascinating. Nothing is more literary than mistakes since they become metaphors, and figurative language is the essence of imaginative literature.

Though the neo-orthodox Eliot and Lewis deprecated reading the Bible as literature, palpably Tanakh is a canonical anthology, and so is the KJB—even more so. Unity is not an attribute of the Bible, Jewish or Protestant. Tanakh is gathered from more than a thousand years of Hebrew literature, and the criteria for selection seem to me to have been surprisingly aesthetic: how else account for the Song of Songs, Ecclesiastes, and Job stripped of its pious editorial conclusion? These three magnificent poems are, respectively, erotic, skeptical, and humanely despairing. Interpretive violence Judaized them, but that is akin to Christianizing *King Lear*. We do them wrong, they being so majestical, to offer them the show of violence.

Nietzsche's pragmatic question was, Who is the interpreter and what power does he seek to gain over the text? The KJB translators, like their forerunners Tyndale and the men of the Geneva Bible, sought to appropriate the Hebrew text for a Protestant Christ. Their fascinating literalism, which almost brought Hebrew over into English, represented a drive to subsume the ancient Jewish language even as they had transformed Tanakh into that shanghaied work the Old Testament. Only a literary reading can hope to restore Tanakh, the as it were Original Testament.

Rabbi Akiba, the founder of normative Judaism, prevailed on the other sages of the second century C.E. to retain the Song of Songs in the canon, insisting that it counted for more than all the rest of Scripture. We do not have his own allegory of interpreting the Song, yet it seems to have been the ancestor of all subsequent spiritualizations. Kabbalah saw Akiba as reading the Sinai Revelation of all Torah in the Song, so that the beloved is Yahweh, whose shape is thus made manifest.

For those to whom the KJB is the Truth, rock of their faith, a literary appreciation is redundant. I write however for the common reader, who can be moved by the Bible's eloquence and beauty. Originally the culmination of one strand of Renaissance English culture, the KJB became a basic source of American literature: Walt Whitman, Herman Melville, Emily Dickinson are its children, and so are William Faulkner, Ernest Hemingway, Cormac McCarthy. The KJB and Shakespeare fuse into a style of language that enabled the emergence of *Leaves of Grass, Moby-Dick, As I Lay Dying, Blood Meridian.* Whitman's verse and Hemingway's prose alike stem from the KJB.

It should in time seem as odd to speak of "the Bible as literature" as to say "Shakespeare as literature." Shakespeare *is* literature, as are the Bible, Homer, Dante, Cervantes, Montaigne, Milton, Proust, Joyce. Literature, in this high sense, is the Blessing: it represents the fullness of life and can give more life. If you read the KJB as revelation then no one can gainsay you. I myself address the common reader who quests for more life.

The Hebrew Bible

The Five Books of Moses

Genesis

THE FIVE SCROLLS (*PENTATEUCH*, from the Greek) or Books of Moses long ago were called the Torah, mistranslated by Christians as "the Law." Accurately, *Torah* means "the Teachings," and mostly it is a story, from the Creation on to the death of Moses, who is not allowed by God to enter the Promised Land.

Though the Pentateuch early assumed Judaic primacy, it was not the first part of the Hebrew Bible to be composed. An archaic text like the magnificent War Song of Deborah (Judges 5) comes out of a world where Moses is absent and the Twelve Tribes of Israel are dominant entities. Sages and rabbis labored to control our perspective, and the Five Scrolls of Moses represent as successful a usurpation of our consciousness as does the Christian conversion of the Hebrew Bible into the Old Testament.

Genesis traditionally is divided by scholars into the Primeval History, chapters 1–13, and the Patriarchal Story, 14–62, which itself separates out into Abraham, 14–32; Jacob, 33–48; and Joseph and his brothers, 49–62. In Hebrew, Genesis takes the title *Bereshit,* the first word of the scroll: "In the beginning."

We do not know when Genesis was put together: it evidently was part of the enormous labor performed by the great Redactor in the Babylonian Exile of the sixth century B.C.E. I have already dismissed the currently fashionable views that fragments of textual tradition were somehow pasted into the tales of Jacob or of Moses. Anyone who can read aesthetically should recognize the narrative style of the Yahwist, or J Writer, who possibly composed during the long reign of Solomon.

Genesis 1:1–2:3 offers a Priestly prose hymn of the cosmological event of Creation, possibly written six hundred years *after* the Yahwist's very different vision of origins in 2:4–3:24. It is difficult to overpraise either account of Creation, Priestly or Yahwistian. Each touches the limits of literature, the sublime in the Priestly Writer, and a strange, homely uncanny in the J Writer. The Hebrew texts compete in power with each other, and neither is quite captured by Tyndale, whose Genesis nevertheless is a magnificent narrative, taken over first by the Geneva men and then by the KJB revisionists.

The height of the Priestly Creation is 1:26–28:

> 26 ¶And God said, Let us make man in our image, after our likeness: and let them have dominion over the fish of the sea, and over the fowl of the air, and over the cattle, and over all the earth, and over every creeping thing that creepeth upon the earth.
>
> 27 So God created man in his *own* image, in the image of God created he him; male and female created he them.
>
> 28 And God blessed them, and God said unto them, Be fruitful, and multiply, and replenish the earth, and subdue it: and have dominion over the fish of the sea,

and over the fowl of the air, and over every living thing that moveth upon the earth.

"Let us make" implies that the Elohim, "divine beings" of the E Writer or God of the Priestly Writer, are a conclave acting together to create, though this can be read also as a royal "we." "Man" is *Adam* in Hebrew, meaning also humankind, and "image" is *zelem* in Hebrew, a term of enormous richness, perpetually evocative in later Jewish commentary, particularly in Kabbalah.

The Yahwist's account of Creation is the very different vision of Eden, in 2:4–25:

> in the day that the LORD God made the earth and the heavens,
>
> 5 And every plant of the field before it was in the earth, and every herb of the field before it grew: for the LORD God had not caused it to rain upon the earth, and *there was* not a man to till the ground.
>
> 6 But there went up a mist from the earth, and watered the whole face of the ground.
>
> 7 And the LORD God formed man *of* the dust of the ground, and breathed into his nostrils the breath of life; and man became a living soul.
>
> 8 ¶ And the LORD God planted a garden eastward in Eden; and there he put the man whom he had formed.
>
> 9 And out of the ground made the LORD God to grow every tree that is pleasant to the sight, and good for food; the tree of life also in the midst of the garden, and the tree of knowledge of good and evil.
>
> 10 And a river went out of Eden to water the garden; and from thence it was parted, and became into four heads.
>
> 11 The name of the first *is* Pison: that *is* it which compasseth the whole land of Havilah, where *there is* gold;

12 And the gold of that land *is* good: there *is* bdellium and the onyx stone.

13 And the name of the second river *is* Gihon: the same *is* it that compasseth the whole land of Ethiopia.

14 And the name of the third river *is* Hiddekel: that *is* it which goeth toward the east of Assyria. And the fourth river *is* Euphrates.

15 And the Lord God took the man, and put him into the garden of Eden to dress it and to keep it.

16 And the Lord God commanded the man, saying, Of every tree of the garden thou mayest freely eat:

17 But of the tree of the knowledge of good and evil, thou shalt not eat of it: for in the day that thou eatest thereof thou shalt surely die.

18 ¶ And the Lord God said, *It is* not good that the man should be alone; I will make him an help meet for him.

19 And out of the ground the Lord God formed every beast of the field, and every fowl of the air; and brought *them* unto Adam to see what he would call them: and whatsoever Adam called every living creature, that *was* the name thereof.

20 And Adam gave names to all cattle, and to the fowl of the air, and to every beast of the field; but for Adam there was not found an help meet for him.

21 And the Lord God caused a deep sleep to fall upon Adam, and he slept: and he took one of his ribs, and closed up the flesh instead thereof;

22 And the rib, which the Lord God had taken from man, made he a woman, and brought her unto the man.

23 And Adam said, This *is* now bone of my bones, and flesh of my flesh: she shall be called Woman, because she was taken out of Man.

24 Therefore shall a man leave his father and his mother, and shall cleave unto his wife: and they shall be one flesh.

25 And they were both naked, the man and his wife, and were not ashamed.

Instead of the Priestly celebration of a blazing glory, we are in a harsh, parched Judean spring, suddenly vivified by a mist welling up from the earth. Adam is formed from the red clay of the *adamah,* the soil, rather as though this playful Yahweh fashioned a mud figurine and then breathed life into it until it became a living being. Eden, used as a place name, also means "delight" in Hebrew. When Yahweh in verse 16 says, You may freely eat, the statement is ambiguous.

The creation of Eve is Yahweh's triumph, aesthetically superior to that of Adam, since she is fashioned out of life and not from clay. Tyndale rendered verse 18 as:

And the Lord God said: it is not good that man should be alone, I will make him an helper to bear him company.

Geneva gave:

Also the Lord God said, It is not good that the man should be himself alone: I will make him an help meet for him.

The KJB omits that awkward "himself" and changes "Also" to "And" but otherwise adopts Geneva. "Helpmeet," our now out-of-fashion term, is a poor version of the Hebrew for "helper parallel to him," though the literal meaning is "opposed to him," which bears some dark pondering.

That is a hint of the opposing agent proper, the serpent of chapter 3:

1 Now the serpent was more subtil than any beast of the field which the Lord God had made. And he said unto

the woman, Yea, hath God said, Ye shall not eat of every tree of the garden?

2 And the woman said unto the serpent, We may eat of the fruit of the trees of the garden:

3 But of the fruit of the tree which *is* in the midst of the garden, God hath said, Ye shall not eat of it, neither shall ye touch it, lest ye die.

4 And the serpent said unto the woman, Ye shall not surely die:

5 For God doth know that in the day ye eat thereof, then your eyes shall be opened, and ye shall be as gods, knowing good and evil.

6 And when the woman saw that the tree *was* good for food, and that it *was* pleasant to the eyes, and a tree to be desired to make *one* wise, she took of the fruit thereof, and did eat, and gave also unto her husband with her; and he did eat.

7 And the eyes of them both were opened, and they knew that they *were* naked; and they sewed fig leaves together, and made themselves aprons.

For verse 4 Geneva gives, "Ye shall not die at all," while Tyndale wonderfully has, "tush ye shall not die." J's irony is that Yahweh has created the serpent to be more fully conscious than man or woman. It is important to be aware that the Yahwist is not Saint John the Divine, for whom the snake is Satan in Revelation. J's serpent is an enigma, a mischief maker without apparent motivation. Rather than translate him as "subtle," I prefer "smooth" in our American vernacular sense. J plays punningly on the Hebrew *arom,* "naked," and *arum,* "sly."

Yahweh's stage-managing of what Christianity names the Fall is adroit and rather reprehensible. It can be viewed as a bad father's deliberate blunder, since Adam and Eve essentially are children. I recall saying that J's point is "When we were children, we were terribly punished for being children." In the entire Hebrew Bible, this supposed Fall is never mentioned again.

Yahweh imposes mortality as a punishment, which makes him something of a hanging judge who thus concludes a children's story inappropriately. What mitigates Yahweh's harshness is that we are not reading narrative theology but a family romance that crosses over into tragicomedy. J's irony, too pervasive to be noticed, makes me wonder at the near-contradiction of a withdrawal from mortals of a freedom they never had. J knows nothing about immortality. The expulsion from Eden is therefore an eloquent puzzle:

> 22 ¶ And the LORD God said, Behold, the man is become as one of us, to know good and evil: and now, lest he put forth his hand, and take also of the tree of life, and eat, and live for ever:
>
> 23 Therefore the LORD God sent him forth from the garden of Eden, to till the ground from whence he was taken.
>
> 24 So he drove out the man; and he placed at the east of the garden of Eden Cherubims, and a flaming sword which turned every way, to keep the way of the tree of life.
>
> [3:22–24]

Can J's Yahweh really fear that Adam will become one of the Elohim by devouring fruit of the tree of life? Something is missing here, but then J can be as elliptical as Dante or the later Shakespeare.

Noah and the Flood, intricately mixed together out of J and P by the Redactor, has been solemnized by tradition as Yahweh's first

Covenant with mankind, "the children of Noah." The J Writer's share in the composite text is marked by deliberate hilarity:

> 20 And Noah began *to be* an husbandman, and he planted a vineyard:
>
> 21 And he drank of the wine, and was drunken; and he was uncovered within his tent.
>
> 22 And Ham, the father of Canaan, saw the nakedness of his father, and told his two brethren without.
>
> 23 And Shem and Japheth took a garment, and laid *it* upon both their shoulders, and went backward, and covered the nakedness of their father; and their faces *were* backward, and they saw not their father's nakedness.
>
> 24 And Noah awoke from his wine, and knew what his younger son had done unto him.
>
> 25 And he said, Cursed *be* Canaan; a servant of servants shall he be unto his brethren.
>
> [9:20–25]

In his Norton edition of the English Bible, Herbert Marks corrects the KJB in verse 20, where the Hebrew reads, "Noah, a man of the ground, was the first planter of a vineyard." Readings differ after that, but evidently Ham sodomizes his drunken father at the moment Noah has intercourse with his wife. The delightfully circumspect behavior of Shem and Japheth has an outrageous humor, worthy of the J Writer. A similar wild spirit of comedy energizes the Tower of Babel, Genesis 11:1–9:

> 1 And the whole earth was of one language, and of one speech.
>
> 2 And it came to pass, as they journeyed from the east, that they found a plain in the land of Shinar; and they dwelt there.

3 And they said one to another, Go to, let us make brick, and burn them throughly. And they had brick for stone, and slime had they for morter.

4 And they said, Go to, let us build us a city and a tower, whose top *may reach* unto heaven; and let us make us a name, lest we be scattered abroad upon the face of the whole earth.

5 And the LORD came down to see the city and the tower, which the children of men builded.

6 And the LORD said, Behold, the people *is* one, and they have all one language; and this they begin to do: and now nothing will be restrained from them, which they have imagined to do.

7 Go to, let us go down, and there confound their language, that they may not understand one another's speech.

8 So the LORD scattered them abroad from thence upon the face of all the earth: and they left off to build the city.

9 Therefore is the name of it called Babel; because the LORD did there confound the language of all the earth: and from thence did the LORD scatter them abroad upon the face of all the earth.

Following Tyndale and Geneva, the KJB valiantly attempts to render the Yahwist at her or his most untranslatable. Satirizing Babylonian cultural aspirations, the J Writer dazzles with a Joycean wordplay that exuberantly mocks Babylonian cosmic structures. J's Yahweh, who closed up Noah's ark with his own hands, descends in person to make his own on-the-ground inspection and delights in his trickster aspect, bringing the tower down by a confusing of tongues, a kind of reverse Pentecost.

With Abram, who becomes Abraham, the Patriarchal Age begins. "Get thee out of" is Yahweh's injunction to Abram, as it will be to Moses, and to most Jews since. Through Ishmael, his son by Hagar, Abraham is the father of the Arabs as well as of the Jews. A purely legendary figure, he nevertheless had to be invented, since his Covenant with Yahweh in Genesis 17 is the foundation of Judaism, and ultimately of Christianity and Islam.

The story of Abraham, powerful in Tanakh, retains its strength in the KJB. Yahweh, totally a personality, speaks to Abraham face to face and argues with him almost as an equal. And yet the incommensurateness always abides, and with it a sense of awe. Emily Dickinson called her God, in whom she nimbly disbelieved, by the name awe. The keynote of awesomeness is heard fully in Genesis 15:12–17:

> 12 And when the sun was going down, a deep sleep fell upon Abram; and, lo, an horror of great darkness fell upon him.
>
> 13 And he said unto Abram, Know of a surety that thy seed shall be a stranger in a land *that is* not theirs, and shall serve them; and they shall afflict them four hundred years;
>
> 14 And also that nation, whom they shall serve, will I judge: and afterward shall they come out with great substance.
>
> 15 And thou shalt go to thy fathers in peace; thou shalt be buried in a good old age.
>
> 16 But in the fourth generation they shall come hither again: for the iniquity of the Amorites *is* not yet full.
>
> 17 And it came to pass, that, when the sun went down, and it was dark, behold a smoking furnace, and a burning lamp that passed between those pieces.

At Yahweh's command, Abram sacrifices heifer, goat, ram, turtle-dove, and pigeon. Then deep sleep falls upon him, and he goes into a trance. Pre-Judaic magic clearly is involved in that smoking oven and burning torch (to keep the fire going in the brazier), both of which intimate the flames associated with Yahweh's state of being. Images of cutting a covenant prepare for the miraculous begetting of Isaac by divine fiat in the wonderful opening half of chapter 18:

1 And the LORD appeared unto him in the plains of Mamre: and he sat in the tent door in the heat of the day;

2 And he lift up his eyes and looked, and, lo, three men stood by him: and when he saw *them,* he ran to meet them from the tent door, and bowed himself toward the ground,

3 And said, My Lord, if now I have found favour in thy sight, pass not away, I pray thee, from thy servant:

4 Let a little water, I pray you, be fetched, and wash your feet, and rest yourselves under the tree:

5 And I will fetch a morsel of bread, and comfort ye your hearts; after that ye shall pass on: for therefore are ye come to your servant. And they said, So do, as thou hast said.

6 And Abraham hastened into the tent unto Sarah, and said, Make ready quickly three measures of fine meal, knead *it,* and make cakes upon the hearth.

7 And Abraham ran unto the herd, and fetcht a calf tender and good, and gave *it* unto a young man; and he hasted to dress it.

8 And he took butter, and milk, and the calf which he had dressed, and set *it* before them; and he stood by them under the tree, and they did eat.

9 ¶ And they said unto him, Where *is* Sarah thy wife? And he said, Behold, in the tent.

10 And he said, I will certainly return unto thee according to the time of life; and, lo, Sarah thy wife shall have a son. And Sarah heard *it* in the tent door, which *was* behind him.

11 Now Abraham and Sarah *were* old *and* well stricken in age; *and* it ceased to be with Sarah after the manner of women.

12 Therefore Sarah laughed within herself, saying, After I am waxed old shall I have pleasure, my lord being old also?

13 And the LORD said unto Abraham, Wherefore did Sarah laugh, saying, Shall I of a surety bear a child, which am old?

14 Is any thing too hard for the LORD? At the time appointed I will return unto thee, according to the time of life, and Sarah shall have a son.

15 Then Sarah denied, saying, I laughed not; for she was afraid. And he said Nay; but thou didst laugh.

Yahweh, accompanied by two angels of destruction, is on the way to extinguish Sodom and Gomorrah, but is happy to stop for a hearty picnic beneath the terebinth trees. Offended by Sarah's sensible derision, he reminds her and us that nothing is too difficult for him. This is charming yet is surpassed by the rest of the chapter. Abraham courageously argues Yahweh down from his plan so that even ten righteous inhabitants would suffice to save Sodom. As there will be only Lot and his family, Sodom must be overthrown. This one time our father Abraham manifests exemplary moral courage. Knowing that he is nothing in himself, Adamic dust and ashes, Abraham stubbornly attempts to speak and act as if he were everything.

Though Proust would have been surprised to think it, Sodom is not destroyed on account of sexual orientation but rather for inhospitality and contempt, toward strangers and also toward Yahweh. We remember the story most for the seriocomic mishaps of the survivors: that unfortunate lady Lot's wife looks back and ends up as a pillar of salt, while Lot's daughters take turns seducing their drunken father so as to achieve pregnancy.

The culmination of the Abraham saga comes in 22:1–19, with the notorious *aqedah,* or Binding of Isaac. I follow E. A. Speiser's Anchor Yale Bible Genesis (1963) and John Van Seters's *Abraham in History and Tradition* (1975) in judging that J originally wrote this text, and what we now have is a severely censored story. Abraham, who strove to save the dreadful inhabitants of Sodom, hardly would have sacrificed his son's life without a considerable agon.

Rather touchingly, Isaac and Ishmael, Isaac's Arab half-brother, son of the Egyptian Hagar, cooperate in the burial of their father, Abraham.

Genesis achieves a new greatness in its tales of Jacob, the only other biblical protagonist whose personality and character are as comprehensive, vivid, and endless to meditation as the heroic David, who was a new kind of man. Jacob, though persistent in his quest for the Blessing, was hardly heroic except in his amazing all-night struggle with the Angel of Death at Penuel. And Jacob was an old kind of man, as wily a trickster as Yahweh himself.

J's Jacob is a survivor above all else, which is how he becomes Israel, now both a nation and a people of survivors. One can nominate Jacob, more than David or Moses, as the Jewish consciousness proper, archetype of Freud, Kafka, and Einstein, the modern representatives of Jewish genius. Though Christianity rarely saw Jacob as an intimation of Jesus, I would argue that Jesus, rightly called by Father John P. Meier a grand embodiment of Jewish genius, in many respects shows affinities with Jacob, who became Israel.

The best aid I know to interpreting the Yahwist's Jacob is Thomas Mann's comic masterpiece, the fifteen-hundred-page narrative tetralogy *Joseph and His Brothers,* written between 1926 and 1942. If you cannot read German, avoid H. T. Lowe-Porter's involuntary parody of the KJB in her unfortunate rendering and instead experience the superb translation by John E. Woods (2005). Mann's Jacob, particularly in the first volume, *The Stories of Jacob,* is an authentic enlargement of J's Jacob, sublime scamp of the Blessing. Though a gifted ironist, Mann was also one of the last humanists, and his authorial spirit reincarnated in him the heritage of the J Writer. Jacob, holder of the Blessing, passed it on both to his fourth son, Judah, and in a literary sense to Paul Thomas Mann, exiled to America by the rise of Hitler and then self-exiled from the United States to Switzerland by the rise of Senator Joseph McCarthy.

Mann's Jacob, increasingly as he ages, ponders his own stories, seeking to gain power over their interpretation. For him they all are stages leading to the Blessing, best shown by his beloved Rachel. But I define the Blessing by more than time. In the Priestly Writer and the Deuteronomists, the Blessing is divinely simple: "Be fruitful and multiply." In the Yahwist (and in Mann) I read the Blessing as "More life into a time without boundaries." If you have the Blessing, your name will not be scattered but will live on in communal memory. Without remembrance, no Blessing. Ironies abound (in J and in Mann), usurpations are frequent, and cunning rather than holiness is the pragmatic qualification for election.

Jacob's quest for the Blessing starts literally during the act of birth, and continues figuratively by an act of fraud:

25 And the first came out red, all over like an hairy garment; and they called his name Esau.

26 And after that came his brother out, and his hand took hold on Esau's heel; and his name was called Jacob: and Isaac *was* threescore years old when she bare them.

27 And the boys grew: and Esau was a cunning hunter, a man of the field; and Jacob *was* a plain man, dwelling in tents.

28 And Isaac loved Esau, because he did eat of *his* venison: but Rebekah loved Jacob.

29 ¶ And Jacob sod pottage: and Esau came from the field, and he *was* faint:

30 And Esau said to Jacob, Feed me, I pray thee, with that same red *pottage;* for I *am* faint: therefore was his name called Edom.

31 And Jacob said, Sell me this day thy birthright.

32 And Esau said, Behold, I *am* at the point to die: and what profit shall this birthright do to me?

33 And Jacob said, Swear to me this day; and he sware unto him: and he sold his birthright unto Jacob.

34 Then Jacob gave Esau bread and pottage of lentils; and he did eat and drink, and rose up, and went his way: thus Esau despised his birthright.

[Genesis 25:25–34]

"Heel" in verse 26 is a characteristic pun of J's, playing *aqeb* against *yaaqob*. Since *aqeb* can mean someone who cheats, this idea of a "heel" is little changed after many ages. The stolen birthright is joined by the Blessing in 27:19–37:

19 And Jacob said unto his father, I *am* Esau thy firstborn; I have done according as thou badest me: arise, I pray thee, sit and eat of my venison, that thy soul may bless me.

20 And Isaac said unto his son, How *is it* that thou hast

found *it* so quickly, my son? And he said, Because the LORD thy God brought *it* to me.

21 And Isaac said unto Jacob, Come near, I pray thee, that I may feel thee, my son, whether thou *be* my very son Esau or not.

22 And Jacob went near unto Isaac his father; and he felt him, and said, The voice *is* Jacob's voice, but the hands *are* the hands of Esau.

23 And he discerned him not, because his hands were hairy, as his brother Esau's hands: so he blessed him.

24 And he said, *Art* thou my very son Esau? And he said, I *am*.

25 And he said, Bring *it* near to me, and I will eat of my son's venison, that my soul may bless thee. And he brought *it* near to him, and he did eat: and he brought him wine, and he drank.

26 And his father Isaac said unto him, Come near now, and kiss me, my son.

27 And he came near, and kissed him: and he smelled the smell of his raiment, and blessed him, and said, See, the smell of my son *is* as the smell of a field which the LORD hath blessed.

28 Therefore God give thee of the dew of heaven, and the fatness of the earth, and plenty of corn and wine:

29 Let people serve thee, and nations bow down to thee: be lord over thy brethren, and let thy mother's sons bow down to thee: cursed *be* every one that curseth thee, and blessed *be* he that blesseth thee.

30 ¶ And it came to pass, as soon as Isaac had made an end of blessing Jacob, and Jacob was yet scarce gone out from the presence of Isaac his father, that Esau his brother came in from his hunting.

31 And he also had made savoury meat, and brought it unto his father, and said unto his father, Let my father arise, and eat of his son's venison, that thy soul may bless me.

32 And Isaac his father said unto him, Who *art* thou? And he said, I *am* thy son, thy firstborn Esau.

33 And Isaac trembled very exceedingly, and said, Who? where *is* he that hath taken venison, and brought *it* me, and I have eaten of all before thou camest, and have blessed him? yea, *and* he shall be blessed.

34 And when Esau heard the words of his father, he cried with a great and exceeding bitter cry, and said unto his father, Bless me, *even* me also, O my father.

35 And he said, Thy brother came with subtilty, and hath taken away thy blessing.

36 And he said, Is not he rightly named Jacob? for he hath supplanted me these two times: he took away my birthright; and, behold, now he hath taken away my blessing. And he said, Hast thou not reserved a blessing for me?

37 And Isaac answered and said unto Esau, Behold, I have made him thy lord, and all his brethren have I given to him for servants; and with corn and wine have I sustained him: and what shall I do now unto thee, my son?

High comedy is enriched here by the marvelous pathos of verse 38:

And Esau said unto his father, Hast thou but one blessing, my father? bless me, even me also, O my father. And Esau lifted up his voice, and wept.

Isaac is not a memorable patriarch, but everyone holds on to his "The voice is Jacob's voice, but the hands are the hands of Esau." A complex kind of sympathy for Jacob returns in chapter 28, when he experiences the great dream vision of a ladder set up between earth and heaven with angels going up and down. Yahweh, standing above the stairs, reaffirms the Blessing, however it was obtained.

Thomas Mann, elaborating the dream, splendidly describes Jacob's repose as "a sturdy and proud sleep full of private laughter." That pride carries Jacob through his celebrated relationship with Laban, and the brief but absolute joy of his marriage with Rachel, Joseph's mother. The great epiphany of Jacob comes in chapter 32, one of the glories of the KJB, following after its strong precursors Tyndale and Geneva. Always influential, the vision of the wrestling Jacob has obsessed many of the best readers of our time:

> 22 And he rose up that night, and took his two wives, and his two womenservants, and his eleven sons, and passed over the ford Jabbok.
>
> 23 And he took them, and sent them over the brook, and sent over that he had.
>
> 24 ¶ And Jacob was left alone; and there wrestled a man with him until the breaking of the day.
>
> 25 And when he saw that he prevailed not against him, he touched the hollow of his thigh; and the hollow of Jacob's thigh was out of joint, as he wrestled with him.
>
> 26 And he said, Let me go, for the day breaketh. And he said, I will not let thee go, except thou bless me.
>
> 27 And he said unto him, What *is* thy name? And he said, Jacob.
>
> 28 And he said, Thy name shall be called no more Jacob, but Israel: for as a prince hast thou power with God and with men, and hast prevailed.
>
> 29 And Jacob asked *him,* and said, Tell *me,* I pray thee,

thy name. And he said, Wherefore *is* it *that* thou dost ask after my name? And he blessed him there.

30 And Jacob called the name of the place Peniel: for I have seen God face to face, and my life is preserved.

31 And as he passed over Penuel the sun rose upon him, and he halted upon his thigh.

32 Therefore the children of Israel eat not *of* the sinew which shrank, which *is* upon the hollow of the thigh, unto this day: because he touched the hollow of Jacob's thigh in the sinew that shrank.

Tyndale and Geneva both are very close to this; all the KJB adds is a little brushwork. The power of this incident partly depends on the unrevealed identity of that nameless one among the Elohim whom Jacob-Israel holds to a standoff. Is it Yahweh himself playing the role of the Angel of Death? We are not told, yet this is no loving embrace; Jacob will limp for the rest of his long life. Why does the angel so dread the dawn?

You could say that nothing in Jacob's life previously has prepared him (or us) for this rugged courage and strength, or again that everything has been prelude to this transformation. The Blessing materializes as the triumphant new name, Israel, only ambiguously translated as "the Almighty strives," and probably meaning something closer to "Israel strives with the Almighty." Much turns on verse 28: "for as a prince hast thou power with God and with men, and hast prevailed." Tyndale has "For thou hast wrestled with God and with men and hast prevailed." Geneva gives "because thou hast had power with God, thou shalt also prevail with men." The KJB men evidently knew the rabbinic reading of "strive" as "to rule over" or "to be a prince."

After this numinous encounter, Jacob-Israel has to be urgently different. For me the finest moment in Mann's *The Stories of Jacob* comes in Jacob's reminiscences:

> What had caused the old man to fall into his current and manifest state of pondering were memories that his son's chatter about "names" had awakened in his mind—lofty and panicky memories with the weight of a dream but from days long past, when in great fear for his life he had been awaiting yet another encounter with his desert-dwelling brother, whom he had tricked and who was doubtlessly thirsting for revenge. For he had so fervently longed for spiritual power that for the sake of a name he had wrestled with the extraordinary man who had attacked him. It was a heavy, terrible, and highly sensual dream of desperate sweetness, not something airy and transient that leaves no traces, but a dream so hot with body heat, so dense with reality that it had left behind a twofold lifelong legacy, like creatures of the sea stranded by the ebbing tide: first, the lameness in Jacob's hip, in the hollow of his thigh, put out of joint by that extraordinary man, leaving him halt; and second, the name—not the name of that peculiar stranger, which had been denied him with might and main, until dawn, until that painfully dangerous moment when it would have been too late, no matter how insistently, violently the hot, panting Jacob had demanded it of him; no, not that name, but his own other and second name, the surname the stranger had bequeathed to him in battle in order to prevent a delay that would have proved most painful and to depart before sunrise, the title of honor that people had used ever since, whenever they wanted to flatter him and see him smile: Yizrael, "God goes to war" . . . He saw the ford

of the Jabbok before him again, where he had remained among the bushes on the near side after having first led across his wives, eleven sons, and the flocks he had selected as a gift of atonement for Esau; saw the unsettled, cloudy night, in which, restless as the sky itself, he had wandered about after two attempts at sleep, still trembling, despite the passable outcome of his encounter with Rachel's outfoxed father, and tormented now by his grave concern at the approach of yet another man he had duped and defrauded. How he had admonished the Elohim in his prayers, more or less declaring it Their duty to stand beside him. And he also saw that man—with whom he had unexpectedly found himself, God knew why, wrestling for his life—by the garish light of that night's moon as it had suddenly emerged from behind the clouds—saw him again so close, almost breast to breast, with his wide-set ox eyes that never blinked, with that face, and those shoulders, shining like polished stone. And entering his heart again was something like the ghastly lust he had felt while his groaning whispers demanded that name. . . . How strong he had been—with the desperate strength of dreams, with the stamina of unexpected reserves of energy in his soul. He had held out the whole night, until dawn, until he saw that it had now grown too late for the distraught man, until he heard him beg, "Let me go!" Neither had prevailed over the other, but had that not meant victory for Jacob, who was no extraordinary man, but a man from here and now, born of man's seed? It seemed to him as if the wide-eyed stranger had had his doubts. That painful blow when he had grabbed his hip had felt like an examination. Maybe it had been meant to determine if there was a ball and socket there, a mobile joint, not one fixed and ill fashioned for sitting, like those of his own kind. . . . And then the man had been clever enough to turn things around so that although he did not yield up his own name, he bestowed one upon Jacob instead. He could hear, as clearly as he had that morning, the high and brazen voice that had spoken to him: "Henceforth you shall be called Yizrael"—whereupon he had released the owner of that extraordinary voice from his arms, in the hope that the stranger might just barely still make it in time.

[Translated by John E. Woods; ellipses in original]

Terror and comedy mingle here in tribute to Mann's mastery. If Israel is the alternative name of the nameless angel, then Jacob has usurped the identity of what, following Wallace Stevens and Freud, could be called the angel of reality. The Blessing pragmatically means survival; Jacob has postponed dying, though not of course the eventual necessity of dying. Perhaps he has made friends with that necessity, a presage of what Freud regarded as reality-testing.

Joseph, whom Jacob loves as fiercely as he did Rachel, may be, as I have suggested in *The Book of J* (1990), the J Writer's surrogate for David the King. He is by any interpretation a favored soul. I always remember Tyndale's delightful "And the Lord was with Joseph, and he was a lucky fellow."

What is luck? In the Hebrew Bible it is the whim of Yahweh, who prefers his charming chosen, Jacob, Joseph, and David, to the more recalcitrant Abraham and Moses. The Olympian gods, notorious for playing favorites, are surpassed by the awesome Yahweh, whose preferences are at once morally outrageous and aesthetically persuasive. The divine Oscar Wilde nominated Jesus as the Supreme Aesthete (or the Supreme Fiction). An idolater of Oscar, I assign the role to an even greater narcissist, Yahweh, the creator-by-catastrophe.

A lifelong exegete, I cannot leap into the freedom of celebrating Yahweh because he causes me too many anxieties. Better to extol Joseph, whose exuberance and joy of being takes him through every trial into a glorious career. That splendor is not historical since Joseph may never have existed. He is a romance hero, and his story is a major prose fiction, a saga of the favorite son of a marvelous father. Yahweh's Blessing cannot be passed on formally from Jacob to Joseph. It goes to Judah, the fourth son, after the first three disqualify themselves by lust or violence. Joseph does not compete for it; he is not an agonist but a born diplomat-politician, exploiting his personal charm. Even as a dream interpreter he is a pragmatist, finding what will suffice, whether for himself or for all Egypt.

Tolstoy, well before Mann, had a passionate attachment to the story of Joseph. He found it to be both Tolstoyan and aesthetically superior to all of Western literature, Tolstoy and Homer included. Certainly it has a completeness in representing reality that rivals the narrative masters of *War and Peace* and the *Iliad*. There is also no fuller account of a father-son loving relationship in any literary work I have absorbed.

Tyndale translated the Hebrew *qetonet* that Jacob gives Joseph as "a coat of many colours" (37:3), a lovely conceit but not what the original means. Elsewhere in the Bible it is an elaborate long-sleeved tunic worn by a royal princess (2 Samuel 13:18), so here Jacob is implying that a royal quality is suitable for his favorite son. Mann goes further, making it a veiled garment embroidered with legends, initially worn by Rachel, Joseph's mother. Ironically, after Joseph's brothers have sold him into what will become his exalted Egyptian career, the coat, soaked with animal blood, convinces the grief-shattered Jacob that a wild beast has devoured his lost son.

The narrative of Joseph in Egypt, Genesis 39–50, is unlike anything else in the Hebrew Bible. Despite the many references to him, Yahweh appears only in 46:3–4, and he does not intervene directly. Weirdly we have a novel by Mann perhaps three thousand years before the time of the author of *The Magic Mountain* and *Doktor Faustus*. J's ironies are as incessant and lovely as Mann's, and Joseph charms us equally in Genesis and in *Joseph and His Brothers*. E. A. Speiser in his Anchor Genesis remarks that the tale is personal and secular, a story told for its own sake. Its grand climax is one of the KJB's great moments; when the brothers return from Egypt to tell Jacob-Israel the extraordinary good news:

> 25 ¶ And they went up out of Egypt, and came into the land of Canaan unto Jacob their father,
>
> 26 And told him, saying, Joseph *is* yet alive, and he *is* governor over all the land of Egypt. And Jacob's heart fainted, for he believed them not.
>
> 27 And they told him all the words of Joseph, which he had said unto them: and when he saw the wagons which Joseph had sent to carry him, the spirit of Jacob their father revived:
>
> 28 And Israel said, *It is* enough; Joseph my son *is* yet alive: I will go and see him before I die.
>
> [45:25–28]

Tyndale came a little short of such eloquence:

> And they departed from Egypt and came into the land of Canaan unto Jacob their father, and told him saying, Joseph is yet alive and is governor over all the land of Egypt. And Jacob's heart wavered, for he believed them

not. And they told him all the words of Joseph which he had said unto them. But when he saw the chariots which Joseph had sent to carry him, then his spirits revived. And Israel said: I have enough, if Joseph my son be yet alive: I will go and see him, ere that I die.

Geneva improved upon Tyndale:

25 ¶ Then they went up from Egypt, and came unto the land of Canaan unto Jacob their father,
26 And told him, saying, Joseph *is* yet alive, and he also is governor over all the land of Egypt, and *Jacob's* heart failed: for he believed them not.
27 And they told him all the words of Joseph, which he had said unto them: but when he saw the chariots, which Joseph had sent to carry him, then the spirit of Jacob their father revived.
28 And Israel said, *I have* enough: Joseph my son *is* yet alive: I will go and see him ere I die.

Israel's eloquence has perfect pitch in the KJB, a decorum maintained in the poignant reunion of Joseph and Israel:

29 And Joseph made ready his chariot, and went up to meet Israel his father, to Goshen, and presented himself unto him; and he fell on his neck, and wept on his neck a good while.
30 And Israel said unto Joseph, Now let me die, since I have seen thy face, because thou *art* yet alive.

[46:29–30]

Joseph momentarily becomes a child again while Jacob's composure does not alter, since as always he is a superb actor playing the role of Israel, the last Patriarch, in front of his people.

There are unresolved enigmas as the story of Joseph ends. As vizier of Egypt, Joseph had the power and the means to have informed his father many years earlier that Rachel's first-born lived and prospered. His long silence is inexplicable. More hurtful even is the account in 47:13–26 of Joseph's fleecing of the Egyptian populace on behalf of the Pharaoh. Perhaps it is one more assertion of the reality principle as Genesis nears its close.

Exodus

For the Children of Abraham—Jews, Christians, Muslims—Exodus is a book of revelation, of the Sinai theophany. For the modern world's liberation movements, Exodus has a primary message: Let my people go!

The unheroic hero Moses has little in common with Abraham, Jacob, Joseph, or King David, yet more than anyone else he is the central man of Judaic tradition. Was he an actual historical personage? Did the Exodus take place? We do not know and perhaps never will.

The second scroll of Torah in Hebrew begins, *ve-ellah shemot* (And these are the names), and so is known as *Shemot* (The names). In Greek this was named *exodos,* the "way out," *exodus* in Latin. Exodus is so epic in scope that I am surprised when I reflect that it is shorter than Genesis—forty chapters in fifty-four pages, compared to fifty chapters in sixty-five. But then Genesis goes from the Creation to Israel's descent into Egypt, while Exodus concludes with Yahweh's radiance ("glory") moving from Sinai to the sanctuary of the Tabernacle.

These two scrolls, though they are in sequence, are very different in spiritual and aesthetic ways, and seem to me impossible to compare with each other. The covenants of Yahweh with Noah, Abraham, and Jacob pertain to individuals and their families. In

Exodus, Moses mediates between an entire people and God, and covenant is subsumed in revelation. Like its descendants Christianity and Islam, Judaism is a revealed religion, however rationalized by a cosmos of subsequent commentary.

The grand protagonists of Exodus, Moses and Yahweh, are problematic because there are three principal authors at work depicting them, and the Redactor scarcely bothers to disentangle his sources. The J Writer's Moses is viewed with ironic sympathy, while the Priestly Writer is cautiously reserved. Only the Elohist regards Moses with reverent awe, anticipating the prophet's exaltation in Deuteronomy. As for Yahweh, J is always prepared to be surprised, unlike the gaze of worship in P and E.

J's Moses accurately doubts his own qualifications for leadership. He lacks patience, calm, and self-confidence. Nor is he an orator; his mouth is "heavy" ("slow of speech," in KJB Exodus 4:10). It may be that he is a stammerer, though that is unclear. Four separate times he evades Yahweh's prophetic call. Such reluctance cannot turn God from his choice. Why Yahweh has chosen this unlikely hero is never clarified for us, but that is aesthetically very satisfying. When at last Moses is allowed only a view of Canaan and denied entrance, it is superbly appropriate that the prophet should be buried by Yahweh's own hands in an unmarked grave, its location forever unknown to us.

Chapter 3, verses 1–6, of Exodus is one of the great epiphanies in the KJB:

> 1 Now Moses kept the flock of Jethro his father in law, the priest of Midian: and he led the flock to the backside of the desert, and came to the mountain of God, *even* to Horeb.
>
> 2 And the angel of the LORD appeared unto him in a

flame of fire out of the midst of a bush: and he looked, and, behold, the bush burned with fire, and the bush *was* not consumed.

3 And Moses said, I will now turn aside, and see this great sight, why the bush is not burnt.

4 And when the LORD saw that he turned aside to see, God called unto him out of the midst of the bush, and said, Moses, Moses. And he said, Here *am* I.

5 And he said, Draw not nigh hither: put off thy shoes from off thy feet, for the place whereon thou standest *is* holy ground.

6 Moreover he said, I *am* the God of thy father, the God of Abraham, the God of Isaac, and the God of Jacob. And Moses hid his face; for he was afraid to look upon God.

Fire contrasts with desolate Mount Horeb, which is also called Sinai, perhaps from the thornbush, *seneh,* that dots it. A flaming thornbush that cannot be consumed is a message unmistakably marked as Yahweh's. The reluctance of Moses to accept the call is phrased perfectly as "Who am I?" That leads to perhaps the most extraordinary exchange in all the Hebrew Bible:

13 And Moses said unto God, Behold, *when* I come unto the children of Israel, and shall say unto them, The God of your fathers hath sent me unto you; and they shall say to me, What *is* his name? what shall I say unto them?

14 And God said unto Moses, I AM THAT I AM: and he said, Thus shalt thou say unto the children of Israel, I AM hath sent me unto you.

Tyndale has Yahweh say, "I will be what I will be," but Geneva gives the powerful though misleading "I Am That I Am," which the KJB adopts. I prefer Tyndale since the Hebrew *ehyeh asher ehyeh* can be translated "I will be who I will be" or "I bring into being what I bring into being." Sublimely punning upon his own name, Yahweh tells Moses (and all of us) that he will be present wherever and whenever he chooses to be. Unfortunately this contains the implication that he will be absent wherever and whenever he decides to be.

Persuaded despite his sizable misgivings, Moses has to survive the ordeal of Yahweh's murderousness:

> 24 ¶ And it came to pass by the way in the inn, that the LORD met him, and sought to kill him.
>
> 25 Then Zipporah took a sharp stone, and cut off the foreskin of her son, and cast *it* at his feet, and said, Surely a bloody husband *art* thou to me.
>
> 26 So he let him go: then she said, A bloody husband *thou art,* because of the circumcision.
>
> [4:24–26]

The Hebrew gives *malon,* the night lodging, which prompted the great orthodox Jewish exegete Rashi to a desperate absurdity: Moses tarried at an inn rather than tumbling down into Egypt! We cannot surmise Yahweh's motive; does he have one? He wills what he wills, and backs away from Zipporah's bitter courage. The J Writer, as William H. C. Propp shrewdly notes in volume 1 of the Anchor Yale Bible Exodus (1999), takes no interest in circumcision, and the Redactor interpolates the Priestly Writer in 4:26. Alas, Propp is too anxious to find a motive for Yahweh's murderousness and so discovers it in Exodus 2:12, where Moses slays an Egyptian, an act Yahweh cannot be expected to censure! Samuel Taylor Coleridge memorably wrote of "Iago's motiveless malignity." Though Coleridge may have been wrong since Iago's motives were ontological, this prods me to analyze Yahweh's motiveless malignity. A God who names himself by punning upon "being" may act violently in defense of his ontological priority over even his chosen prophet. Martin Buber in his book on Moses oddly says of Yahweh's outrageousness in this incident: "He claims the entirety of the one he has chosen." Murder is surely not a useful way of asserting such a claim.

Aaron, brother to and spokesman for Moses, unsurprisingly is emphasized in the Priestly portions of the saga. Since he can be regarded as the first priest (depending upon which of the Exodus sources is invoked), he is close ally to the prophet Moses yet also potentially an antithetical rival.

Not even the combined force of Moses and Aaron can bend Pharaoh until Yahweh afflicts the Egyptians with the ten proverbial plagues. In the Priestly text, the plagues are supernatural emblems but not yet full marks of Yahweh's power. The secular texts, Yahwist and Elohist, make the plagues an agon between Moses and Pharaoh, in which both behave rather dubiously.

After the account in 12:1–13:16 of the first Passover, Exodus moves to its visionary climax in 13:17–15:21: the crossing of the Reed Sea (*yam suf*) and Moses' and Miriam's great song of triumph, equal to the War Song of Deborah in its antiquity and extraordinary poetic power. In 14:26–30, the KJB adds very little to Tyndale and Geneva, but it would be difficult to better Tyndale's narrative swiftness and economy, which matches the Hebrew original:

> When now Moses stretched forth his hand over the sea, the Lord carried away the sea with a strong east wind that blew all night, and made the sea dry land and the water divided itself. And the children of Israel went in through the midst of the sea upon the dry ground. And the water was a wall unto them, both on their right hand and on

their left hand. And the Egyptians followed and went in after them to the midst of the sea, with all Pharao's horses, and his chariots and his horsemen.

And in the morning watch, the Lord looked unto the host of the Egyptians out of the fiery and cloudy pillar, and troubled their host and smote off their chariot wheels and cast them down to the ground. Then said the Egyptians: Let us flee from Israel, for the Lord fighteth for them against us. Then said the Lord unto Moses: stretch out thine hand over the sea, that the water may come again upon the Egyptians upon their chariots and horsemen. Then stretched forth Moses his hand over the sea, and it came again to his course early in the morning, and the Egyptians fled against it. Thus the Lord overthrew the Egyptians in the midst of the sea, and the water returned and covered the chariots and the horsemen: so that of all the host of Pharao that came into the sea after them, there remained not one. But the children of Israel went upon dry land in the midst of the sea, and the water was a wall unto them: both on the right hand of them and also on the left.

Thus the Lord delivered Israel the selfsame day out of the hand of the Egyptians, and Israel saw the Egyptians dead upon the sea side.

[14:7–9]

The Song of the Sea (15:1–18) is composed in so difficult and archaic a Hebrew as to daunt me. I am not equal to judging the aesthetic contrast between the original and the KJB version, particularly since Handel's setting of it (*Israel in Egypt*) will not leave my inner ear. Let us start with Propp's literal rendering in the Anchor Exodus:

¹Then sang Moses and Israel's Sons this song of
    Yahweh, and they said, saying:
I would sing of Yahweh, for he acted exaltedly,
    exaltedly!
Horse and his driver he hurled into the Sea.

²My strength and my power/music is Yah;
And he was for me as salvation.

This is my god, and I exalt him,
My father's deity, and I elevate him:
³Yahweh Man of War, Yahweh is his name.

⁴Pharaoh's chariots and his force he cast into the Sea.
And the choice of his *thirds* were sunk in the Suph
    Sea.

⁵Deeps, they cover them;
They went down in the depths like stone.

⁶Your right hand, Yahweh, strong in might,
Your right hand, Yahweh, you shatter enemy.

⁷And in your pride's greatness you break down your
    uprisers.
You release your anger; it consumes them as straw.

⁸And with your nostrils' breath waters were piled;
Streams stood like a heap.
Deeps congealed in Sea's heart.

⁹Enemy said,
"I'll pursue, overtake,
Apportion spoil.

My gullet will be full of them.

I'll *empty* my sword.
My hand will dispossess thezm."

¹⁰You blew with your breath; Sea covered them.
They sank like lead in strong waters.

¹¹Who as you among gods, Yahweh,
Who as you is strong in holiness,
Dreadful of glory, worker of wonder?

¹²You extended your right arm;
Earth swallows them.

¹³You led by your grace the people which you
    redeemed;
You guided by your might to your holiness's pasture/
    camp/tent.

¹⁴Peoples heard. They shudder.
Convulsion seized Philistia's inhabitants.

¹⁵Then perturbed were Edom's princes.
Moab's *rams,* quaking seizes them.
Liquefied were all Canaan's inhabitants.

¹⁶Upon them fall fear and terror.
At your limb's greatness they are still as stone,

Till crosses your people, Yahweh,
Till crosses the people which you have gotten.

¹⁷May you bring them and plant them in your property
    mountain,
The firm seat for your sitting/throne/dwelling you
    devised, Yahweh,
The sanctum, my Lordship, your hands founded.

[18]Yahweh, he will reign, ever and eternity.

[19]For Pharaoh's horse, with his chariotry and his horse-men, entered the Sea, and Yahweh brought back upon them the Sea's waters. But Israel's Sons walked on the dry land in the Sea's midst. [20]And Miriam the prophetess, Aaron's sister, took the drum in her hand, and all the women went forth behind her with drums and with dances. [21]And Miriam sang back to them:

"Sing of Yahweh, for he acted exaltedly, exaltedly!
Horse and his driver he hurled into the Sea."

The aesthetic limitations of a literal translation from archaic Hebrew are palpable, yet Propp labors to be useful, and he is. Tyndale, marvelously transforming lyric into narrative, necessarily loses the song and gives us the fierce ecstasy:

Then Moses and the children of Israel sang this song unto the Lord and said:

Let us sing unto the Lord, for he is become glorious, the horse and him that rode upon him hath he overthrown in the sea.

The Lord is my strength and my song, and is become my salvation.

He is my God and I will glorify him, he is my father's God and I will lift him up on high.

The Lord is a man of war, Jehovah is his name: Pharao's chariots and his host hath he cast into the sea.

His jolly captains are drowned in the Red sea, the deep waters have covered them: they sank to the bottom as a stone.

Thine hand Lord is glorious in power, thine hand Lord hath all to-dashed the enemy.

The Hebrew Bible

And with thy great glory thou hast destroyed thine adversaries, thou sentest forth thy wrath and it consumed them: even as stubble.

With the breath of thine anger the water gathered together and the floods stood still as a rock, and the deep water congealed together in the midst of the sea.

The enemy said, I will follow and overtake thee and will divide the spoil: I will satisfy my lust upon them: I will draw my sword and mine hand shall destroy them.

Thou blewest with thy breath and the sea covered them, and they sank as lead in the mighty waters.

Who is like unto thee O Lord among gods: who is like thee so glorious in holiness, fearful, laudable and that showest wonders?

Thou stretchedest out thy right hand, and in the earth swallowed them.

And thou carriedest with thy mercy this people which thou deliveredest, and broughtest them with thy strength unto thy holy habitation.

The nations heard and were afraid, pangs came upon the Philistines.

Then the dukes of the Edomites were amazed, and trembling came upon the mightiest of the Moabites, and all the inhabiters of Canaan waxed faint-hearted.

Let fear and dread fall upon them through the greatness of thine arm, and let them be as still as a stone, while thy people pass through O Lord, while the people pass through, which thou hast gotten.

Bring them in and plant them in the mountains of thine inheritance, the place Lord which thou hast made for thee to dwell in, the sanctuary Lord which thy hands have prepared.

The Lord reign ever and always.

For Pharao went in on horseback with his chariots and horsemen into the sea, and the Lord brought the waters of the sea upon them. And the children of Israel went on dry land through the midst of the sea.

And Miriam a prophetess the sister of Aaron took a timbrel in her hand, and all the women came out after her with timbrels in a dance. And Miriam sang before them: sing ye unto the Lord, for he is become glorious indeed: the horse and his rider hath he overthrown in the sea.

[15:1–24]

Who would want to lose "His jolly captains" and much else in this exuberant vernacular? The Geneva men, rather than Tyndale, proved the model for the matchless KJB refinement of the martyr's rough prose music:

1 Then sang Moses and the children of Israel this song unto the Lord, and spake, saying, I will sing unto the Lord, for he hath triumphed gloriously: the horse and his rider hath he thrown into the sea.

2 The Lord *is* my strength and song, and he is become my salvation: he *is* my God, and I will prepare him an habitation; my father's God, and I will exalt him.

3 The Lord *is* a man of war: the Lord *is* his name.

4 Pharaoh's chariots and his host hath he cast into the sea: his chosen captains also are drowned in the Red sea.

5 The depths have covered them: they sank into the bottom as a stone.

6 Thy right hand, O Lord, is become glorious in power: thy right hand, O Lord, hath dashed in pieces the enemy.

7 And in the greatness of thine excellency thou hast

overthrown them that rose up against thee: thou sentest forth thy wrath, *which* consumed them as stubble.

8 And with the blast of thy nostrils the waters were gathered together, the floods stood upright as an heap, *and* the depths were congealed in the heart of the sea.

9 The enemy said, I will pursue, I will overtake, I will divide the spoil; my lust shall be satisfied upon them; I will draw my sword, my hand shall destroy them.

10 Thou didst blow with thy wind, the sea covered them: they sank as lead in the mighty waters.

11 Who *is* like unto thee, O LORD, among the gods？ who *is* like thee, glorious in holiness, fearful *in* praises, doing wonders？

12 Thou stretchedst out thy right hand, the earth swallowed them.

13 Thou in thy mercy hast led forth the people *which* thou hast redeemed: thou hast guided *them* in thy strength unto thy holy habitation.

14 The people shall hear, *and* be afraid: sorrow shall take hold on the inhabitants of Palestina.

15 Then the dukes of Edom shall be amazed; the mighty men of Moab, trembling shall take hold upon them; all the inhabitants of Canaan shall melt away.

16 Fear and dread shall fall upon them; by the greatness of thine arm they shall be *as* still as a stone; till thy people pass over, O LORD, till the people pass over, *which* thou has purchased.

17 Thou shalt bring them in, and plant them in the mountain of thine inheritance, *in* the place, O LORD, *which* thou hast made for thee to dwell in, *in* the Sanctuary, O Lord, *which* thy hands have established.

18 The LORD shall reign for ever and ever.

19 For the horse of Pharaoh went in with his chariots and with his horsemen into the sea, and the LORD brought again the waters of the sea upon them; but the children of Israel went on dry *land* in the midst of the sea.

20 ¶ And Miriam the prophetess, the sister of Aaron, took a timbrel in her hand; and all the women went out after her with timbrels and with dances.

21 And Miriam answered them, Sing ye to the LORD, for he hath triumphed gloriously; the horse and his rider hath he thrown into the sea.

The Yahweh of Exodus is a man of war, and this song celebrates *his* victory and scants Moses. In 15:11 "the gods" presumably are the angels of Yahweh's heavenly court. Like most victory odes, the Song of Moses offers exultation at the cost of wisdom and can leave the wary reader a little chilled.

After liberation, we are subject to the trials of wilderness wandering until the Sinai revelation in chapter 19, which continues through chapter 24. In a sense, the rest of Exodus, and all of Numbers after it, is a continual juxtaposition between revelation and wilderness. Since my long-ago childhood, I have wondered at a forty years' wandering back and forth in the Sinai, between the symbolic extremes of Egypt and Canaan. The outrageousness of what Yahweh imposes upon his wretched chosen people somehow has escaped commentary, ancient and modern, rabbinical and scholarly. Who can journey forty years in the waste lands without anguish and discontent? Is that part of the Blessing?

The theophany on the mountain (19:16) is a composite J-E text, given here in the KJB:

And it came to pass on the third day in the morning, that there were thunders and lightnings, and a thick cloud upon the mount, and the voice of the trumpet exceeding loud; so that all the people that *was* in the camp trembled.

Propp attempts to disengage the two sources:

J. [16]And it happened on the third day at morning's happening, [18]and Mount Sinai, it smoked, all of it, forasmuch as Yahweh had descended upon it in fire, and its smoke ascended like furnace smoke, and all the mountain quaked greatly. [20]And Yahweh descended onto Mount Sinai, to the mountain's head, and Yahweh called Moses to the mountain's head. And Moses ascended.

E. [16]And there were sounds and lightnings and a heavy cloud on the mountain and a horn's sound, very strong. And all the people who were in the camp quaked. [17]And Moses took the people out to meet the Deity from the camp, and they stationed themselves at the mountain's bottom. [19]And the horn's sound was going and strengthening greatly; Moses, he would speak, and the Deity, he would answer him with sound.

[Anchor Yale Bible Exodus 19–40 (2006)]

The J Writer creates irony through a fusion of ellipsis and acute literalization. Yahweh, already given to irritation, is unhappy with his covenanted obligation to extend his Blessing to all of the people at the foot of his Holy Mountain. He suddenly becomes self-contradictory: he *cannot* be seen by the people, and yet he will be seen, since he will come down upon Sinai in the sight of all the people:

20 And the LORD came down upon mount Sinai, on the top of the mount: and the LORD called Moses up to the top of the mount; and Moses went up.

21 And the LORD said unto Moses, Go down, charge the

people, lest they break through unto the Lord to gaze, and many of them perish.

22 And let the priests also, which come near to the Lord, sanctify themselves, lest the Lord break forth upon them.

23 And Moses said unto the Lord, The people cannot come up to mount Sinai: for thou chargedst us, saying, Set bounds about the mount, and sanctify it.

24 And the Lord said unto him, Away, get thee down, and thou shalt come up, thou, and Aaron with thee: but let not the priests and the people break through to come up unto the Lord, lest he break forth upon them.

25 So Moses went down unto the people, and spake unto them.

The astonishing climax comes in chapter 24:

9 ¶ Then went up Moses, and Aaron, Nadab, and Abihu, and seventy of the elders of Israel:

10 And they saw the God of Israel: and *there was* under his feet as it were a paved work of a sapphire stone, and as it were the body of heaven in *his* clearness.

11 And upon the nobles of the children of Israel he laid not his hand: also they saw God, and did eat and drink.

The KJB, refining Geneva, phrases this so nobly that we are likely to glide over the shock of what we are being told. Seventy-four eminences of Israel sit upon Sinai, picnicking as guests of their Creator, and stare at him while he stares back. He says nothing (unique in Tanakh) and presumably himself does not eat. Propp charmingly wonders *what* they ate, but then Yahweh demands so many burnt offerings that a surplus must be available at all times. We know from Mamre, where Sarah fed him, that Yahweh decidedly is not a vegetarian.

After the Sinai theophany, the Redactor so confounds his sources with one another that little coherence obtains. The commandments, whatever their moral value, need not be considered in an aesthetic appreciation, nor do the instructions for confecting the Tabernacle and the Ark.

Though the doctrinal and metaphorical importance and vitality of Exodus are beyond question, it hardly seems to me the literary equal of Genesis, whether in the Hebrew Bible or the KJB. The great personalities of Genesis, Jacob and Joseph, are sadly lacking in Exodus, where Moses is a somewhat confused enigma. And the Yahweh of Genesis, human-all-too-human and approachable, has a dramatic intensity not achieved—except in spasms—by the jealous overlord of Exodus.

Numbers

Herbert Marks accurately calls Numbers "the Bible's most unruly book." Since it opens with a census, it is termed "Numbers" in the English Bible, following Greek and Latin. One prefers "In the Wilderness" (*Bamidbar*), the Hebrew naming.

As a reader, I remain always unhappy with Numbers, an endless Priestly castigation of the suffering Israelite host. They behave no better than they should as they are marched by Moses for forty years through the desolate places, all too frequently parched and famished. Yahweh monstrously punishes their murmurings with flaming serpents or just plain fire, and also by the plague. Liking this god or trusting him seems beyond human compass, yet he will not just go away. His personality endures.

The Priestly redactors, after returning from exile in Babylon, evidently put together much of Numbers, more or less in the spirit of Leviticus, which I find unreadable. Chapters 11–25 are a J-E amalgam, refreshingly so, while chapters 26–39, though heavily edited by the Priestly scribes, still retain narrative rigor from their secular origins.

For much of what I can apprehend about Numbers, I am indebted to the splendid Anchor Yale Bible exegesis by Baruch Levine (1993, 2000). He emphasizes that the Priestly Writers altered the character of Numbers, ultimately attributing all that mattered to the Sinai theophany. They also exchanged evident history for cultic purposes, thus manifesting what Levine calls "a loaded agenda." Narrative, in their rescension, continually yields to ritual, and to a positive relish for Yahweh's savage retributions.

What in KJB Numbers is of authentic literary value? I would say, wherever traces of the J Writer's voice emerge: in 10:29–36, 13, 16, 22–24, 25:1–5, and two passages reft away into Deuteronomy, 31:14–15, 31:23, and 34:1h–5a, 6, and 10. The story of Balaam the Seer, 22–24, is almost sufficient in itself to redeem Numbers, since it is both a comic triumph and a critique of the shifting borderlines where magic and prophecy meet and mingle.

Balaam's name *may* mean "destruction by being swallowed." He is bad news: a hired gun of a prophet, skilled alike at curses and blessings. Retained by the king of Moab to curse the advancing and too-numerous Israelites, Balaam involuntarily blesses them. The story's heroine is Balaam's amiable and ill-treated donkey, who in chapter 22 saves the great charlatan from riding blindly into the sword of destruction wielded by Yahweh's angel:

> 21 And Balaam rose up in the morning, and saddled his ass, and went with the princes of Moab.
> 22 ¶ And God's anger was kindled because he went: and the angel of the LORD stood in the way for an adversary

against him. Now he was riding upon his ass, and his two servants *were* with him.

23 And the ass saw the angel of the Lᴏʀᴅ standing in the way, and his sword drawn in his hand: and the ass turned aside out of the way, and went into the field: and Balaam smote the ass, to turn her into the way.

24 But the angel of the Lᴏʀᴅ stood in a path of the vineyards, a wall *being* on this side, and a wall on that side.

25 And when the ass saw the angel of the Lᴏʀᴅ, she thrust herself unto the wall, and crushed Balaam's foot against the wall; and he smote her again.

26 And the angel of the Lᴏʀᴅ went further, and stood in a narrow place, where *was* no way to turn either to the right hand or to the left.

27 And when the ass saw the angel of the Lᴏʀᴅ, she fell down under Balaam: and Balaam's anger was kindled, and he smote the ass with a staff.

28 And the Lᴏʀᴅ opened the mouth of the ass, and she said unto Balaam, What have I done unto thee, that thou hast smitten me these three times?

29 And Balaam said unto the ass, Because thou hast mocked me: I would there were a sword in mine hand, for now would I kill thee.

30 And the ass said unto Balaam, *Am* not I thine ass, upon which thou hast ridden ever since *I was* thine unto this day? was I ever wont to do so unto thee? And he said, Nay.

31 Then the Lᴏʀᴅ opened the eyes of Balaam, and he saw the angel of the Lᴏʀᴅ standing in the way, and his sword drawn in his hand: and he bowed down his head, and fell flat on his face.

32 And the angel of the Lord said unto him, Wherefore hast thou smitten thine ass these three times‽ behold, I went out to withstand thee, because *thy* way is perverse before me:

33 And the ass saw me, and turned from me these three times: unless she had turned from me, surely now also I had slain thee, and saved her alive.

34 And Balaam said unto the angel of the Lord, I have sinned; for I knew not that thou stoodest in the way against me: now therefore, if it displease thee, I will get me back again.

35 And the angel of the Lord said unto Balaam, Go with the men: but only the word that I shall speak unto thee, that thou shalt speak. So Balaam went with the princes of Balak.

The lovely irony of the donkey who sees all too well as opposed to her rider, a professional seer who cannot see, is presented here with a humor too grand for a common reader to resist. Learning his own survival lesson, Balaam blesses rather than curses the Israelites. His blessings are constituted by archaic poems, which are at moments very powerful:

5 How goodly are thy tents, O Jacob, *and* thy tabernacles, O Israel!

6 As the valleys are they spread forth, as gardens by the river's side, as the trees of lign aloes which the Lord hath planted, *and* as cedar trees beside the waters.

7 He shall pour the water out of his buckets, and his seed *shall be* in many waters, and his king shall be higher than Agag, and his kingdom shall be exalted.

8 God brought him forth out of Egypt; he hath as it were the strength of an unicorn: he shall eat up the nations

his enemies, and shall break their bones, and pierce *them* through with his arrows.

9 He couched, he lay down as a lion, and as a great lion: who shall stir him up? Blessed *is* he that blesseth thee, and cursed *is* he that curseth thee.

[24:5–9]

Equally strong, a further blessing inspires the KJB translators to capital lettering, implying that the prophecy foretells Jesus Christ:

17 I shall see him, but not now: I shall behold him, but not nigh: there shall come a Star out of Jacob, and a Sceptre shall rise out of Israel, and shall smite the corners of Moab, and destroy all the children of Sheth.

18 And Edom shall be a possession, Seir also shall be a possession for his enemies; and Israel shall do valiantly.

19 Out of Jacob shall come he that shall have dominion, and shall destroy him that remaineth of the city.

[24:17–19]

After the Balaam episode, the most memorable passages in Numbers concern Aaron, whom the book seems to prefer over Moses. Harshness is the characteristic trait of Yahweh in Numbers; like the multitudes in the wilderness, he at times seems half-crazed. The flowering of Aaron's rod (17:1–11) is an emblem that only the priesthood flourishes in Numbers. Moses and the people endure suffering piled upon suffering, but these do not placate an angry God.

Deuteronomy

In Hebrew tradition the book of Deuteronomy (Greek for "second law") was called *Mishneh Torah* (copy of the law) but also *Devarim* (the Words). Its literary interest is considerable in chapters 1–11; in chapter 32, the Song of Moses; and in the final chapter, 34, the death of Moses.

After David, the Hebrew Bible exalts two kings of Judah, Hezekiah (2 Kings 18:1–8) and Josiah (2 Kings 23:4–25). Deuteronomy, in its original form, emerged from their militantly pious reigns in the seventh century B.C.E. In 2 Kings 22:8–11, the young king Josiah receives the original book of Deuteronomy from the high priest:

> 8 ¶ And Hilkiah the high priest said unto Shaphan the scribe, I have found the book of the law in the house of the LORD. And Hilkiah gave the book to Shaphan, and he read it.
>
> 9 And Shaphan the scribe came to the king, and brought the king word again, and said, Thy servants have gathered the money that was found in the house, and have delivered it into the hand of them that do the work, that have the oversight of the house of the LORD.
>
> 10 And Shaphan the scribe shewed the king, saying, Hilkiah the priest hath delivered me a book. And Shaphan read it before the king.
>
> 11 And it came to pass, when the king had heard the words of the book of the law, that he rent his clothes.

My polite skepticism is somewhat disarmed by current scholarship, which asserts that the book hidden in the Temple was very likely a brief first version of Deuteronomy, composed earlier in the seventh century B.C.E. under Hezekiah. Moshe Weinfeld, the Israeli authority on Deuteronomy, has a useful caution concerning our anachronistic notion of "composing" a book:

> Today when we speak of a book, we mean a composition written by a certain person at a specific place and time:

every line is impressed with the personality of the author and the period and milieu in which it was written. Such was not the case in Israel or in the ancient East. Even in the book of Ecclesiastes, which comes closer to the concept of a modern book, we find sections of which similar examples can be found in Babylonian and Egyptian literature from the first half of the second millennium B.C.E. . . . The author of ancient times was generally a collector and compiler of traditions rather than a creator of literature, and was certainly not an author in the modern sense of the term. Even if the book of Deuteronomy had been put into writing in the days of Hezekiah-Josiah, that does not mean to say that all of its contents reflect that period, for in the book of Deuteronomy there have been preserved for us very ancient laws, especially in sections that have no connection with the subject of the centralization of the cult, such as chaps. 21–25. Even the laws that have as their basis the idea of the centralization of the cult, such as the regulations of the firstfruits, the firstborn animals, and tithes, the festival of the Passover, and other festivals are not in themselves within the category of an innovation, for they comprised some of the most ancient precepts of Israel; only, during the period of Hezekiah and Josiah, they were adapted to the principle of the centralization of the cult and were written anew. We can comprehend this process of adaptation by way of a comparison of these laws with the other collections of ancient laws. . . . It is impossible to come to a decision concerning the date of Deuteronomy without comparing every individual law included in it with the same law as it appears in the other collections, in the book of covenant and the holiness code.

[Anchor Yale Bible Deuteronomy 1–11 (1991)]

There are other problems the reader should consider. Deuteronomy centers upon an event that never happened, the assembly of all the Israelites in Moab, across the Jordan, where they are addressed—at considerable length—by Moses. They will cross over into Canaan (or their children will), but Moses will die in Transjordan. We listen to oracular oratory, much of it pitched rather high, in which the history of the Hebrews is recast from a priestly perspective that insists upon the centralization of Yahweh's cult in the Jerusalem Temple.

Severely revisionist, Deuteronomy confines the Sinai revelation to the Ten Commandments, reserving all the rest of Torah to Moses the proclaimer at the Moab assembly. In a sense, Deuteronomy begins that strong misreading of earlier texts that will culminate with the rabbis of Akiba's circle in the second century of the Common Era. The religion of Akiba, our normative Judaism, stems more from Deuteronomy than from the Covenant code of Exodus 20:23–23:19. Since the sequence of "histories" from Joshua on through Judges and Samuel to Kings was shaped by the school of Deuteronomists, they are the precursors of Akiba.

The KJB, itself baroque as to rhetorical temper, in some ways is closer in spirit to the Hebrew Deuteronomy's elevated style than is Tyndale's sinewy narrative or the Geneva Bible's earnest rendering of an inspired Moses. Contrast the magnificent KJB Song of Moses, 32:1–15, with its English precursors:

> 1 Give ear, O ye heavens, and I will speak; and hear, O earth, the words of my mouth.
> 2 My doctrine shall drop as the rain, my speech shall distil as the dew, as the small rain upon the tender herb, and as the showers upon the grass:

3 Because I will publish the name of the LORD: ascribe ye greatness unto our God.

4 *He is* the Rock, his work *is* perfect: for all his ways *are* judgment: a God of truth and without iniquity, just and right *is* he.

5 They have corrupted themselves, their spot *is* not *the spot* of his children: *they are* a perverse and crooked generation.

6 Do ye thus requite the LORD, O foolish people and unwise? *is* not he thy father *that* hath brought thee? hath he not made thee, and established thee?

7 ¶ Remember the days of old, consider the years of many generations: ask thy father, and he will shew thee; thy elders, and they will tell thee.

8 When the most High divided to the nations their inheritance, when he separated the sons of Adam, he set the bounds of the people according to the number of the children of Israel.

9 For the LORD's portion *is* his people; Jacob *is* the lot of his inheritance.

10 He found him in a desert land, and in the waste howling wilderness; he led him about, he instructed him, he kept him as the apple of his eye.

11 As an eagle stirreth up her nest, fluttereth over her young, spreadeth abroad her wings, taketh them, beareth them on her wings:

12 *So* the LORD alone did lead him, and *there was* no strange god with him.

13 He made him ride on the high places of the earth, that he might eat the increase of the fields; and he made him to suck honey out of the rock, and oil out of the flinty rock;

14 Butter of kine, and milk of sheep, with fat of lambs, and rams of the breed of Bashan, and goats, with the fat of kidneys of wheat; and thou didst drink the pure blood of the grape.

15 ¶ But Jeshurun waxed fat, and kicked: thou art waxen fat, thou art grown thick, thou art covered *with fatness;* then he forsook God *which* made him, and lightly esteemed the Rock of his salvation.

[KJB]

Hear O heaven, what I shall speak and hear O earth the words of my mouth.

My doctrine drop as doth the rain, and my speech flow as doth the dew, as the mizzling upon the herbs, and as the drops upon the grass. For I will call on the name of the Lord: Magnify the might of our God.

He is a rock and perfect are his deeds, for all his ways are with discretion. God is faithful and without wickedness, both righteous and just is he.

The froward and overthwart generation hath marred themselves to him-ward, and are not his sons for their deformities' sake.

Dost thou so reward the Lord? O foolish nation and unwise. Is not he thy father and thine owner? hath he not made thee and ordained thee?

Remember the days that are past: consider the years from time to time. Ask thy father and he will shew thee, thine elders and they will tell thee.

When the most highest gave the nations an inheritance, and divided the sons of Adam, he put the borders of the nations, fast by the multitude of the children of Israel.

For the Lord's part is his folk, and Israel is the portion of his inheritance.

He found him in a desert land, in a void ground and a roaring wilderness. He led him about and gave him understanding, and kept him as the apple of his eye.

As an eagle that stirreth up her nest and fluttereth over her young, he stretched out his wings and took him up and bare him on his shoulders.

The Lord alone was his guide, and there was no strange god with him.

He set him up upon an high land, and he ate the increase of the fields. And he gave him honey to suck out of the rock, and oil out of the hard stone.

With butter of the kine and milk of the sheep, with fat of the lambs and fat rams and he goats with fat kidneys and with wheat. And of the blood of grapes thou drunkest wine.

And Israel waxed fat and kicked. Thou wast fat, thick and smooth. And he let God go that made him and despised the rock that saved him.

[Tyndale]

1   Hearken, ye heavens, and I will speak: and let the earth hear the words of my mouth.
2   My doctrine shall drop as the rain, *and* my speech shall still as doeth the dew, as the shower upon the herbs, and as the great rain upon the grass.
3   For I will publish the Name of the Lord: give ye glory unto our God.
4   Perfect is the work of the mighty God: for all his ways *are* judgment. God is true, and without wickedness: just, and righteous is he.

5   They have corrupted them selves toward him by their vice, not being his children, *but* a frowarde and crooked generation.

6   Do ye so reward the Lord, o foolish people and un-wise? is not he thy father, that hath bought thee? he hath made thee, and proportioned thee.

7   Remember the days of old: consider the years of so many generations: ask thy father, and he will shew thee: thine Elders, and they will tell thee.

8   When the most high *God* divided to the nations their inheritance, when he separated the sons of Adam, he appointed the borders of the people according to the number of the children of Israel.

9   For the Lord's portion *is* his people: Jacob *is* the lot of his inheritance.

10   He found him in the land of the wilderness, in a waste, and roaring wilderness: he led them about, he taught him, *and* kept him as the apple of his eye.

11   As an eagle stirreth up her nest, fluttereth over her birds, stretcheth out her wings, taketh them, *and* beareth them on her wings,

12   *So* the Lord alone led him and there was no strange god with him.

13   He carried him up to the high places of the earth, that he might eat the fruits of the fields, and he caused him to suck honey out of the stone and oil out of the hard rock.

14   Butter of kine, and milk of sheep with fat of the lambs, and rams fed in Bashan and goats, with the fat of the grains of wheat, and the red liquor of the grape hast thou drunk.

15   But *he that should have been* upright, when he waxed

fat, spurned with his heel: thou art fat, thou art gross, thou art laden with fatness: therefore he forsook God *that* made him, and regarded not the strong God of his salvation.

[Geneva]

As rhetoric the KJB is far stronger here than Tyndale and Geneva, and its Song of Moses has opened magnificently. "Doctrine" in verse 2 is *torah* in the Hebrew, while "spot" in 5 is read by Marks as "blemish." "Bought" in the next verse should be "created," while the famous "apple of his eye" in 10 is "little man of his eye" in Hebrew, meaning the reflection in the pupil. "Fat . . . of wheat" is the best wheat, and *Jeshurun* is "straight" or "upright," used for Israel in Isaiah 44:2, though its employment here is palpable irony. I myself, superb as I find the Song of Moses to be, resent the sarcasm it manifests toward the hapless Israelites.

Tyndale is wonderful in his vernacular exuberance in verse 15: "And Israel waxed fat and kicked. Thou wast fat, thick, and smooth." The KJB, more dignified, might be speaking of Sir John Falstaff. Geneva here seems preferable to both Tyndale and the KJB:

But he *that should have been* upright, when he waxed fat, spurned with his heel: thou art fat, thou art gross, thou art laden with fatness.

Shakespeare, imbued with the Geneva Bible, may have Prince Hal recalling that remonstrance in his castigations of Falstaff. So vigorous are all three—Tyndale, Geneva, KJB—that they challenge their Hebrew original.

Deuteronomy concludes majestically with chapter 34, where Yahweh grants Moses his Pisgah sight from Mount Nebo of the Promised Land:

4 And the Lord said unto him, This *is* the land which I sware unto Abraham, unto Isaac, and unto Jacob, saying, I will give it unto thy seed: I have caused thee to see *it* with thine eyes, but thou shalt not go over thither.

5 ¶ So Moses the servant of the Lord died there in the land of Moab, according to the word of the Lord.

6 And he buried him in a valley in the land of Moab, over against Beth-peor: but no man knoweth of his sepulchre unto this day.

7 ¶ And Moses *was* an hundred and twenty years old when he died: his eye was not dim nor his natural force abated.

Buried in an unmarked grave, unknown forever, Yahweh's greatest prophet cannot be made into a shrine, a site for pilgrimages. The final tribute is beyond ambiguity:

And there arose not a prophet since in Israel like unto Moses, whom the Lord knew face to face.

[34:10]

Four Heroines

Deborah (Judges 5)

WE REMEMBER THE BOOK OF JUDGES for its most eminent leaders:
Deborah, Gideon, Samson. The historical era depicted is Iron Age
(1200–1100 B.C.E.), yet we are not given history but highly pic-
turesque fiction. An anonymous scribe, writing during the Babylonian Exile, puts together both traditional and recent material.
But I am concerned with Deborah and her magnificent War Song,
which must be the oldest poem in the Hebrew Bible, going back
to at least 1200 B.C.E.

The prophetess Deborah (whose very name means "utter-
ance") dominates her stalwart general, Barak ("lightning"), who
will not risk battle without her heroic presence. Though the
KJB describes her as "the wife of Lapidoth," that should probably be rendered as "the woman of torches," no husband being
in sight. A northern fighter from lower Galilee, Barak leads the
soldiers of Zebulon and Naphtali, warlike Galilean tribes. I know
no verse in the KJB more thrilling than Deborah's great outcry
(Judges 5:18):

Zebulun and Naphtali *were* a people *that* jeoparded their
lives unto the death in the high places of the field.

Literally the archaic Hebrew might be rendered

Zebulon is a force that scorned death; Naphtali also on
the heights of the field.

Tyndale translated this as

Zebulon is a people that put their lives in jeopardy of
death, and Nephthalim in like manner, even unto the
top of the fields.

Geneva gave the KJB the material it molded:

But the people of Zebulon and Naphtali have jeoparded
their lives unto the death in the hye places of the field.

With a marvelous ear, the KJB men transposed that, but here I
want the context to the entire War Song in the KJB version:

1 Then sang Deborah and Barak the son of Abinoam on
that day, saying,
2 Praise ye the LORD for the avenging of Israel, when the
people willingly offered themselves.
3 Hear, O ye kings; give ear, O ye princes; I, *even* I, will sing
unto the LORD; I will sing *praise* to the LORD God of Israel.
4 LORD, when thou wentest out of Seir, when thou
marchedst out of the field of Edom, the earth trembled,
and the heavens dropped, the clouds also dropped water.
5 The mountains melted from before the LORD, *even* that
Sinai from before the LORD God of Israel.
6 In the days of Shamgar the son of Anath, in the days
of Jael, the highways were unoccupied, and the travelers
walked through byways.

7 *The inhabitants of* the villages ceased, they ceased in Israel, until that I Deborah arose, that I arose a mother in Israel.

8 They chose new gods; then *was* war in the gates: was there a shield or spear seen among forty thousand in Israel?

9 My heart *is* toward the governors of Israel, that offered themselves willingly among the people. Bless ye the Lord.

10 Speak, ye that ride on white asses, ye that sit in judgment, and walk by the way.

11 *They that are delivered* from the noise of archers in the places of drawing water, there shall they rehearse the righteous acts of the Lord, *even* the righteous acts *toward the inhabitants* of his villages in Israel: then shall the people of the Lord go down to the gates.

12 Awake, awake, Deborah: awake, awake, utter a song: arise, Barak, and lead thy captivity captive, thou son of Abinoam.

13 Then he made him that remaineth have dominion over the nobles among the people: the Lord made me have dominion over the mighty.

14 Out of Ephraim *was there* a root of them against Amalek; after thee, Benjamin, among thy people; out of Machir came down governors, and out of Zebulun they that handle the pen of the writer.

15 And the princes of Issachar *were* with Deborah; even Issachar, and also Barak: he was sent on foot into the valley. For the divisions of Reuben *there were* great thoughts of heart.

16 Why abodest thou among the sheepfolds, to hear the bleatings of the flocks? For the divisions of Reuben *there were* great searchings of heart.

17 Gilead abode beyond Jordan: and why did Dan remain in ships? Asher continued on the sea shore, and abode in his breaches.

18 Zebulun and Naphtali *were* a people *that* jeoparded their lives unto the death in the high places of the field.

19 The kings came *and* fought, then fought the kings of Canaan in Taanach by the waters of Megiddo; they took no gain of money.

20 They fought from heaven; the stars in their courses fought against Sisera.

21 The river of Kishon swept them away, that ancient river, the river Kishon. O my soul, thou hast trodden down strength.

22 Then were the horsehoofs broken by the means of the pransings, the pransings of their mighty ones.

23 Curse ye Meroz, said the angel of the LORD, curse ye bitterly the inhabitants thereof; because they came not to the help of the LORD, to the help of the LORD against the mighty.

24 Blessed above women shall Jael the wife of Heber the Kenite be, blessed shall she be above women in the tent.

25 He asked water, *and* she gave *him* milk; she brought forth butter in a lordly dish.

26 She put her hand to the nail, and her right hand to the workmen's hammer; and with the hammer she smote Sisera, she smote off his head, when she had pierced and stricken through his temples.

27 At her feet he bowed, he fell, he lay down: at her feet he bowed, he fell: where he bowed, there he fell down dead.

28 The mother of Sisera looked out at a window, and cried through the lattice, Why is his chariot *so* long in coming? why tarry the wheels of his chariots?

29 Her wise ladies answered her, yea, she returned answer to herself,

30 Have they not sped? have they *not* divided the prey; to every man a damsel *or* two; to Sisera a prey of divers colours, a prey of divers colours of needlework, of divers colours of needlework on both sides, *meet* for the necks of *them that take* the spoil?

31 So let all thine enemies perish, O LORD: but *let* them that love him *be* as the sun when he goeth forth in his might. And the land had rest forty years.

The satiric contrast between the tribes that evaded the challenge and those that fought is magnificently caught in the transition between verses 17 and 18. In verse 20, the KJB wins another triumph:

> From heaven came battle: for the stars being in their course, fought against Sisara.
>
> [Tyndale]

> They fought from heaven, *even* the stars in their courses fought against Sisera.
>
> [Geneva]

> They fought from heaven; the stars in their courses fought against Sisera.
>
> [KJB]

Omit "even" (not in the Hebrew) and it is enough to make the sentence perfect.

Samuel Taylor Coleridge particularly admired verse 27 of the KJB's song of Deborah:

> At her feet he bowed, he fell, he lay down: at her feet he bowed, he fell: where he bowed, there he fell down dead.

There Tyndale and Geneva clearly are surpassed, though the Hebrew is stronger: "He sank between her feet," with its overtones both of birth and intercourse.

The brutal execution of Sisera by Jael emphasizes again Deborah's assertion of her power over Barak, who indeed will not go into battle without her prophetic presence. Compared to the other "judges" (charismatic leaders, actually) Deborah is a torch; Gideon is initially timorous, and Samson an absurd fool in regard to Delilah. "A mother in Israel," in every sense except the literal, she is as resolute and certain as any prophet after her. Deborah's magnificent War Song, ironic and controlled, invokes Yahweh as a warrior whose stormy advent returns us to Sinai.

The women of the J Writer, as we have seen, are more admirable than the men, from Sarah and Rebecca through Rachel and Tamar. Deborah is in their tradition. I see no reason to doubt that her song, like Miriam's Song of the Sea, was composed by a woman. We never will know the identity of the strongest writer in Tanakh, the Yahwist. However she or he is scattered by fresh waves of scholiasts, her or his voice remains. Feminists have accused me of the sin of "essentialism" but the Yahwist's mode of irony seems to me more a woman's than a man's.

Ruth

The brief, perfect book of Ruth may be the most beautiful work in all the Hebrew Bible, and it maintains that high place in the KJB. Its poetic heirs include John Keats in his "Ode to a Nightingale" and Victor Hugo in a poem of equal splendor, "Boaz Asleep." A kind of narrative poem in prose, rather than a short story, Ruth memorializes much that is humane in Judaic tradition, and retains its normative vitality even today.

Whoever composed Ruth, he or she probably lived no later

than about 700 B.C.E., and this pastoral idyll may be even older, contemporary with the Yahwist of 950 B.C.E. or so. So direct and integral is the book of Ruth that we could believe its admirable heroine is contemporary with us.

Herbert Marks, as always the Bible's best literary critic, accurately praises the art of Ruth's design in his Norton edition of the English Bible:

> From a formal perspective, the plot is the most skillfully balanced in the Hebrew Bible. The four chapters are organized about four main scenes, alternately private and public: the road back to Bethlehem, where Ruth makes her crucial decision to follow Naomi; Boaz's field, where she meets her future "redeemer"; the threshing floor at night, where she wins his love; and the city gate, where he secures public endorsement for the marriage. Each scene is flanked (or in chapter four followed) by two shorter episodes, which prepare the main action and comment on it. Following the austere account of migration and widowhood in the first five verses, the plot moves with seeming inerrancy toward the providential union, running a gamut of impediments which heighten the dramatic interest: the threat that Ruth will yield to Naomi's logic and remain in Moab; the revelation that there is a kinsman with a claim prior to Boaz's; and the suspense as the kinsman momentarily chooses to exercise his right of redemption. Superimposed on this progressive movement from "emptiness" (1:21) to "restoration" (4:15) is a second chiastic or concentric pattern, which balances the ten generations born in Israel (4:18–22) against the ten years of barrenness in Moab (1:4), the elders' public blessing (4:11–12) against Naomi's public plaint (1:20–21), the kins-

man's decision to preserve his estate (4:6) against Orpah's preference for the security of home (1:14), and Naomi's service in providing a husband for Ruth (chap. 3) against Ruth's selflessness in providing for Naomi (chap. 2).

Marks catches also the fundamental theme of Jewish redemption through migration. The injunction "get thee out of"—Abram from Ur of the Chaldees, Moses from Egypt into the Land of the Promise—is acted out again by Ruth and Naomi, returning from Moab to Israel. Marks calls their trek "a journey back to everything one has had to renounce," with the benign patriarch Boaz representing the "second chance" that Yahweh implicitly permits to the steadfast.

More even than most biblical books, Ruth employs proper names to convey character. The name Ruth means a "friend," a refreshment of life; while Naomi means "sweet," a meaning that is momentarily put aside when in her sorrow she calls herself Mara, "bitterness." Boaz can be interpreted as "strength" in the particular sense of "shrewdness."

The covenant love that springs up between Ruth and Boaz moves us with no ambiguities or anxieties, yet it is matched by the love between Naomi and Ruth, really mother and daughter rather than in-law relations:

> 16 And Ruth said, Intreat me not to leave thee, *or to* return from following after thee: for whither thou goest, I will go; and where thou lodgest, I will lodge: thy people *shall* be my people, and thy God my God:
>
> 17 Where thou diest, will I die, and there will I be buried: the Lord do so to me, and more also, *if ought* but death part thee and me.
>
> [1:16–17]

This love that binds is *hesed,* loyalty to Covenant, and the fable of Ruth is a paean to the women of Covenant: Rachel, Leah, the remarkable Tamar, and here Naomi and Ruth, who through her marriage to Boaz will bear Obed, grandfather of King David. Ruth's seduction (to call it that) of the willing Boaz repeats in a finer tone Tamar's shrewdly deceiving seduction of the unwary Judah. As the ancestress of Boaz, Tamar thus also establishes what will be the line of David and Solomon.

Though absorbed into Tanakh, the book of Ruth remarkably varies and indeed opens up this concept of hesed, since the convert Ruth is a Moabite even as Solomon will be the son of a Hittite woman, Bathsheba. Tamar appears to have been a Canaanite, like Judah's wife before her, and so David is of Canaanite and Moabite lineage as well as Hebrew. Many scholars want to date the book of Ruth as late as the fifth century B.C.E., after the return from Babylonian exile, since the campaign for ethnic purity in Ezra and Nehemiah therefore would be confuted.

To appreciate the KJB book of Ruth is to further admire the Geneva Bible, whose text is altered only slightly in the KJB. That returns me to my realization that to write a literary appreciation of the KJB is necessarily to compose an aesthetic estimate of the English Bible: Tyndale, Coverdale, Geneva, and finally the Authorized Version. After that, all the British versions have been so much dross.

I find myself reluctant to leave Ruth, one of my favorite books in the Bible. Keats's tribute in his "Ode to a Nightingale" will be already familiar to most of my readers. I quote instead from a marvelous translation of Victor Hugo's "Boaz Asleep" from the titanic *The Legend of the Ages.* Boaz is clearly the grand Victor Hugo himself, ageless seducer of regiments of women:

While he was sleeping, Ruth, a Moabite,
Came to his feet and, with her breast bared, lay
Hoping for some unknown uncertain ray
When, suddenly, they would waken into light.

Though she was near, Boaz was unaware;
And what God planned for her, Ruth couldn't tell.
Cool fragrance rose from the tufts of asphodel,
And over Galgala, night stirred the air.

The shade was a deep, nuptial, solemn thing;
Angels were flying dimly there, no doubt;
Here and there, in the night, could be made out
Some blueness that appeared to be a wing.

Boaz's breathing mingled in his rest
With muffled streams running through mossy ways.
These things occurred in Nature's gentlest days,
And every hill had lilies on its crest.

The grass was dark; he slept, and she could think;
Some flock-bells tinkled now and then by chance;
Abundant blessings fell from the expanse.
It was the peaceful hour when lions drink.

All slumbered in Jerimadeth and Ur;
The stars enameled the deep, somber sky;
Westward a slender crescent shone close by
Those flowers of night, and Ruth, without a stir,

Wondered—with parting eyelids half revealed
Beneath her veils—what stray god, as he cropped
The timeless summer, had so idly dropped
That golden sickle in the starry field.

[Translated by E. H. and A. M. Blackmore]

The Hebrew Bible

Esther

Most enlightened Bible readers do not much like the book of Esther, as it is a rather savage performance. It also is scarcely religious, historically absurd, and rarely acceptable to Christians. But it goes with the joyous festival of Purim and is an admirably wrought story. I have a particular fondness for Esther because Martin Luther loathed the book, which indeed is never mentioned in the New Testament.

Esther was written when Daniel 1–6 was composed, the fourth century before the Common Era, and it reflects the Maccabean revolution against the Syrian-Hellenes (2 Maccabees 15:36). Herbert Marks suggestively terms Esther the inaugural text of Diaspora Judaism, since Purim seems to have begun as a celebration among those who chose to stay in Babylon.

There is a brazen flamboyance in the story of Esther, conveyed by an energetic, somewhat roistering narrative style. Purim in its origins was refreshingly pagan, and Esther's tale is splendidly secular. It is grimly funny in places and presumably was written for the Jews at ease in Babylon, not for those of the return to Zion. As with Judith in her book, Esther exudes a sexual power that cannot be resisted. The narrative drive of her book depends upon her erotic magnetism.

The enjoyment of Esther involves yielding to the story's extravagance, its self-indulgence in mingling together blood, wine, sex, danger, ironic humor—all ingredients of the grotesque. Both the Persian emperor and Queen Esther host absurdly overflowing banquets, and the arch-villain Haman is a melodramatic bogeyman who admirably suits a context of excess. More even than Daniel or Jonah, Esther is an odd work to discover in the canonical Bible.

Whoever wrote Esther affected a matter-of-fact style, as if

to establish the veracity of this fantastic tale. Mordecai the Jew adopts as his daughter the beautiful Esther, his orphaned cousin. The Persian king, having deposed Vashti, his queen, for refusing to appear naked to his guests, replaces her with Esther. Haman, the king's vizier, is refused homage by Mordecai. As retribution, Haman resolves that Mordecai and all the Persian Jews are to be slain. Earlier, Mordecai had saved the king from a plot against his life, but the king seems to have forgotten this extraordinary service. But then he recalls it, commands Haman to honor Mordecai, and then learns from Esther that her people, Mordecai included, were to be slaughtered at Haman's command. A slaughter follows of Haman and *his* people. Purim is decreed, and all concludes joyously. The tone is rambunctious even if the stance is rather bloody-minded.

It would be a literary mistake to take this heavily. *The Arabian Nights* is a clear analogue of this gaudy Jewish folklore. Haman is a melodramatic villain, but not an embodiment of the wicked Gentile, and Purim is almost a Feast of Fools, joyous and irresponsible, not exactly another Passover, being quite close to pagan festivals.

What matters most about the book of Esther is the heroine herself, who transcends Mordecai in her bold epiphany, based only upon the power of her beauty, self-assurance, and sexual allure. There is no withstanding her, an impression strengthened by the enigma of her personality, concerning which the narrator tells us almost nothing. At the story's close, the greatness of Mordecai is proclaimed and Esther goes unmentioned, but that scarcely matters, since it always has remained her book and not his.

Judith

The affinities between the books of Esther and of Judith are read-ily apparent, though the KJB places Judith among the Apocrypha ("hidden" works). Judith's tale is later in composition than Esther's, whose first version could have been as early as the fourth century B.C.E. Judas Maccabeus is implicit in the story of Judith, a glorifica-tion of a resurrected Jewish nationhood. Carey A. Moore, in the Anchor Yale Bible Judith (1995), plausibly suggests that Judith was written toward the end of the rule of John Hyrcanus I (135–104 B.C.E.), the first king of the line descended from Simon the brother of Judas Maccabeus. The attitude and tone of Judith suggests early Pharisaism, before the reign of the anti-Pharisaic warrior king Alexander Janneus.

Moore sensibly argues that the literary mode of Judith is irony. I have shown that the Yahwist is the most ironical of biblical au-thors, and Judith indeed exploits several of the J Writer's modes. The book's largest irony, given and never explained, is that the all-but-saintly Judith is so astonishingly audacious, capable of planning the murder of Holofernes and carrying it through.

Judith has more in common with Jael, who destroys Sisera, than with Esther, who does not herself venture into physical vio-lence. Yet we know little of Jael and everything knowable about Judith. She does not enter her own story until chapter 8, a finely delayed narrative device, and then totally dominates the rest of the book. The most pious and self-denying of widows, "very beautiful to behold," she is wealthy and patriotic, a paragon. Her fierce fast-ing evidently has not excessively diminished her sexually compel-ling appearance, nor her energy in calling upon God:

> 9 Behold their pride, and send thy wrath upon their heads: give into mine hand, which am a widow, the power that I have conceived.

Four Heroines: Judith

93

10 Smite by the deceit of my lips the servant with the prince, and the prince with the servant: break down their stateliness by the hand of a woman.

11 For thy power standeth not in multitude, nor thy might in strong men: for thou art a God of the afflicted, an helper of the oppressed, an upholder of the weak, a protector of the forlorn, a saviour of them that are without hope.

[9:9–11]

Deceit, sanctioned by God, shall be one instrument for the death of Holofernes, as will her beauty:

1 Now after that she had ceased to cry unto the God of Israel, and had made an end of all these words,

2 She rose where she had fallen down, and called her maid, and went down into the house, in the which she abode in the sabbath days, and in her feast days,

3 And she pulled off the sackcloth which she had on, and put off the garments of her widowhood, and washed her body all over with water, and anointed herself with precious ointment, and braided the hair of her head, and put on a tire upon it, and put on her garments of gladness, wherewith she was clad during the life of Manasses her husband.

4 And she took sandals upon her feet, and put about her bracelets, and her chains, and her rings, and her earrings, and all her ornaments, and decked herself bravely, to allure the eyes of all men that should see her.

[10:1–4]

The irony of her seduction of Holofernes is splendidly set forth:

5 Then Judith said unto him, Receive the words of thy servant, and suffer thine handmaid to speak in thy presence, and I will declare no lie to my lord this night.

6 And if thou wilt follow the words of thine handmaid, God will bring the thing perfectly to pass by thee; and my lord shall not fail of his purposes.

[11:5–6]

Judith, whose goal after all is decapitation, nevertheless avoids unlawful food, while the infatuated Holofernes becomes quite drunk and so cooperates in his demise:

6 Then she came to the pillar of the bed, which was at Holofernes' head, and took down his fauchion from thence,

7 And approached to his bed, and took hold of the hair of his head, and said, Strengthen me, O Lord God of Israel, this day.

8 And she smote twice upon his neck with all her might, and she took away his head from him,

9 And tumbled his body down from the bed, and pulled down the canopy from the pillars; and anon after she went forth, and gave Holofernes his head to her maid.

[13:6–9]

Direct and merciless as this already is, Judith goes beyond it by coolly taking the head out of the bag and showing it to her people. Inspired by Judith, her nation takes arms, rushes upon their disconcerted enemies, and triumphs.

Consistent with her career, Judith—though much desired—continues in her widowhood and dies at age 105, still faithful to her deceased husband.

We are left to ironic speculation as to the psychology of this most formidable of women, godly and lethal, virtuous and deadly. Deborah rouses Israel to battle, while Jael obliterates Sisera. Esther manifests her own ferocity by requesting an additional day for slaughtering the enemies of the Jews. Judith is well beyond Jael and Esther in her pugnacity. You can think of her as a saintly avenger, remarkably akin to Jezebel, except that she is Yahweh's instrument and not his enemy, as was Jezebel. Her story surges on, aesthetically impressive in a violent glory rather like that of the Icelandic sagas.

David
(1 and 2 Samuel to 1 Kings 2)

THE DOMINANT FIGURES IN TANAKH after Yahweh are Moses the prophet and David the king. They are the central heroes of Hebrew tradition, transcending even the glory of the patriarchs Abram/Abraham and Jacob/Israel. David's story is closer to us because so large a part of European secular literary tradition stems from him. Of all the Bible's protagonists, David is the most novelistic, though no great novel has yet been founded upon him to rival Thomas Mann's tetralogy *Joseph and His Brothers*. But then, as I read and interpret the J Writer, her Joseph is a surrogate for the beloved David and shares his charisma.

David's story is concluded in 1 Kings and told again in 1 Chronicles, while much of the book of Psalms is ascribed improbably to his authorship or perhaps pertains to him. Like Moses, he never is far away in Jewish tradition, though neither of them is confirmed by extrabiblical ancient reference. One can doubt that the Exodus actually occurred, yet it seems likely that much of David's career could be historical, making allowances for hyperboles and legendary elaborations. A great writer, generally called the Court Historian, composed the book of Samuel, possibly in the days of the J Writer. However powerful the Court Historian's imagination, the complexity of his portraits of David, Saul, and Samuel—multiple character faults included—can plausibly be ascribed to models that perhaps were directly observed, or were reported on a generation or so earlier.

It hardly would be possible to compose an extensive account of the personality and character of Moses, whether in the Yahwist's or the Deuteronomist's model. Of all the figures in Tanakh, David seems the most Shakespearean, inward and multi-selved. As with the Shakespearean protagonists most endless to meditation—Falstaff, Hamlet, Iago, Edgar, Cleopatra—David cannot be thought through, since always there is more to be considered. (Samuel is curiously ill-tempered, and his authentic prophetic call does not free him from dangerous self-interest and considerable pomposity.)

Saul is one of the darkest souls in all of the Hebrew Bible. David is his bad luck, which is to say that Yahweh's caprice destroys Saul by degrees. To be the initial king of the Hebrews is a dreadful destiny. Nothing that Saul could perform or leave undone will lift his doom. The narrator gives Saul no way out. His rages cannot prevail against what can be termed David's charismatic duplicities, which charm Yahweh and beguile Saul's children, Michal and Jonathan.

Saul's descent culminates in his most notorious enterprise, the raising up of Samuel's ghost by the Witch of Endor at the king's command:

> 11 Then said the woman, Whom shall I bring up unto thee? And he said, Bring me up Samuel.
> 12 And when the woman saw Samuel, she cried with a loud voice: and the woman spake to Saul, saying, Why hast thou deceived me? for thou *art* Saul.

13 And the king said unto her, Be not afraid: for what sawest thou? And the woman said unto Saul, I saw gods ascending out of the earth.

14 And he said unto her, What form *is* he of? And she said, An old man cometh up; and he *is* covered with a mantle. And Saul perceived that it *was* Samuel, and he stooped with *his* face to the ground, and bowed himself.

15 ¶ And Samuel said to Saul, Why hast thou disquieted me, to bring me up? And Saul answered, I am sore distressed; for the Philistines make war against me, and God is departed from me, and answereth me no more, neither by prophets, nor by dreams: therefore I have called thee, that thou mayest make known unto me what I shall do.

16 Then said Samuel, Wherefore then dost thou ask of me, seeing the LORD is departed from thee, and is become thine enemy?

17 And the LORD hath done to him, as he spake by me: for the LORD hath rent the kingdom out of thine hand, and given it to thy neighbour, *even* to David:

18 Because thou obeyedst not the voice of the LORD, nor executedst his fierce wrath upon Amalek, therefore hath the LORD done this thing unto thee this day.

19 Moreover the LORD will also deliver Israel with thee into the hand of the Philistines: and to morrow *shalt* thou and thy sons *be* with me: the LORD also shall deliver the host of Israel into the hand of the Philistines.

[1 Samuel 28:11–19]

Throughout the books of Samuel, the KJB, like Geneva, simply takes over Tyndale, with only minor changes in wording. After the death of Saul and Jonathan in their losing battle against the Philistines, David's magnificent lament (2 Samuel 1) is one of the

KJB's glories, and contrasts superbly with its strong forerunners in Tyndale and Geneva:

17 ¶ And David lamented with this lamentation over Saul and over Jonathan his son:

18 (Also he bade them teach the children of Judah *the use of* the bow: behold, *it is* written in the book of Jasher.)

19 The beauty of Israel is slain upon thy high places: how are the mighty fallen!

20 Tell *it* not in Gath, publish *it* not in the streets of Askelon; lest the daughters of the Philistines rejoice, lest the daughters of the uncircumcised triumph.

21 Ye mountains of Gilboa, *let there be* no dew, neither *let there be* rain, upon you, nor fields of offerings: for there the shield of the mighty is vilely cast away, the shield of Saul, *as though he had* not *been* anointed with oil.

22 From the blood of the slain, from the fat of the mighty, the bow of Jonathan turned not back, and the sword of Saul returned not empty.

23 Saul and Jonathan *were* lovely and pleasant in their lives, and in their death they were not divided: they were swifter than eagles, they were stronger than lions.

24 Ye daughters of Israel, weep over Saul, who clothed you in scarlet, with *other* delights, who put on ornaments of gold upon your apparel.

25 How are the mighty fallen in the midst of the battle! O Jonathan, *thou wast* slain in thine high places.

26 I am distressed for thee, my brother Jonathan: very pleasant hast thou been unto me: thy love to me was wonderful, passing the love of women.

27 How are the mighty fallen, and the weapons of war perished!

Tyndale, whose genius was for narrative, not lyric, astonishes me by converting David's elegy into story:

> And David sang this song of mourning over Saul and Jonathas his son, and bade to teach the children of Israel the staves thereof. And behold it is written in the book of the righteous. The glory of Israel is slain upon the high hills: Oh how were the mighty overthrown? Tell it not in Geth: nor publish it in the streets of Askalon: lest the daughters of the Philistines rejoice, and that the daughters of the uncircumcised triumph thereof. Ye mountains of Gelboe, upon you be neither dew nor rain, nor fields whence heave offerings come. For there the shields of the mighty were cast from them: the shield of Saul as though he had not been anointed with oil. The bow of Jonathas and the sword of Saul turned never back again empty, from the blood of the wounded and from the fat of the mighty warriors.
>
> Saul and Jonathas lovely and pleasant in their lives, were in their deaths not divided, men swifter than eagles and stronger than lions. Ye daughters of Israel, weep over Saul, which clothed you in purple and garments of pleasure, and bordered your raiment with ornaments of gold. How were the mighty slain in battle? Jonathas on the high hills was wounded to death: woe is me for thee my brother Jonathas: delectable to me wast thou exceeding. Thy love to me was wonderful, passing the love of women. How were the mighty overthrown, and how were the weapons of war forlorn.

The Geneva Bible, very close to the KJB, does not quite match its cadences:

17 Then David mourned with this lamentation over Saul, and over Jonathan his son,

18 (Also he bade them teach the children of Judah to shoot, as it is written in the book of Jasher)

19 O noble Israel, he is slain upon thy high places: how are the mighty overthrown?

20 Tell it not in Gath, nor publish it in the streets of Ashkelon, lest the daughters of the Philistines rejoice, lest the daughters of the uncircumcised triumph.

21 Ye mountains of Gilboa, upon you *be* neither dew nor rain, nor *be there* fields of offerings: for there the shield of the mighty is cast down, the shield of Saul, as though he had not been anointed with oil.

22 The bow of Jonathan never turned back, neither did the sword of Saul return empty from the blood of the slain, and from the fat of the mighty.

23 Saul and Jonathan were lovely and pleasant in their lives, and in their deaths they were not divided: they were swifter than eagles, they were stronger than lions.

24 Ye daughters of Israel, weep for Saul, which clothed you in scarlet, with pleasures, and hanged ornaments of gold upon your apparel.

25 How were the mighty slain in the midst of battle? O Jonathan, thou wast slain in thine high places.

26 Woe is me for thee, my brother Jonathan: very kind hast thou been unto me: thy love to me was wonderful, passing the love of women: how are the mighty overthrown, and the weapons of war destroyed?

There are no substantive changes made here either to Tyndale or Geneva, yet the literary improvement is considerable. The Hebrew original is an extraordinary poem, but the honors can be divided between it and the KJB version. As for the nature of David's love for Jonathan, we can doubt any homosexual orientation, if only because there is political duplicity in the poem. It overstates David's affection for both Saul *and* Jonathan, and reminds us that his authentic love will be for his son Absalom, and perhaps for Bathsheba, whom he so fiercely desires.

The hidden nature of David's affective life persists throughout his career, enhances his interest as a literary representation, and is an undoubted aid in his extraordinary rise to royal power. More of an improviser than a machiavel, David is a sublime opportunist, unlike Jonathan, who is constant yet conflicted in his loyalty both to his father and to his friend.

Fleeing Saul, David becomes the chief of a company of freebooters. His relations with the Philistines, which would have destroyed the popularity of any other Hebrew hero, include a period of vassalage. Since he finally will end the Philistine menace, as Saul could not, tradition has forgiven him. The Court Historian celebrates David without apparent reservations, though his narrative also asks to be read between the lines, where David is scarcely exemplary. Yet that enhances the literary strength of the book of Samuel, which competes with the J Writer's share in Genesis, Exodus, Numbers. These are the narrative masterpieces of Tanakh, fit rivals to Homer and Tolstoy. The Yahwist's saga is the epic of a people, while the story of David is another kind of fiction, perhaps the first portrait of an artist who is also a national leader, beloved of God.

Poet and musician, usurper and anointed monarch, alternately ruthless and expediently compassionate, David anticipates Hamlet as a masterpiece of contraries. Like Hamlet, he inspires our love yet does not return it. Hamlet is the hero of Western consciousness, and disputes with David the crown of personality, but David is also a religious figure, which may make him even more complex.

The analogies between David and Hamlet haunt me, and I suspect that Shakespeare, immersed in the Geneva Bible, was aware of the affinities between these two charismatic royal personages. Jewish tradition envisioned a messiah descended from David, and Christianity found that messiah in Jesus. Retrospectively, both traditions enhance the aura already evident in the second Jewish king.

The biblical David is an incarnate poem, whether dancing before the Ark or grieving for a slain son. Since the KJB closely follows Geneva in Samuel, and Geneva relies heavily upon Tyndale, I leap over the Geneva text here and juxtapose the KJB with Tyndale. In 2 Samuel 11 David, having enjoyed Bathsheba, the wife of the warrior Uriah the Hittite, arranges for Uriah to die in battle. In chapter 12, the prophet Nathan tells David a parable that the king fails to understand, about a wealthy man who steals the ewe lamb of a poor victim:

> 5 And David's anger was greatly kindled against the man; and he said to Nathan, *As* the LORD liveth, the man that hath done this *thing* shall surely die:
>
> 6 ¶ And he shall restore the lamb fourfold, because he did this thing, and because he had no pity.
>
> 7 And Nathan said to David, Thou *art* the man. Thus saith the LORD God of Israel, I anointed thee king over Israel, and I delivered thee out of the hand of Saul;
>
> 8 And I gave thee thy master's house, and thy master's wives into thy bosom, and gave thee the house of Israel and of Judah; and if *that had been* too little, I would moreover have given unto thee such and such things.
>
> 9 Wherefore hast thou despised the commandment of the LORD, to do evil in his sight? thou hast killed Uriah the Hittite with the sword, and hast taken his wife *to*

be thy wife, and hast slain him with the sword of the children of Ammon.

10 Now therefore the sword shall never depart from thine house; because thou hast despised me, and hast taken the wife of Uriah the Hittite to be thy wife.

[KJB]

And David was exceeding wroth with the man, and said to Nathan: as surely as the Lord liveth the fellow that hath done this thing is the child of death and shall restore the lamb fourfold because he did this thing and because he had no pity. Then Nathan said to David: thou art the man. Thus saith the Lord God of Israel: I anointed thee king over Israel and rid thee out of the hands of Saul. And I gave thee thy master's house and thy master's wives into thy bosom, and gave thee the house of Israel and of Juda, and would if that had been too little have given thee twice so much more. Wherefore hast thou despised the commandment of the Lord, to do wickedness in his sight? thou hast killed Urias the Hethite with the sword and has taken his wife to thy wife, and hast slain him with the sword of the children of Ammon.

Now therefore the sword shall never depart from thine house, because (saith the Lord) thou hast despised me and taken the wife of Urias the Hethite, to be thy wife.

[Tyndale]

I prefer Tyndale here for the directness of his passion—the great phrase is originally his: "thou art the man." Tyndale again is stronger in the superb recovery of David from his grief at the death of the boy he has begotten upon Bathsheba:

David

Then said David unto Nathan: I have sinned against the Lord. And Nathan said again to David: the Lord hath put away thy sin, thou shalt not die. Howbeit because in doing this deed thou hast given the enemies of the Lord a cause to rail, the child that is born thee shall die surely. And Nathan departed unto his house. And the Lord struck the child that Urias' wife bare David and it sickened. And David besought God for the boy and fasted and went and lay all night upon the earth. And the elders of his house arose and went to him to take him up from the earth. But he would not, neither yet eat meat with them.

And it happened the seventh day that the child died. But the servants of David durst not tell him that the child was dead. For they said: see, while the child was yet alive, we spake unto him, and he would not hearken unto our voice. How much more will he vex himself if we tell him that the child is dead? But David saw his servants whispering and thereby perceived that the child was dead, and said unto his servants: is the child dead? And they said yea. Then David arose from the earth and washed and anointed himself and changed his apparel, and went into the house of the Lord and prayed, and after came to his own house and bade that they should set meat before him, and he did eat. Then said his servants unto him: what is this that thou hast done? Thou fastedest and weepest for the child while it was alive, and as soon as it was dead thou didst rise up and didst eat meat. And he answered: while the child was alive, I fasted and wept. For I this thought: who can tell whether God will have mercy on me that the child may live? But now seeing it is dead wherefore should I fast? can I bring him again any more? I shall go to him: but he shall not come again to me.

The Hebrew Bible

The swiftness of Tyndale's plain style is somewhat diffused here by the KJB:

13 And David said unto Nathan, I have sinned against the LORD. And Nathan said unto David, The LORD also hath put away thy sin; thou shalt not die.

14 Howbeit, because by this deed thou hast given great occasion to the enemies of the LORD to blaspheme, the child also *that is* born unto thee shall surely die.

15 ¶ And Nathan departed unto his house. And the LORD struck the child that Uriah's wife bare unto David, and it was very sick.

16 David therefore besought God for the child; and David fasted, and went in, and lay all night upon the earth.

17 And the elders of his house arose, *and went* to him, to raise him up from the earth: but he would not, neither did he eat bread with them.

18 And it came to pass on the seventh day, that the child died. And the servants of David feared to tell him that the child was dead: for they said, Behold, while the child was yet alive, we spake unto him, and he would not hearken unto our voice: how will he then vex himself, if we tell him that the child is dead?

19 But when David saw that his servants whispered, David perceived that the child was dead: therefore David said unto his servants, Is the child dead? And they said, He is dead.

20 Then David arose from the earth, and washed, and anointed *himself,* and changed his apparel, and came into the house of the LORD, and worshipped: then he came to his own house; and when he required, they set bread before him, and he did eat.

David

21 Then said his servants unto him, What thing *is* this that thou hast done? thou didst fast and weep for the child, *while it was* alive; but when the child was dead, thou didst rise and eat bread.

22 And he said, While the child was yet alive, I fasted and wept: for I said, Who can tell *whether* God will be gracious to me, that the child may live?

23 But now he is dead, wherefore should I fast? can I bring him back again? I shall go to him, but he shall not return to me.

This is David at his most revelatory, in equal control of his grief and his acceptance of loss. Saul is a tragic figure, but David incarnates the whole truth of our contrary existences. James Joyce said that Homer's Odysseus was the most complete man represented in literature, but I venture that David rivals the wily, metamorphic protagonist of the *Odyssey*. Compared to David, even such grand personages as Jacob, Joseph, and Moses seem truncated. Jacob endlessly pursues the Blessing, Joseph (in Tyndale's phrasing) was a "lucky fellow," while the J Writer's Moses labors to keep up with the caprices of Yahweh. Only David gratuitously receives the Blessing, masters his own fortunes, makes his own luck through opportunism, and cannot lose Yahweh's love whether he merits it or not.

David's saga attains its fullest power from 2 Samuel 13 through 1 Kings 2, the Secession Narrative of the transition from David to Solomon, another son by Bathsheba. The center of this sequence is the rebellion of Absalom, David's favorite son, in an attempt to usurp the kingdom. Absalom, a kind of reincarnation of the young David, reverses his father's knack of good fortune and is destroyed despite the king's desperate wistfulness in instructing that the *naar* (lad) be spared.

In the extraordinarily vivid recital of Absalom's revolt and death, both the Geneva and the KJB translators added very little to Tyndale. On the whole, I again prefer straight Tyndale to his revisionists. In 2 Samuel 16:21 Absalom has intercourse with all ten of his father's concubines in a tent set up on the roof of David's palace, signifying his possession of the throne:

> 21 And Ahithophel said unto Absalom, Go in unto thy father's concubines, which he hath left to keep the house; and all Israel shall hear that thou art abhorred of thy father: then shall the hands of all that *are* with thee be strong.
> 22 So they spread Absalom a tent upon the top of the house; and Absalom went in unto his father's concubines in the sight of all Israel.

Tyndale wonderfully had rendered "and all Israel shall hear that thou art abhorred of thy father" as: "For when all Israel shall hear that thou hast made they father to stink." David's lament for the slain Absalom (18:33) is pruned a touch by the KJB:

> And the king was much moved, and went up to the chamber over the gate, and wept: and as he went, thus he said, O my son Absalom, my son, my son Absalom! would God I had died for thee, O Absalom, my son, my son!

Again, I prefer Tyndale, who catches better the wildness of David's grief.

> And the king was moved and went up to a chamber over the gate and wept. And as he went thus he said: my son Absalom, my son, my son, my son Absalom, would to God I had died for thee Absalom, my son, my son.

After Absalom's death, the remainder of David's story is what John Milton might have called a long day's dying to ease his pain. The first two chapters of Kings leave unclear whether the queen mother Bathsheba and the prophet Nathan manipulate the failing David into naming Solomon as his successor or if this always was David's future vision.

Solomon, second in prestige only to David among all Jewish kings, is an ambiguous figure in Tanakh. He builds the Temple but otherwise is famous for his curious triad of eros, wealth, and wisdom. David is an endlessly fascinating personality, but Solomon is a cipher. The book of Kings scarcely conceals its ambivalence toward him, and the ascription of the Song of Songs and Koheleth (Ecclesiastes) to him is transparently absurd.

The account of Solomon in 1 Kings 1–11 is frequently ironic, though very measured, and is capable of antithetical readings. However his story is interpreted, he makes no claim upon our affection. The contrast to David is palpable and may be the narrator's true point. Worldly glory alone cannot substitute for not possessing a charismatic personality.

The Prophets

THE HEBREW PROPHETS NECESSARILY are distorted in any Christian context, such as the KJB. Tanakh goes from Torah on to the Nevi'im and only then on to the Kethuvim, which includes Daniel, who is not a prophet in Jewish views. Nobody knows why Joshua, Judges, Samuel, and Kings came to be called "the former prophets," preceding Isaiah, Jeremiah, Ezekiel, and the Twelve Minor Prophets ("minor" only in regard to the brevity of their texts). Joshua, though chosen by Moses, is a soldier, and only Deborah of the so-called Judges has prophetic status. Samuel is a prophet, but his two books center upon David; Kings, a cavalcade of disasters, does give the stories of Elijah and Elisha.

The Hebrew word *navi* is misleadingly translated by the Greek *prophetes,* a go-between who interprets an oracle. But the navi himself is the oracle, called by God, who begins by asserting: "The Yahweh-word was to me." The Hebrew for "word," *davar,* fundamentally means an act, so the prophet starts out saying that an action by Yahweh prompts him.

That the prophets have been tamed by canonical inclusion is absurd yet inevitable. Making Amos into Scripture is an act of violence toward him. Institutionalizing prophecy is betrayal. I prefer First Isaiah and Amos to Jeremiah and Ezekiel because Yahweh becomes much more extreme in the latter two, particularly in the disturbed Ezekiel. Yet I know that my response to the prophets is questionable because I rebel against their incessant denunciations of their own people.

Prophecy is one mode of poetry but only one, though most deep readers have trouble sorting out the aesthetic and spiritual strands in their response to the Bible. This difficulty is inevitable since prophecy is meaningless without Yahweh, an outrageous, uncanny, unpredictable God, human all too human. He proclaims his ethos, which is always questionable, while his logos scarcely exists in comparison to his exuberant pathos.

To be Yahweh's man is a fearsome fate, as the careers of Jeremiah and Ezekiel indicate. Counting up the prophets in Tanakh is, for me, a confusing process. The sages said there were fifty-five true or canonical prophets, but I cannot locate that many. The prophet of prophets is taken to be Moses, but if Elijah and the first Isaiah are prophets, then Moses is something else. He is primarily a literary character, but so are Elijah and Isaiah, and so in mere fact are Yahweh and Jesus. William Blake described religion as choosing forms of worship from poetic tales, and who can refute him?

The prophets are depicted as extraordinary personalities, Jeremiah and Ezekiel in particular. Some regard Jeremiah as a hero: he seems to me a great poet and a bipolar case history, though compared to the psychotic Ezekiel, another major poet, he may be closer to our fathomings. If Jeremiah and Ezekiel are prophets, then Amos, Micah, and Isaiah of Jerusalem are something else, and better, because social justice is the burden of their message.

Elijah and Elisha (1 Kings 17 to 2 Kings)

Oral prophecy is difficult to grasp, yet I still find it odd that only Isaiah of Jerusalem seems as much of a historical personage as the more legendary Elijah and Elisha. Despite the vivid representations of Ezekiel and Jeremiah, they seem to me extraordinary literary characters, a category dominated by the West's major literary characters, Yahweh and Jesus.

Robert Carroll and Stephen Prickett, editors of Oxford's World's Classics KJB, remark on the curious omission in 1 and 2 Kings of the classical writing prophets (except Isaiah) whose works make up the prophetic books of the Hebrew Bible. When we think of the prophets Elijah, Elisha, and the first Isaiah, we naturally pass on to Jeremiah and Ezekiel and to Amos, Hosea, and Micah. Were they simply unknown to the writers of Kings? If unknown, does that argue a fictive status or something else? There is a fine, circular irony in this: the Talmud says that Jeremiah was the author of Kings!

Elijah and his disciple Elisha are uncanny persons: miracle workers and adepts at resurrection. Elisha, who is something of a blunderer, seems a more archaic figure than the high transcendental Elijah, always a harbinger of the visionary future. The prestige of Elijah is enormous and almost rivals the eminence of Moses. I still recall my childhood awe at the wineglass set aside for *Eliahu hanavi* at every Passover seder, with my sleepy fantasies that indeed he had come by to drain it! It is wonderfully appropriate that Elijah does not die but ascends to Yahweh in a chariot of fire. In contrast, the anxious disciple Elisha returns to the earth at his close.

Kings is not one of the Tanakh's great books, except for Elijah and for that vivid couple King Ahab and Queen Jezebel. *Ahab* was appropriated by Herman Melville as the name for his awesome captain of the whaler *Pequod,* whose revenge tragedy pivots upon

Moby-Dick, a version of Job's Leviathan. *Jezebel* is now a common word for a wickedly dangerous woman; no one names a daughter Jezebel (alas). I always tell my students that the Macbeths have the happiest marriage in Shakespeare, and that may be true of Ahab and Jezebel in the Bible. Of course there are Jacob and Rachel, Joseph's mother, but she dies early giving birth to Benjamin. Like the Macbeths, Ahab and Jezebel come to individual bad ends, but their solidarity never is shaken.

We do not know the identities of the authors and redactors of Kings, but whoever among them first created the enmity between Elijah and Ahab (and his queen) had the potential to be an extraordinary dramatist. Elijah is portrayed as sublimely abrupt, driven by a quasi-divine impetus, appropriate to a prophet whose own name fuses *El,* "the almighty," and *Yahweh*. Tradition has seen Elijah as a second Moses, but that would be the Moses of Deuteronomy and not of the J Writer. The vision of the Deuteronomists clearly provides the contexts of Kings, and Elijah centers that vision.

With wonderful swiftness Elijah comes before us in the narrative style of William Tyndale, whose version of Kings essentially is taken over first by the Geneva translators and then by the KJB, which I quote here:

> 1 And Elijah the Tishbite, *who was* of the inhabitants of Gilead, said unto Ahab, *As* the LORD God of Israel liveth, before whom I stand, there shall not be dew nor rain these years, but according to my word.
>
> 2 And the word of the LORD came unto him, saying,
>
> 3 Get thee hence, and turn thee eastward, and hide thyself by the brook Cherith, that *is* before Jordan.
>
> 4 And it shall be, *that* thou shalt drink of the brook; and I have commanded the ravens to feed thee there.
>
> 5 So he went and did according unto the word of the

LORD: for he went and dwelt by the brook Cherith, that
is before Jordan.

6 And the ravens brought him bread and flesh in the
morning, and bread and flesh in the evening; and he
drank of the brook.

[1 Kings 17:1–6]

Baal, Yahweh's enemy, is a rain god. Elijah erupts from no back-
ground; nobody knows anything of the unknown village of
Tishbe. Speaking with Yahweh's authority, his prophet Elijah
proclaims drought. His entire career will be one long miracle until
his ascension in the flaming chariot. Far more than his New Testament imitator John the Baptist, Elijah is a Yahweh-like paradox,
wholly transcendent yet altogether immanent, at once divine fire
and "a hairy man."

A pure solitary until he accepts Elisha as his disciple, Elijah is
a forbidding precursor for the entire prophetic tradition. His ferocity can be terrifying, as when he personally slaughters Jezebel's
prophets of Baal. Something of Yahweh himself is manifested
in and by Elijah: call it a scary otherness. No other prophet, not
Moses himself, seems nearly so theomorphic. I cannot think of
Elijah as someone who had a mother and a father. He emerges out
of Yahweh's matrix, challenging all in Yahweh's name.

Elijah's most illustrious challenge is to Jezebel's 450 prophets of Baal, augmented by 400 prophets of Asherah, mother of
the gods of Canaan. Upon Mount Carmel the contest is joined
between 1 and 850, whom the satiric Elijah reduces to absurdity:

21 And Elijah came unto all the people, and said, How
long halt ye between two opinions? if the LORD *be* God,
follow him: but if Baal, *then* follow him. And the people
answered him not a word.

22 Then said Elijah unto the people, I, *even* I only, re-

main a prophet of the LORD; but Baal's prophets are four hundred and fifty men.

23 Let them therefore give us two bullocks; and let them choose one bullock for themselves, and cut it in pieces, and lay *it* on wood, and put no fire *under:* and I will dress the other bullock, and lay *it* on wood, and put no fire *under:*

24 And call ye on the name of your gods, and I will call on the name of the LORD: and the God that answereth by fire, let him be God. And all the people answered and said, It is well spoken.

[1 Kings 18:21–24]

Few passages in the Bible match the ironic splendor of Elijah's derision when Baal fails to respond:

27 And it came to pass at noon, that Elijah mocked them, and said, Cry aloud: for he *is* a god; either he is talking, or he is pursuing, or he is in a journey, *or* peradventure he sleepeth, and must be awaked.

28 And they cried aloud, and cut themselves after their manner with knives and lancets, till the blood gushed out upon them.

29 And it came to pass, when midday was past, and they prophesied until the *time* of the offering of the *evening* sacrifice, that *there was* neither voice, nor any to answer, nor any that regarded.

30 And Elijah said unto all the people, Come near unto me. And all the people came near unto him. And he repaired the altar of the LORD *that was* broken down.

[18:27–30]

When Yahweh's fire descends, the hopeless agon ends, to be followed by an even grander conclusion. His life threatened by the vengeance of Jezebel, Elijah flees south of Beersheba into the wilderness of the Negev. He stands at the last upon Horeb, Yahweh's sacred mountain, and a great epiphany ensues:

> 9 ¶ And he came thither unto a cave, and lodged there; and, behold, the word of the LORD *came* to him, and he said unto him, What doest though here, Elijah?
> 10 And he said, I have been very jealous for the LORD God of hosts: for the children of Israel have forsaken thy covenant, thrown down thine altars, and slain thy prophets with the sword; and I, *even* I only, am left; and they seek my life, to take it away.
> 11 And he said, Go forth, and stand upon the mount before the LORD. And, behold, the LORD passed by, and a great and strong wind rent the mountains, and brake in pieces the rocks before the LORD; *but* the LORD *was* not in the wind: and after the wind an earthquake; *but* the LORD *was* not in the earthquake:
> 12 And after the earthquake a fire; but the LORD was not in the fire: and after the fire a still small voice.
>
> [19:9–12]

The Hebrew *qol demmanah daqah* is an oxymoron, and might be rendered as "a small voice of silence," "a soundless stillness," or perhaps better "a voice of thin silence." But here the KJB triumphs absolutely: "a still small voice." Tyndale gives "a small still voice," while Geneva has "a still and soft voice." All three are lovely, but the palm has to be awarded to the KJB. That "still small voice" should last forever.

There are two perspectives for apprehending Elijah, that of Ahab and Jezebel, and that of Elisha. Ahab is too frightened of Elijah to dare execute him, but the ferocious Jezebel would risk anything. Both end as Elijah prophesied: Ahab is slain in battle "and the dogs licked up his blood," while Jezebel is defenestrated and most of her carcass is devoured by dogs.

Elisha in some respects is more enigmatic even than Elijah. Though the disciple of the solitary Elijah, he gathers around him a host of "sons of the prophets" and becomes a war advisor to the royal court. His incessant miracles compel (in me anyway) more annoyance than awe. A curious figure, allied with kings and their military policies, Elisha is a strange continuator for Elijah to have chosen. The blood-curdling Jehu, sanctioned by Elisha, is the ironic culmination of Elijah's tradition in the Tanakh.

Jehu destroys the entire family of Ahab and Jezebel, a carnage that earns the approval of the redactors of Kings, who probably were Deuteronomists. The historical Ahab seems to have been a remarkably strong king, whose military and political successes were of no interest to Deuteronomists. I do not believe in his wickedness or even in that of Jezebel, who after all was not a Hebrew but a Phoenician princess, probably of the same family as Dido of Carthage. But then Kings is not history but religious propaganda and possesses a kind of value as such.

Isaiah

Matthew Arnold, on the basis of the KJB's Isaiah, asserted that the Hebrew prophet stood with Homer among the poets, upon an eminence beyond even Shakespeare and Milton. I am unimpressed by fashions in biblical scholarship, which currently dissolve the Yahwist into a mosaic of fragments. Isaiah is now even more atomized. Not all of chapters 1–39 are now ascribed to First Isaiah: he has been divested, in part or in whole, of chapters 2, 10, 11, 13–14, 24–27, 31–33, 34–35. That leaves him twenty-four chapters, held together by no apparent continuity. The poet-prophet Isaiah has been replaced by three centuries (eighth to fifth B.C.E.) of disciples gathered together in an anthology. Where can we hear the voice of the visionary statesman Isaiah of Jerusalem, the strong rival to Plato of Athens? Have the sages from Matthew Arnold to Leo Strauss been self-deceived?

The largest literary failure of the KJB, as I keep noting, is the tonal uniformity its baroque style imposes upon very different writers. And yet the Hebrew text itself, particularly in Isaiah, is a wilderness of linguistic and textual difficulties. The power of Isaiah's stance engendered a company of enthusiasts who passionately imitated their forerunner.

Isaiah of Jerusalem, of royal blood and connected both to court and temple, prophesied during the kingships of Ahaz and Hezekiah in the later years of the eighth century B.C.E. Assyria was the region's dominant power and ended the northern Kingdom of Israel in 721 B.C.E. A younger contemporary of Amos and of Hosea, Isaiah continued their northern denunciations, turning these against the wealthy in southern Judah, who feasted upon the poor of the land.

The famous chapter 6 is the true foreboding of Isaiah's quest and necessary failure:

> 1 In the year that king Uzziah died I saw also the Lord sitting upon a throne, high and lifted up, and his train filled the temple.
>
> 2 Above it stood the seraphims: each one had six wings; with twain he covered his face, and with twain he covered his feet, and with twain he did fly.
>
> 3 And one cried unto another, and said, Holy, holy, holy, *is* the LORD of hosts: the whole earth *is* full of his glory.
>
> 4 And the posts of the door moved at the voice of him that cried, and the house was filled with smoke.
>
> 5 ¶ Then said I, Woe *is* me! for I am undone; because I *am* a man of unclean lips, and I dwell in the midst of a

people of unclean lips: for mine eyes have seen the King, the LORD of hosts.

6 Then flew one of the seraphims unto me, having a live coal in his hand, *which* he had taken with the tongs from off the altar:

7 And he laid *it* upon my mouth, and said, Lo, this hath touched thy lips; and thine iniquity is taken away, and thy sin purged.

8 Also I heard the voice of the Lord, saying, Whom shall I send, and who will go for us? Then said I, Here *am* I; send me.

9 ¶ And he said, Go, and tell this people, Hear ye indeed, but understand not; and see ye indeed, but perceive not.

10 Make the heart of this people fat, and make their ears heavy, and shut their eyes; lest they see with their eyes, and hear with their ears, and understand with their heart, and convert, and be healed.

11 Then said I, Lord, how long? And he answered, Until the cities be wasted without inhabitant, and the houses without man, and the land be utterly desolate,

12 And the LORD have removed men far away, and *there be* a great forsaking in the midst of the land.

13 ¶ But yet in it *shall be* a tenth, and it shall return, and shall be eaten: as a teil tree, and as an oak, whose substance *is* in them, when they cast *their leaves: so* the holy seed *shall be* the substance thereof.

Unlike the KJB, the Hebrew here names Yahweh twice, and the fright of gazing upon the Holy gives a more pervasive sense of dread in the original. Though this might seem the prophetic call, why did the redactors place it after the first five chapters?

Evidently the School of Isaiah did not regard this as the summoning of Isaiah to his vocation but as the start of a sequence (6–8) that absolves him from the failure of a crucial mission in 734 B.C.E. (or so). Sent to alert the people of Judah to the threat of invasion by the Assyrians and their vassals in the northern state of Israel, the prophet speaks to the deaf, and the vision of Yahweh in his throne room means more to us than to Isaiah's disciples; the epiphany of Yahweh is stunning. No one disputes that the visionary here is Isaiah of Jerusalem, directly called by Yahweh in his temple, and I wish that the prophet's disciples had placed it first in the book. Yet the redacted Isaiah seems concentric in design—a brilliant suggestion by Herbert Marks. Its great poems are dispersed; in my judgment they are chapters 5:1–7, 13, 32, 35, 40:1–11, 42:1–9, 45, 54, 60, 62. Of these, 13, 32, and 35 probably are not by Isaiah of Jerusalem, and of course from 40 on they are by Second Isaiah or later. In these ten poems and the throne vision of chapter 6, the KJB fully matches the splendor of the Hebrew.

I must add that more accurately "the English Bible" matches Tanakh, since the KJB's Isaiah is almost entirely taken from the Geneva Bible, though with embellishments.

Isaiah of Jerusalem, royal statesman, prophet, and priest of the Temple, counsels the kings of Judah in their perpetually hopeless situation of contending with the vastly more powerful nation-states Assyria and Babylon, more than thirty years apart in their aggressions. King Uzziah, Isaiah's first cousin, died in 734 B.C.E., during the Assyrians' attack upon Judah. In 701, Sennacherib led a campaign against King Hezekiah. A century later, Judah's independence ended, a few years after the death of King Josiah. Isaiah's public career ended in 701, after more than thirty years of applying prophecy to international politics. The great seer did not have to suffer the Babylonian Captivity of the elite among his people.

The common reader, unlike the historical scholar, values

Isaiah and his school for the poetry and not the pragmatics of applied prophecy. As for "the theology of Isaiah," that is a Christian formulation and is foreign to Tanakh, and to the Jews before Maimonides. Theology, a Greek word and idea, is contrary to prophetic trust in Yahweh.

To what extent does the poetry of Isaiah and his tradition merit at best a portion of Arnold's over-praise? It is hardly superior to Dante, Shakespeare, or Milton, and has nothing in common with Homer: Odysseus and Achilles are alien to the Tanakh's aesthetic sensibility. Yet I see what so moved Arnold, as here in chapter 32, verses 1–8, almost certainly composed long after Isaiah of Jerusalem:

> 1 Behold, a king shall reign in righteousness, and princes shall rule in judgment.
>
> 2 And a man shall be as an hiding place from the wind, and a covert from the tempest; as rivers of water in a dry place, as the shadow of a great rock in a weary land.
>
> 3 And the eyes of them that see shall not be dim, and the ears of them that hear shall hearken.
>
> 4 The heart also of the rash shall understand knowledge, and the tongue of the stammerers shall be ready to speak plainly.
>
> 5 The vile person shall be no more called liberal, nor the churl said *to be* bountiful.
>
> 6 For the vile person will speak villany, and his heart will work iniquity, to practice hypocrisy, and to utter error against the LORD, to make empty the soul of the hungry, and he will cause the drink of the thirsty to fail.
>
> 7 The instruments also of the churl *are* evil: he deviseth wicked devices to destroy the poor with lying words, even when the needy speaketh right.

8 But the liberal deviseth liberal things; and by liberal things shall he stand.

The Hebrew in verse 2 says "each," not "a man," and so the reference is to idealized rulers of Judah, who shall be "as the shadow of a great rock in a weary land," a phrase that is a great poem in itself. One of the Geneva group (Coverdale perhaps, who sat in with them, since the accent is his) gloriously hit upon this, troping the Hebrew for "arid" to the wonderful "weary." How all of us wish for a president who could be the shadow of a great rock in our own weary land.

Chapter 5, likely to be the work of Isaiah himself, opens extraordinarily as the Song of the Vineyard:

1 Now will I sing to my wellbeloved a song of my beloved touching his vineyard. My wellbeloved hath a vineyard in a very fruitful hill:

2 And he fenced it, and gathered out the stones thereof, and planted it with the choicest vine, and built a tower in the midst of it, and also made a winepress therein: and he looked that it should bring forth grapes, and it brought forth wild grapes.

3 And now, O inhabitants of Jerusalem, and men of Judah, judge, I pray you, betwixt me and my vineyard.

4 What could have been done more to my vineyard, that I have not done in it? wherefore, when I looked that it should bring forth grapes, brought it forth wild grapes?

5 And now go to; I will tell you what I will do to my vineyard: I will take away the hedge thereof, and it shall be eaten up; *and* break down the wall thereof, and it shall be trodden down:

6 And I will lay it waste: it shall not be pruned, nor digged; but there shall come up briers and thorns: I

will also command the clouds that they rain no rain upon it.

7 For the vineyard of the LORD of hosts *is* the house of Israel, and the men of Judah his pleasant plant: and he looked for judgment, but behold oppression; for righteousness, but behold a cry.

8 ¶ Woe unto them that join house to house, *that* lay field to field, till *there be* no place, that they may be placed alone in the midst of the earth!

Rarely has a love song yielded as rapidly to divine denunciation. There is always something abrupt about Isaiah's own voicings. Here Yahweh's love for the Jews is rebuffed and fury ensues. This bears out the illuminating perspective of Herbert Marks: "The Reader of Isaiah needs to be particularly sensitive to these disjunctions and shifts, for where other prophetic books tend to arrange their judgments and promises successively along a temporal axis, Isaiah arranges them concentrically, making destruction and salvation not successive stages but simultaneous possibilities which together bear on the historical moment. In such context, salvation is not the sequel to suffering but implicit within it, as the burnt stump contains the new messianic shoot (11:1)." The key phrase is "simultaneous possibilities," which is the essence of Hebraic prophetic proclamation. Each navi cries (however emphatically): "The Yahweh-word is to me!" The Hebrew *davar* is at once word, thing, and act, and it drives forward something held back in the self. Isaiah and his disciples can be allegorized by the Freudian drives of love and death, simultaneously caught up in a struggle.

In Isaiah 13 and 14 (certainly *not* by the Jerusalem statesman) a great voice proclaims the ruin of Babylon:

9 Hell from beneath is moved for thee to meet *thee* at thy coming: it stirreth up the dead for thee, *even* all the chief

ones of the earth; it hath raised up from their thrones all the kings of the nations.

10 All they shall speak and say unto thee, Art thou also become weak as we? art though become like unto us?

11 Thy pomp is brought down to the grave, *and* the noise of thy viols: the worm is spread under thee, and the worms cover thee.

12 How art thou fallen from heaven, O Lucifer, son of the morning! *how* art thou cut down to the ground, which didst weaken the nations!

13 For thou hast said in thine heart, I will ascend into heaven, I will exalt my throne above the stars of God: I will sit also upon the mount of the congregation, in the sides of the north:

14 I will ascend above the heights of the clouds; I will be like the most High.

15 Yet thou shalt be brought down to hell, to the sides of the pit.

16 They that see thee shall narrowly look upon thee, *and* consider thee, *saying, Is* this the man that made the earth to tremble, that did shake kingdoms;

17 *That* made the world as a wilderness, and destroyed the cities thereof; *that* opened not the house of his prisoners?

[14:9–17]

Hell is a Christian idea; the Hebrew says *sheol,* akin to Homeric Dis or Hades, while "the dead" in the original are "the powerless." "Lucifer" in the Hebrew is *helel,* the shining morning star Venus, called Ishtar by the Babylonians, and adopted by Milton as Satan's name before he fell.

Isaiah 32–33, again later, ventures messianic tonalities, even as these call upon the women of Jerusalem to perform ritual lamentation. The passage to Second Isaiah, in chapter 40, is equally sublime in the Hebrew and in the KJB:

1 Comfort ye, comfort ye my people, saith your God.

2 Speak ye comfortably to Jerusalem, and cry unto her, that her warfare is accomplished, that her iniquity is pardoned: for she hath received of the LORD's hand double for all her sins.

3 ¶ The voice of him that crieth in the wilderness, Prepare ye the way of the LORD, make straight in the desert a highway for our God.

4 Every valley shall be exalted, and every mountain and hill shall be made low: and the crooked shall be made straight, and the rough places plain:

5 And the glory of the LORD shall be revealed, and all flesh shall see *it* together: for the mouth of the LORD hath spoken *it*.

6 The voice said, Cry. And he said, What shall I cry? All flesh *is* grass, and all the goodliness thereof *is* as the flower of the field:

7 The grass withereth, the flower fadeth: because the spirit of the LORD bloweth upon it: surely the people *is* grass.

8 The grass withereth, the flower fadeth: but the word of our God shall stand for ever.

9 ¶ O Zion, that bringest good tidings, get thee up into the high mountain; O Jerusalem, that bringest good tidings, lift up thy voice with strength; lift *it* up, be not afraid; say unto the cities of Judah, Behold your God!

10 Behold, the Lord GOD will come with strong *hand,* and his arm shall rule for him: behold, his reward *is* with him, and his work before him.

11 He shall feed his flock like a shepherd: he shall gather the lambs with his arm, and carry *them* in his bosom, *and* shall gently lead those that are with young.

Many reading this hear Handel, who was equal to such greatness. The grand trope flesh is grass perfectly suits with the grandeur of Yahweh and the vulnerability of a restored Jerusalem. Walt Whitman's superb fantasia on the grass in "Song of Myself" is the most significant development of this text in Isaiah but "All flesh is grass" reverberates throughout poetic tradition.

Even that superb metaphor is surpassed by the figure of the Suffering Servant throughout chapters 49–55. The Persian king Cyrus had failed to fulfill prophetic hopes, and the Servant takes his place. For the KJB as for all other Christian Bibles, the Suffering Servant is Jesus Christ. For the Jewish School of Isaiah, he is intended as an image of apotheosis surmounting natural degradation. A powerful determination is set up between this Servant song and a new group of songs of Zion.

Chapters 60 and 62 are for me the poetic summit of Isaiah, whether in Tanakh or the English Bible. Here is chapter 60:

1 Arise, shine; for thy light is come, and the glory of the LORD is risen upon thee.

2 For, behold, the darkness shall cover the earth, and gross darkness the people: but the LORD shall arise upon thee, and his glory shall be seen upon thee.

3 And the gentiles shall come to thy light, and kings to the brightness of thy rising.

4 Lift up thine eyes round about, and see: all they gather themselves together, they come to thee: thy sons shall come from far, and thy daughters shall be nursed at *thy* side.

5 Then thou shalt see, and flow together, and thine heart shall fear, and be enlarged; because the abundance of

the sea shall be converted unto thee, the forces of the Gentiles shall come unto thee.

There one accepts Matthew Arnold's invocation of Shakespeare and Milton. Even more splendid is chapter 62:

> 1 For Zion's sake will I not hold my peace, and for Jerusalem's sake I will not rest, until the righteousness thereof go forth as brightness, and the salvation thereof as a lamp *that* burneth.
>
> 2 And the Gentiles shall see thy righteousness, and all kings thy glory: and thou shalt be called by a new name, which the mouth of the LORD shall name.
>
> 3 Thou shalt also be a crown of glory in the hand of the LORD, and a royal diadem in the hand of thy God.
>
> 4 Thou shalt no more be termed Forsaken; neither shall thy land any more be termed Desolate: but thou shalt be called Hephzi-bah, and thy land Beulah: for the LORD delighteth in thee, and thy land shall be married.
>
> 5 ¶ For *as* a young man marrieth a virgin, so shall thy sons marry thee: and *as* the bridegroom rejoiceth over the bride, *so* shall thy God rejoice over thee.

Beulah, the land married to Yahweh, receives exultant response in American chants such as "Beulah Land," a Protestant hymn, and dozens of others, and in William Blake, where it is both illusory and finally redeemed. As I read them, the "Zion songs" are prompted by the Isaiah School's anxiety of influence in regard to Jeremiah, whose accent is heard throughout the Suffering Servant songs.

The sages of the Jewish oral tradition necessarily repudiated the Christian appropriation of the Suffering Servant. To them the Servant was Moses or Jeremiah or the people of Israel enduring the Exile, which seems to me the most persuasive identification. Victory through suffering is a dark formula, but the failure of expectations about Cyrus of Persia stimulated desperate imaginings. The Servant transmutes and fuses Jeremiah and Job. Bipolar in his anguish, Jeremiah is actually an unlikely figure to associate with Job, except that each retains his integrity in ghastly circumstances.

The ultimate paradox of the book of Isaiah is how different it becomes over the centuries from its heroic inception to its anguished and wistful closure. Isaiah of Jerusalem, stern champion of Yahweh alone, has nothing in common with the Suffering Servant. The KJB's high rhetoric conceals this, since First, Second, and Third Isaiah, and all their epigoni, homogenize into a common exaltation. Yet so sublime is the consequence that a Matthew Arnold could deceive himself that even Shakespeare and Milton could not consistently attain that intense level of something evermore about to be.

Jeremiah

The longest and bitterest of the prophetic books, Jeremiah is the most personal and perhaps the most influential. We know the man (or think we do) much better than the lofty Isaiah of Jerusalem or the strange visionary Ezekiel. Probably what we know is a skilled literary fiction: the prophet of perpetual travail who sees his kings and his city destroyed and himself dies in Egypt, the dishonored prisoner of his fellow exiles. We associate him with what we still call jeremiads: denunciations foretelling disasters.

Jeremiah for me is very difficult to admire, though I may be eccentric in that regard. His sufferings are extraordinary and vociferous, and for him they constitute the stuff of redemption. That may seem commonplace now, but it was violently original in his own lifetime. As a poet he evades Isaiah and returns to Hosea, a great original of a century earlier. The terrible intimacy of Hosea's oracles makes Jeremiah's amazing inwardness possible. Both prophets are *hurtful:* that is their power and their authority, though this gift of wounding makes me wince and sometimes serves to drive me away.

Addicted as a reader to the personal, I ought to appreciate Jeremiah rather more than I do. But I find in him one of my own faults, which I first came to recognize through reading, teaching, and writing about Shakespeare's *Richard II.* Jeremiah keeps murmuring, "terror all around," and Richard II is addicted to telling sad stories of the death of kings. The proclivity to make calamity yet more unmitigated by expressing it hyperbolically may not be a universal human trait, but few fictive beings exemplify it so fiercely as do Jeremiah and Richard. In their bipolar manias they augment catastrophes with a kind of disagreeable relish.

This is not to deny Jeremiah his hysterical heroism but rather to fend our souls from him. In 586 B.C.E. came the final destruction of Jerusalem by the Babylonians, who pillaged Yahweh's Temple, ending it and exiling a second wave of educated Judahites. What remained were the lower classes, who worked the land, poor and desperate. This is the dreaded event prophesied by Jeremiah throughout forty years, and always foretold in vain since his auditors scorned him.

Despite his ongoing popular renown as poet of doom, Jeremiah was absorbed into later Judaic tradition as a singer of hope, a baffling enough paradox. Presumably this resulted from the so-called Book of Consolation, chapters 30–33. The book of Jeremiah is a vast, sprawling aggregation, and it is useless to speak of its "structure": it has none. Perhaps some passages of it truly *were* dictated by the prophet to his legendary scribe Baruch, but nobody will ever know. We seem to have an anthology founded upon prior anthologies, put together over considerable spans of time by many would-be Jeremiahs.

The KJB's Jeremiah, essentially founded on the Geneva version, is superbly rhetorical, and achieves the sublime in chapter 31, verses 15–21:

> 15 ¶ Thus saith the LORD; A voice was heard in Ramah, lamentation, *and* bitter weeping; Rahel weeping for her children refused to be comforted for her children, because they *were* not.
>
> 16 Thus saith the LORD; Refrain thy voice from weeping, and thine eyes from tears: for thy work shall be rewarded, saith the LORD; and they shall come again from the land of the enemy.
>
> 17 And there is hope in thine end, saith the LORD, that thy children shall come again to their own border.
>
> 18 ¶ I have surely heard Ephraim bemoaning himself *thus;* Thou hast chastised me, and I was chastised, as a bullock unaccustomed *to the yoke:* turn thou me, and I shall be turned; for thou *art* the LORD my God.
>
> 19 Surely after that I was turned, I repented; and after that I was instructed, I smote upon *my* thigh: I was ashamed, yea, even confounded, because I did bear the reproach of my youth.
>
> 20 *Is* Ephraim my dear son? *is he* a pleasant child? for since I spake against him, I do earnestly remember him still: therefore my bowels are troubled for him; I will surely have mercy upon him, saith the LORD.
>
> 21 Set thee up waymarks, make thee high heaps: set thine heart toward the highway, *even* the way *which* thou wentest: turn again, O virgin of Israel, turn again to these thy cities.

Ramah is a town a few miles to the north of Jerusalem, while Rachel is Jacob's beloved wife, the mother of Joseph and of Benjamin. The particular force of this plangent passage increases for Christian readers since it is quoted in Matthew 2:18. "Turn now!" is the burden, for Jeremiah is on the threshold of proclaiming a new, more inward covenant in 31:31–34. Saint Paul strongly misread this as Christ's substitution of the spirit for the letter, thus creating the phrase "the New Testament," which was later applied to the Christian canon. A misreading it certainly was and is: Jeremiah does *not* proclaim a new Torah or Teaching, a growing inner self, or a more inward Torah. Instead he interprets into being a new opposition between inwardness and outwardness, beautifully caught by the KJB in its version of 31:33:

> But this *shall be* the covenant that I will make with the house of Israel; After those days, saith the LORD, I will put my law in their inward parts, and write it in their hearts; and will be their God, and they shall be my people.

The Hebrew does not say "inward parts" but "within them": the opposition is between inwardness and outwardness. Jeremiah's indubitable greatness inheres in his radical originality as a psychological dualist, prophetic of Sigmund Freud. To trace that originality you need to turn back to 4:19–21:

> 19 ¶ My bowels, my bowels! I am pained at my very heart; my heart maketh a noise in me; I cannot hold my peace, because thou hast heard, O my soul, the sound of the trumpet, the alarm of war.
> 20 Destruction upon destruction is cried; for the whole land is spoiled: suddenly are my tents spoiled, *and* my curtains in a moment.

21 How long shall I see the standard, *and* hear the sound
of the trumpet?

"My soul" like "my very heart" refers literally in the Hebrew to
"you, my being, hear." The estrangement from inner self may
be a trance-phenomenon, yet conveys a doubleness incessant in
Jeremiah. He invents what may be the greatest of Judaic (and
subsequently Christian) tropes, the injustice of outwardness.

From chapter 2 on, Jeremiah's oracles center upon a weird, implicit metaphor in which Jerusalem is Yahweh's unfaithful bride,
his to-be-divorced first wife (as it were). Jeremiah himself, rather
shockingly, presents himself as Yahweh's choice of a second wife,
from chapter 20, verse 7, on:

7 ¶ O Lord, thou hast deceived me, and I was deceived:
thou art stronger than I, and hast prevailed: I am in derision daily, every one mocketh me.

8 For since I spake, I cried out, I cried violence and spoil;
because the word of the Lord was made a reproach unto
me, and a derision, daily.

9 Then I said, I will not make mention of him, nor speak
any more in his name. But *his word* was in mine heart as a
burning fire shut up in my bones, and I was weary with
forbearing, and I could not *stay.*

10 ¶ For I heard the defaming of many, fear on every
side. Report, *say they,* and we will report it. All my famil-
iars watched for my halting, *saying,* Peradventure he will
be enticed, and we shall prevail against him, and we shall
take our revenge on him.

11 But the Lord *is* with me as a mighty terrible one:
therefore my persecutors shall stumble, and they shall
not prevail: they shall be greatly ashamed; for they shall

not prosper: *their* everlasting confusion shall never be forgotten.

12 But, O LORD of hosts, that triest the righteous, *and* seest the reins and the heart, let me see thy vengeance on them: for unto thee have I opened my cause.

13 Sing unto the LORD, praise ye the LORD: for he hath delivered the soul of the poor from the hand of evildoers.

14 ¶ Cursed be the day wherein I was born: let not the day wherein my mother bare me be blessed.

15 Cursed *be* the man who brought tidings to my father, saying, A man child is born unto thee; making him very glad.

16 And let that man be as the cities which the LORD overthrew, and repented not: and let him hear the cry in the morning, and the shouting at noontide;

17 Because he slew me not from the womb; or that my mother might have been my grave, and her womb *to be* always great *with me.*

18 Wherefore came I forth out of the womb to see labour and sorrow, that my days should be consumed with shame?

Most exegetes have softened this blasphemous despair, which is to take away from Jeremiah his authentic strength. He accuses Yahweh of unlawful seduction—indeed, of rape. His call is unwilled, from childhood on—he could not be more unlike Isaiah of Jerusalem. Yahweh deprives Jeremiah of everything: childhood, marriage, honor in the community.

In turning away from this outwardness of perpetual loss, Jeremiah creates a new Yahweh, consonant neither with that of the J Writer nor that of Isaiah. Martin Buber, loving Jeremiah, named this new Yahweh "the God of the sufferers." Job, rather than Jesus

Christ or even Second Isaiah's Suffering Servant, seems to me Jeremiah's true heir.

Jeremiah's intimacy with Yahweh is so close that visions seem redundant in regard to him. When he sees visionary flames, they divide into outer—Yahweh's fury—and inner—the prophet's vocation. In 21:12–14, Yahweh's flame is outward:

> 12 O house of David, thus saith the LORD; Execute judgment in the morning, and deliver *him that is* spoiled out of the hand of the oppressor, lest my fury go out like fire, and burn that none can quench *it,* because of the evil of your doings.
>
> 13 Behold, I *am* against thee, O inhabitant of the valley, and rock of the plain, saith the LORD; which say, Who shall come down against us? or who shall enter into our habitations?
>
> 14 But I will punish you according to the fruit of your doings, saith the LORD: and I will kindle a fire in the forest thereof, and it shall devour all things round about it.

Very different is Jeremiah's inward fire:

> Then I said, I will not make mention of him, nor speak any more in his name. But *his word* was in mine heart as a burning fire shut up in my bones, and I was weary with forbearing, and I could not *stay.*
>
> [20:9]

Those two conflagrations are the ultimate emblems of Jeremiah. He lives and suffers between the fury of Yahweh and his own burning fervor against the injustice of all outwardness.

Ezekiel

There is a strangeness to the book of Ezekiel that repeated readings cannot reduce. Since childhood I have been disturbed by it, and old age only augments Ezekiel's effect upon me. Nor can the book be evaded: Ezekiel invents apocalypse. From the book of Revelation on to Dante, Milton, Blake, and Shelley, the symbolism of Ezekiel forms much of poetic and spiritual tradition. Kabbalah in its early form of Merkabah mysticism stems directly from Ezekiel's vision. Though this prophet scarcely seems to have been sane, he can be regarded as the start of Judaism and also as the origin of Christian revelation, a self-contradictory legacy. He makes me unhappy (so does Jeremiah), but perhaps that only means Yahweh makes me unhappy.

Ezekiel's book or books (it breaks into two) is immensely difficult, despite more than two millennia of exegesis. Moshe Greenberg's two admirable volumes of the Anchor Yale Bible series (1983, 1995) are an immense help, and I will rely on them here. Yet I have been thinking about Ezekiel for a half century and will feel free to present my own speculations since they are informed both by poetic and Kabbalistic tradition.

Reading Ezekiel's Hebrew is difficult, because the text is packed with allusion but also too frequently is spasmodic in style. Sometimes the redundancy is incremental, reflecting design, but frequently it seems manic. I can well believe that the prophet himself composed at least the first twenty chapters, with an eloquence punctuated by madness.

Herbert Marks brilliantly observes that Ezekiel's Yahweh is "a God in exile." Since the entire text has been worked over by contrary redactors, we can be a little slow in seeing Ezekiel plain, an impossible prospect anyway. He is more difficult than Dante, Blake, or

Shelley, all hugely influenced by him, but all considerably saner and more balanced. Reading Ezekiel, the trope of splintering always afflicts me: text, prophet, Jerusalem, God. Everything breaks apart.

And yet Ezekiel is obsessed by fixed dates, mapped by Greenberg in his first volume. The dread of time is so intense as to prelude Macbeth's. Prophecy has a timeless aspect in other Hebrew visionaries but not in Ezekiel 1–24. The prophet's career extends from 593 to 571 B.C.E. and takes place entirely during the Babylonian Exile. More than Jeremiah, Ezekiel is a Diaspora phenomenon, though pragmatically the two dark prophets convey the same burden: abandon hope for an immediate restoration of Zion. Only false prophets prate of a rebuilt Jerusalem, except in regard to a vision beyond time.

The KJB Ezekiel, very reliant upon Geneva, is rhetorically powerful though frequently obscure because inaccurate. Added to Ezekiel's own disjunctiveness, this makes for hard though awesome reading. And yet Greenberg's far more correct version does not stand up to the KJB. Here is Ezekiel 1:26–28:

> 26 Above the expanse that was over their heads was the figure of a throne with the appearance of sapphire-stone, and above, on the figure of a throne was a figure with the appearance of a human being. 27 From the appearance of his loins upward I saw the like of *hashmal,* having something with the appearance of fire surrounding it; and from the appearance of his loins downward I saw something with the appearance of fire; and he was surrounded by a radiance. 28 Like the appearance of the bow that is in a cloud on a rainy day such was the appearance of the surrounding radiance. That was the appearance of the figure of the Majesty of YHWH; when I saw it, I fell on my face—
> [Anchor Yale Bible Ezekiel, 1–20]

Prophets: Ezekiel

26 ¶ And above the firmament that *was* over their heads *was* the likeness of a throne, as the appearance of a sapphire stone: and upon the likeness of the throne *was* the likeness as the appearance of a man above upon it.

27 And I saw as the color of amber, as the appearance of fire round about within it, from the appearance of his loins even upward, and from the appearance of his loins even downward, I saw as it were the appearance of fire, and it had brightness round about.

28 As the appearance of the bow that is in the cloud in the day of rain, so *was* the appearance of the brightness round about. This *was* the appearance of the likeness of the glory of the LORD. And when I saw *it,* I fell upon my face, and I heard a voice of one that spake.

[KJB]

Ezekiel's giant metaphor of the chariot-throne is magnificently fecund and seems to demand an oracular rhetoric, pitched incredibly high. Yahweh in Ezekiel is centered upon himself and not the people of Judah. He is in love with his own name and wants to be recognized for his might, not for his Covenant. Ezekiel will not say so but his God is very bad news both for the exiles and for those who will go down with Jerusalem. Ezekiel, whose name means "God strengthens," testifies instead that "God destroys."

The "wheels and their work," merkabah and throne, are related by Greenberg to Mesopotamian and Syrian iconography, but I am not convinced (nor, indeed, is he). Tanakh itself provides much of the materia poetica that Ezekiel transmutes: Exodus 24, and 40, Isaiah 6, Psalm 18. Yet the refiner's fire of Ezekiel's imagination brings forth an amazing apotheosis of all prior visions of Yahweh:

4 ¶ And I looked, and, behold, a whirlwind came out of the north, a great cloud, and a fire infolding itself, and

a brightness *was* about it, and out of the midst thereof as the color of amber, out of the midst of the fire.

5 Also out of the midst thereof *came* the likeness of four living creatures. And this *was* their appearance; they had the likeness of a man.

6 And every one had four faces, and every one had four wings.

7 And their feet *were* straight feet; and the sole of their feet *was* like the sole of a calf's foot: and they sparkled like the color of burnished brass.

8 And *they had* the hands of a man under their wings on their four sides; and they four had their faces and their wings.

9 Their wings *were* joined one to another; they turned not when they went; they went every one straight forward.

10 As for the likeness of their faces, they four had the face of a man, and the face of a lion, on the right side: and they four had the face of an ox on the left side; they four also had the face of an eagle.

11 Thus *were* their faces: and their wings *were* stretched upward; two *wings* of every one *were* joined one to another, and two covered their bodies.

12 And they went every one straight forward: whither the spirit was to go, they went; *and* they turned not when they went.

13 As for the likeness of the living creatures, their appearance *was* like burning coals of fire, *and* like the appearance of lamps: it went up and down among the living creatures; and the fire was bright, and out of the fire went forth lightning.

14 And the living creatures ran and returned as the appearance of a flash of lightning.

15 ¶ Now as I beheld the living creatures, behold one wheel upon the earth by the living creatures, with his four faces.

16 The appearance of the wheels and their work *was* like unto the color of a beryl: and they four had one likeness: and their appearance and their work *was* as it were a wheel in the middle of a wheel.

17 When they went, they went upon their four sides: *and* they turned not when they went.

18 As for their rings, they were so high that they were dreadful; and their rings *were* full of eyes round about them four.

19 And when the living creatures went, the wheels went by them: and when the living creatures were lifted up from the earth, the wheels were lifted up.

20 Whithersoever the spirit was to go, they went, thither *was their* spirit to go; and the wheels were lifted up over against them: for the spirit of the living creature *was* in the wheels.

21 When those went, *these* went; and when those stood, *these* stood; and when those were lifted up from the earth, the wheels were lifted up over against them: for the spirit of the living creature *was* in the wheels.

22 And the likeness of the firmament upon the heads of the living creature *was* as the color of the terrible crystal, stretched forth over their heads above.

23 And under the firmament *were* their wings straight, the one toward the other: every one had two, which covered on this side, and every one had two, which covered on that side, their bodies.

24 And when they went, I heard the noise of their wings, like the noise of great waters, as the voice of the

Almighty, the voice of speech, as the noise of an host: when they stood, they let down their wings.

25 And there was a voice from the firmament that *was* over their heads, when they stood, *and* had let down their wings.

[1:4–25]

As a Jew who does not trust in the Covenant, and who has strong Gnostic tendencies, I nevertheless am overwhelmed by this epiphany of Yahweh. As a literary critic, I yield to its rhetorical authority, and to the great traditions it fostered (Dante, Milton, Blake, Shelley, and Kabbalah). If you want an authentic view of God, this dynamic whirlwind is where Tanakh wants you to turn. Turn it and turn it, for everything of Yahweh is in it.

The emphasis is upon a Yahweh who wants you to know that he *is* the Lord. I hear anxiety in this: a God who endlessly roars, "I am Yahweh!" angrily seems to be reassuring himself. Exiled in Babylon, Ezekiel's friends and relations had to be very uncomfortable with this rabid priest-turned-prophet.

Riding in his chariot, horsed on the "living creatures" or cherubim, Yahweh has a numinosity that is awesome, described as *hashmal,* weakly translated in KJB as "amber" yet untranslatable anyway. A priest in the Jerusalem Temple, Ezekiel participated in the mystery of the Holy of Holies, a bare place, not a chariot-borne throne. Exile can be judged as the context that transformed Isaiah's vision of Yahweh enthroned in the Temple into Ezekiel's far more dynamic vision of the wheels and their work, where the wheels also are angelic.

The prophet Amos had proclaimed that the very soil outside Israel was tainted. Yahweh, appearing to Ezekiel in Babylon, chooses to forget this rough truth.

Instead he makes a triumphal flight over enemy country. *Tri-*

umph is the particular mark of this most elaborate of Yahweh's epiphanies. The insight is not mine but the poets': Dante's Triumphal Chariot of the Church, Petrarch's *Triumphs,* Milton's Chariot of Paternal Divinity, Shelley's *The Triumph of Life,* Blake's *The Four Zoas,* where the Enthroned Man is unfallen Albion.

We hardly think of Ezekiel as a triumphant personality. Isaiah of Jerusalem and Amos can be described so but not the desperately disturbed Ezekiel. Yahweh appears at his most formidable and most triumphant as an expression of his election of the priest Ezekiel as a new kind of prophet. No longer does the navi speak to the moment of crisis and proclaim, "Turn now!" It is far too late for that. Even if the exiles were to forsake their false prophets, it would no longer suffice.

Nothing less than a fully triumphant Yahweh could have demonstrated to the ravaged priest Ezekiel that he had been charged with a prophetic mission. Yet there is a quality of excess in the epiphany that has overflowed into Western poetic tradition and into Kabbalah. Unpacking Ezekiel, one finds chapter 1 virtually impossible. Greenberg usefully cites a midrash to Exodus 15's Song of the Sea:

> Four Kinds of proud beings were created in the world: the proudest of all—man; of birds—the eagle; of domestic animals—the ox; of wild animals—the lion; and all of these are stations beneath the chariot of the Holy One.
>
> [Exodus Rabba 23:13]

Walther Zimmerli, in his vast commentary upon Ezekiel (1969) emphasizes that the prophet's vision is a storm-theophany, akin to Psalm 18. But the feeling-tone of Psalm 18:10–15 is very different from the prophetic theophany:

> 10 And he rode upon a cherub, and did fly: yea, he did fly upon the wings of the wind.

11 He made darkness his secret place; his pavilion round about him *were* dark waters *and* thick clouds of the skies.

12 At the brightness *that was* before him his thick clouds passed, hail *stones* and coals of fire.

13 The LORD also thundered in the heavens, and the Highest gave his voice; hail *stones* and coals of fire.

14 Yea, he sent out his arrows, and scattered them; and he shot out lightnings, and discomfited them.

15 Then the channels of waters were seen, and the foundations of the world were discovered at thy rebuke, O LORD, at the blast of the breath of thy nostrils.

That is an angry, not a triumphant Yahweh; Ezekiel is far more original. But what is his purpose in creating his fourfold cherubim? So baroque are these images (confusedly worked over by the School of Ezekiel) that both poetic and esoteric interpretation touch a limit in venturing upon clarification.

Since the call of the prophet by Yahweh follows directly after, God's triumphal manifestation must be an enabling word/act that would not be so fully persuasive without the singular nature of these cherubim. John Calvin, in his farewell commentary on Ezekiel (he died before finishing it), said that the vision was not lucid and that he scarcely could understand it. Nevertheless, he added that he granted its necessity, because Ezekiel's dire need required "a formidable form of God."

Calvin could have said the same of himself. Dante, a better guide to Ezekiel, emphasized the eyes in the wheels, as Blake did. The wheels, *ophannim* in Hebrew, eventually were raised by exegetes to a third order of angels, ranking behind seraphim and cherubim. This was bound to happen because neither the conveying cherubim nor the wheels actually can provide the force that moves Yahweh, who himself is the origin of all motion. That may be the subtlest import of Ezekiel's vision: the elaborate symbolism of chariot and throne, cherubim and ophannim, is there to proclaim its own redundancy, in contrast to a Yahweh so dynamic as to beggar our human sense of origin and affect.

Ezekiel can be so extreme a prophet as to make even Jeremiah seem moderate, while Ezekiel's is the harshest of Yahwehs, pragmatically alienated from the people he perpetually accuses of having forsaken him. It seems more accurate to observe that Yahweh has abandoned them to their Babylonian Captivity, but that is not Ezekiel's perspective. Clearly it is my own, and so I remind myself that this is a *literary* appreciation of the KJB, and Ezekiel is a large component in that aesthetic splendor, disconcerting as he and Yahweh can be.

What, after the famous opening chapter, are the splendors of the KJB Ezekiel (which is close to identical with the Geneva Ezekiel)? The rhetorical glories and human miseries are closely interwoven, as we ought to expect in a book utterly persuaded that every expectation and event should be for the sake of Yahweh. If, as the Diaspora prophet, Ezekiel has to be regarded as a forerunner of Judaism, that makes me reflect upon Judaism in the spring of 2010, which is when I write. The shadow of the Holocaust still and always falls upon Judaism. How could it not? What would we think of a Hebraic prophet who rose up now to say that the martyrs of the Shoah were abandoned by Yahweh because of their sins against him? The question is obscenely unanswerable. But is Ezekiel less outrageous and less unforgivable? He and his Yahweh *celebrate* the fall of Jerusalem and the slaughter of its inhabitants in chapter 5:

> 1 And thou, son of man, take thee a sharp knife, take
> thee a barber's razor, and cause *it* to pass upon thine head

and upon thy beard: then take thee balances to weigh, and divide the *hair*.

2 Thou shalt burn with fire a third part in the midst of the city, when the days of the siege are fulfilled: and thou shalt take a third part, *and* smite about it with a knife: and a third part thou shalt scatter in the wind; and I will draw out a sword after them.

3 Thou shalt also take thereof a few in number, and bind them in thy skirts.

4 Then take of them again, and cast them into the midst of the fire, and burn them in the fire; *for* thereof shall a fire come forth into all the house of Israel.

5 ¶ Thus said the Lord God; This *is* Jerusalem: I have set it in the midst of the nations and countries *that are* round about her.

6 And she hath changed my judgments into wickedness more than the nations, and my statutes more than the countries that *are* round about her: for they have refused my judgments and my statutes, they have not walked in them.

7 Therefore thus saith the Lord God; Because ye multiplied more than the nations that *are* round about you, *and* have not walked in my statutes, neither have kept my judgments, neither have done according to the judgments of the nations that *are* round about you;

8 Therefore thus saith the Lord God; Behold, I, even I, *am* against thee, and will execute judgments in the midst of thee in the sight of the nations.

9 And I will do in thee that which I have not done, and whereunto I will not do any more the like, because of all thine abominations.

10 Therefore the fathers shall eat the sons in the midst

of thee, and the sons shall eat their fathers; and I will execute judgments in thee, and the whole remnant of thee will I scatter into all the winds.

11 Wherefore, *as* I live, saith the Lord God; Surely because thou hast defiled my sanctuary with all thy detestable things, and with all thine abominations, therefore will I also diminish *thee;* neither shall mine eye spare, neither will I have any pity.

12 ¶ A third part of thee shall die with the pestilence, and with famine shall they be consumed in the midst of thee: and a third part shall fall by the sword round about thee; and I will scatter a third part into all the winds, and I will draw out a sword after them.

13 Thus shall mine anger be accomplished, and I will cause my fury to rest upon them, and I will be comforted: and they shall know that I the Lord have spoken *it* in my zeal, when I have accomplished my fury in them.

14 Moreover I will make thee waste, and a reproach among the nations that *are* round about thee, in the sight of all that pass by.

15 So it shall be a reproach and a taunt, an instruction and an astonishment unto the nations that *are* round about thee, when I shall execute judgments in thee in anger and in fury and in furious rebukes. I the Lord have spoken *it*.

16 When I shall send upon them the evil arrows of famine, which shall be for *their* destruction, *and* which I will send to destroy you: and I will increase the famine upon you, and will break your staff of bread:

17 So will I send upon you famine and evil beasts, and they shall bereave thee; and pestilence and blood shall pass through thee; and I will bring the sword upon thee. I the Lord have spoken *it*.

I don't know whether I am more horrified by verse 13, *and I will be comforted,* or by the very end of this: *I the* LORD *have spoken it.* The aesthetic power of Ezekiel comes at too high a human price, and who needs such a God as his?

Since childhood I have been most appalled by chapter 9, verse 4, which is the basis of William Blake's great lyric "London" in *The Songs of Experience:*

> And the LORD said unto him, Go through the midst of the city, through the midst of Jerusalem, and set a mark upon the foreheads of the men that sigh and that cry for all the abominations that be done in the midst thereof.

The divine chariot-throne returns in chapter 10, verse 14, but with a surprising variation:

> And every one had four faces: the first face *was* the face of a cherub, and the second face *was* the face of a man, and the third the face of a lion, and the fourth the face of an eagle.

The cherub's face has replaced that of the ox, perhaps reflecting the sanctified slaughter, since God in 10:7 commands that the fire to incinerate Jerusalem be taken "from between the wheels, and from between the cherubim." The litany of divinely ordered destruction goes on with fearsome exuberance from chapters 11 through 17. I wince as I reread them and find in their zest an unhealthy, virtually sadomasochistic pleasure on the prophet's part.

Mitigation commences only with chapter 18, which turns upon the already proverbial saying "The fathers have eaten sour grapes, and the children's teeth are set on edge." Jeremiah, envisioning a newly inward Covenant, had quoted this also (31:29–30), but Ezekiel rejects it utterly. But how does one reconcile Ezekiel 11–17 with his earlier proclamations of absolute devastation for all of Jewry? These return anyway, to be followed by dire denunciations of neighboring nations, litanies that attain extraordinary eloquence in regard to Tyre. So zestful are these that they are among the grandest of biblical orations, poems of preternatural eloquence. Chapter 27 sings the fall of the great merchant port:

> 32 And in their wailing they shall take up a lamentation for thee, and lament over thee, *saying,* What *city is* like Tyrus, like the destroyed in the midst of the sea?
>
> 33 When thy wares went forth out of the seas, thou filledst many people; thou didst enrich the kings of the earth with the multitude of thy riches and of thy merchandise.
>
> 34 In the time *when* thou shalt be broken by the seas in the depths of the waters thy merchandise and all thy company in the midst of thee shall fall.
>
> 35 All the inhabitants of the isles shall be astonished at thee, and their kings shall be sore afraid, they shall be troubled in *their* countenance.
>
> 36 The merchants among the people shall hiss at thee; thou shalt be a terror, and never *shalt be* any more.

In Revelation 18, this is torn away and applied to Babylon (that is to say, Rome) but not very persuasively. More fascinating to me personally is the ironic dirge for the prince of Tyre in Ezekiel 28, which alludes brilliantly to Isaiah 14:9–20, the fall of the king of Babylon, and to Psalm 82. One of my touchstones for great poetry, since my childhood, has been Ezekiel 28:11–16:

> 11 ¶ Moreover the word of the LORD came unto me, saying,
>
> 12 Son of man, take up a lamentation upon the king of Tyrus, and say unto him, Thus saith the Lord GOD; Thou sealest up the sum, full of wisdom, and perfect in beauty.

13 Thou hast been in Eden the garden of God; every precious stone *was* thy covering, the sardius, topaz, and the diamond, the beryl, the onyx, and the jasper, the sapphire, the emerald, and the carbuncle, and gold: the workmanship of thy tabrets and of thy pipes was prepared in thee in the day that thou wast created.

14 Thou *art* the anointed cherub that covereth; and I have set thee *so:* thou wast upon the holy mountain of God; thou hast walked up and down in the midst of the stones of fire.

15 Thou *wast* perfect in thy ways from the day that thou wast created, till iniquity was found in thee.

16 By the multitude of thy merchandise they have filled the midst of thee with violence, and thou hast sinned: therefore I will cast thee as profane out of the mountain of God: and I will destroy thee, O covering cherub, from the midst of the stones of fire.

A scholar of William Blake in my far-off youth, I remain fascinated by his figure of the Covering Cherub, a guardian of Eden fallen into a blocking agent, barring our way back into Paradise. Ezekiel's "far-extending" (*mimshach*) cherub is more obscure than Blake's but is fully discussed by Moshe Greenberg in his Anchor Yale Bible commentary on Ezekiel 21–37 (1997).

I find William Blake, though, to be the best imaginative guide to Ezekiel's extraordinary narration upon the fall of Adam. In Blake the Covering Cherub is interpreted as the barrier in each of us between creative desire and artistic completion. I myself once identified the Covering Cherub in Ezekiel and in Blake as the emblem for the anxiety of influence. Blake's Covering Cherub was John Milton; who was Ezekiel's? His terrible density of allusiveness attempts to fuse priestly tradition with prophetic election, and that does not work. Is he not at times more priest than prophet, unlike Isaiah, Amos, Micah, Jeremiah—his own Covering Cherubs?

Since prophecy, unlike priestcraft, is a mode of poetry, I yield up my ambivalence toward Ezekiel each time I read or recite chapter 28. Yahweh speaks, and the poetic authority overwhelms me: "therefore I will cast thee as profane out of the mountain of God: and I will destroy thee, O covering cherub, from the midst of the stones of fire."

Ezekiel rises to the poetic sublime with Yahweh's proclamation of resurrection in the famous chapter 37:

> 1 The hand of the LORD was upon me, and carried me out in the spirit of the LORD, and set me down in the midst of the valley which *was* full of bones,
>
> 2 And caused me to pass by them round about: and, behold, *there were* very many in the open valley; and, lo, *they were* very dry.
>
> 3 And he said unto me, Son of man, can these bones live? And I answered, O Lord GOD, thou knowest.
>
> 4 Again he said unto me, Prophesy upon these bones, and say unto them, O ye dry bones, hear the word of the LORD.
>
> 5 Thus saith the Lord GOD unto these bones; Behold, I will cause breath to enter into you, and ye shall live:
>
> 6 And I will lay sinews upon you, and will bring up flesh upon you, and cover you with skin, and put breath in you, and ye shall live; and ye shall know that I *am* the LORD.
>
> 7 So I prophesied as I was commanded: and as I prophesied, there was a noise, and behold a shaking and the bones came together, bone to his bone.

8 And when I beheld, lo, the sinews and the flesh came up upon them, and the skin covered them above: but *there was* no breath in them.

9 Then said he unto me, Prophesy unto the wind, prophesy, son of man, and say to the wind, Thus saith the Lord GOD; Come from the four winds, O breath, and breathe upon these slain, that they may live.

10 So I prophesied as he commanded me, and the breath came into them, and they lived, and stood up upon their feet, an exceeding great army.

11 ¶ Then he said unto me, Son of man, these bones are the whole house of Israel: behold, they say, Our bones are dried, and our hope is lost: we are cut off for our parts.

12 Therefore prophesy and say unto them, Thus saith the Lord GOD; Behold, O my people, I will open your graves, and cause you to come up out of your graves, and bring you into the land of Israel.

13 And ye shall know that I *am* the LORD, when I have opened your graves, O my people, and brought you up out of your graves,

14 And shall put my spirit in you, and ye shall live, and I shall place you in your own land: then shall ye know that I the LORD have spoken it, and performed it, saith the LORD.

The Resurrection of the Body became a Pharasaic and then a Christian conviction, but I do not sense that Ezekiel sees it as a literal matter. In him, it is a great trope for the political rebirth of Israel (remaining figurative until 1948). The greatest rabbinical exegetes clearly state that Ezekiel's vision is metaphor. I particularly like the (perhaps ironic) comment of Rabbi Eliezer: "The dead

revived by Ezekiel stood up on their feet, sang a hymn and died."
Rashi and even more Kimchi saw exodus from Exile as the true
meaning: a reader—Jewish, Christian, Muslim, secular—is free
to follow his or her own judgment.

The KJB, closely following Geneva, catches almost the precise
note of eloquence in the Hebrew of chapter 37. One verse at least
echoes forever in Western spirituality:

> And he said unto me, Son of man, can these bones live?
> And I answered, O Lord God, thou knowest.

In the Psalms and Proverbs, "dry" bones are emblems of despair.
Ezekiel (or his school), reacting against the prophet's earlier nega-
tivity, attempts an upward movement of the spirit in the later
chapters. How persuasive is this really? Chapters 38 and 39,
scarcely less famous than 37, present the apocalyptic image of
the war against Gog and Magog. Who Gog was, we never will
know, but Alexander the Great will do. Gog is whomever you
fear most. When I was younger, it was whoever headed the Soviet
Union, so far as American fundamentalism concerned itself with
its unread Rock of Ages.

After the fulminations against Gog, the Book of Ezekiel turns
to its own utopianism, beholding a restored Israel, in a vision transcending that of Ezra and Nehemiah. I react coldly to these final
chapters, probably composed by a disciple or disciples of Ezekiel.
Theocracy is the center of this Israel dominated by a new Temple,
and like many other readers I am disheartened at this further
triumph of priest over prophet.

Ezekiel, with all his darkness, is a great visionary poet, and
one of the mixed glories both of Tanakh and of the English Bible.
He has an urgency difficult to resist, even when we doubt his
balance and his humanity. As a poet he yields to none of the

apocalyptic proclaimers who rise in his wake. Later poets found in him a symbolism so answering to their imaginative needs that he became the foundation for the visionary tradition that goes from Dante through Milton on to Blake and Shelley. Esoteric speculation, prompted by him, formed the mode of early Kabbalah and continued in the crucial book Zohar, which largely created classical Kabbalah. Without Ezekiel, Western tradition, both poetic and mystical, would be very different.

Daniel

In my far-off youth, when I was an intoxicated exegete of William Blake, the book of Daniel held enormous fascination for me. In old age I am wary of it, as of all apocalyptic writings. The English Bible, being Protestant Christian, rather weirdly places Daniel as a fourth major prophet, coming after Isaiah, Jeremiah, and Ezekiel. Tanakh regards Daniel as a seer, not a prophet, and stations his book among the Writings, between Esther and Ezra.

Scribes had accomplished a final version of Daniel by 164 B.C.E. (or so), which makes it the last book of Tanakh to be completed. Its stories go back to the sixth century B.C.E. and center upon Daniel, exiled in Babylonia.

The book actually is two works: the first six chapters tell stories of Jewish heroes of the Exile, and the remaining six are first-person visions of apocalypse. Since both Aramaic and Hebrew are employed, there is an unresolved puzzle as to origins. Herbert Marks suggests that "interpretation" (*p-sh-r*) is the salient theme of the book of Daniel. Certainly it interests me more than the pious nobility exalted by its scribes, who opposed Hellenization of Yahweh worship but who declined to join in the violent and successful resistance to Antiochus Epiphanes, the Syrian-Greek ruler who vainly attempted to destroy the religion of Yahweh. Judas Maccabeus and his brothers saved the ancestral Covenant, yet go uncelebrated in the book of Daniel.

Christian exaltation of Daniel founded itself upon a strong misreading of 7:9–14, given here in the KJB version:

> 9 ¶ I beheld till the thrones were cast down, and the Ancient of days did sit, whose garment *was* white as snow, and the hair of his head like the pure wool: his throne *was like* the fiery flame, *and* his wheels *as* burning fire.
>
> 10 A fiery stream issued and came forth from before him: thousand thousands ministered unto him, and ten thousand times ten thousand stood before him: the judgment was set, and the books were opened.
>
> 11 I beheld then because of the voice of the great words which the horn spake: I beheld *even* till the beast was slain, and his body destroyed, and given to the burning flame.
>
> 12 As concerning the rest of the beasts, they had their dominion taken away: yet their lives were prolonged for a season and time.
>
> 13 I saw in the night visions, and, behold, *one* like the Son of man came with the clouds of heaven, and came to the Ancient of days, and they brought him near before him.
>
> 14 And there was given him dominion, and glory, and a kingdom, that all people, nations, and languages, should serve him: his dominion is an everlasting dominion, which shall not pass away, and his kingdom that which shall not be destroyed.

To Christians the "Son of man" prophesied Jesus Christ. And yet an accurate translation would be "one like a son of man," a human being or likeness, and not a beast. Ezekiel endlessly employs "son of man" for a human being, as the English translators had to know.

Jewish commentary chose to identify this human as the angel Michael or as a personified Israel. Yahweh, here the "Ancient one," has aged markedly in this, his final appearance in Tanakh. Jack Miles, Yahweh's Boswell, sees this Ancient of days as Yahweh's last stand before his suicidal sacrifice of himself as Christ. The Christian misprision of Daniel is strongest in chapter 10, where "a certain man" (almost certainly intended as the angel Gabriel) touches Daniel's lips and thus strengthens him. In Revelation 1:13–16 this figure is interpreted as Jesus, "one like unto the Son of man," who comes as Alpha and Omega.

If the book of Daniel is read without this Christian overlay, what force does it yet retain? The legendary strength of the fables in the first six chapters seems eternal: Nebuchadnezzar's dreams; Shadrach, Meshach, and Abednego in the fiery furnace, with "the fourth like the Son of God" (literally "a son of the gods"); Nebuchadnezzar eating grass like an ox; Belshazzar's feast; Daniel in the den of lions. The English Bible, culminating in the KJB, handles this mode of folklore with a sense of entertainment.

The denser visions of the seer Daniel in the book's second half reflect the crisis brought on by Antiochus Epiphanes and cross over from legend into apocalypse. The Aramaic seventh chapter is followed by five in rather bad Hebrew. Once I thrilled to these chapters; now they oppress me. Apocalyptic, whether Jewish or Christian, is a mode that devalues life. Yahweh is the god of the living, not of the dead. The Hebrew Blessing, as I keep observing, means more life into a time without boundaries. There is no blessing in apocalypse.

The book of Daniel relies upon Ezekiel, who in 14:14 and 28:3 had seen Daniel as an exemplary paradigm. Ezekiel's sense of our mortality, each a "son of man," transmutes into Daniel's angelic prophecies in chapter 12 of the resurrection of the dead (though he cannot say when). When 12:2 says that many of us shall wake, we are given the only overt statement of survival after death in Tanakh (though there are intimations in Isaiah and Ezekiel).

Cold as I have become in my later years to the book of Daniel, I confess to being greatly moved by its final verse in the KJB version, 12:13:

> But go thou thy way till the end *be:* for thou shalt rest, and stand in thy lot at the end of the days.

Hosea

A harlot-wife, even metaphorically, remains a startling figure at any time in any culture. Anyone's first thought concerning the prophet Hosea once his book has been read through is speculation as to whether his marriage was literally or symbolically contracted with a whore.

The seven-hundred-page Anchor Yale Bible commentary by Francis I. Andersen and David Noel Freedman (1996) does not resolve this enigma, though the volume is immensely useful for absorbing Hosea, whose book I find very hard to read in the Hebrew. The text has been worked over by revisionists, and one wonders if any of it is Hosea's own words.

Herbert Marks incisively notes, "Where Amos calls for justice, Hosea calls for loyalty; the one evokes God's power to act, the other his capacity to feel." Yahweh's hurt feelings are awesome to contemplate, and Yahweh as a betrayed husband is scary, particularly when he brings three "controversies" (lawsuits founded upon the Covenant) against his "unfaithful" bride, Israel.

The rhetoric of the book of Hosea is intimately disturbing, brilliantly caught by the Geneva Bible, which the KJB closely follows. Domestic betrayals in literature are essential fictions, but in a prophetic context they reverberate as even the wildest adultery in the novel cannot. Of Gomer, Hosea's wife, we are given no personal details whatever. But then we know almost nothing about Hosea either, except that he lived in Israel, the northern kingdom. Except for his misguided marriage, Hosea is merely an anonymous voice taken up by a school of disciples.

An added complexity is the folding or fusing of that prophetic voice into Yahweh's own utterances, so that at moments I cannot tell whether Hosea or Yahweh is expressing his wounded affection, be it for Gomer or for Israel. Marks sinuously praises Hosea's book for "the way it avoids the dangers of anthropomorphism implicit in this absorption into the divine." That puzzles me; Hosea is not the Yahwist who gives us theomorphic women and men. Hosea and *his* Yahweh indeed are human-all-too-human.

There is an erotic and elegiac quality to Hosea's tone, in the original and in the Geneva and KJB versions, that is different from the other prophets. His Yahweh, who will influence Deuteronomy and Jeremiah, seems to me altogether different from the Yahweh of Amos, Micah, and Isaiah of Jerusalem. It is the God of neither the J Writer nor the Priestly Writer or Writers. Hosea's Yahweh is a forsaken husband who still loves Israel, his betraying wife, and a bereaved father still ready to forgive almost all. That loyal love, hesed, can be experienced only by a Yahweh who possesses the quality of inwardness. Such a characteristic is what distinguishes the God who will make a New Covenant with Israel through Jeremiah, and thus will inscribe his Teaching upon our inward parts.

Hosea's three children, begotten by him upon Gomer, carry the dark names of Jezreel, or "Yahweh Will Sow [Destruction]"; Lo-ruhamah, or "Not to Be Pitied"; and Lo-ammi, "Not My People." Yahweh is rarely more volatile than in his abrupt movement between verse 13 and verse 14 in chapter 2 of Hosea:

13 And I will visit upon her the days of Baalim, wherein she burned incense to them, and she decked herself with her earrings and her jewels, and she went after her lovers, and forgat me, saith the LORD.

14 ¶ Therefore, behold, I will allure her, and bring her into the wilderness, and speak comfortably unto her.

15 And I will give her her vineyards from thence, and the valley of Achor for a door of hope: and she shall sing there, as in the days of her youth, and as in the day when she came up out of the land of Egypt.

16 And it shall be at that day, saith the LORD, *that* thou shalt call me Ishi; and shalt call me no more Baali.

There is the thrill of literary strangeness there as suddenly Yahweh speaks to the heart (of Gomer and of Israel) and she reciprocates in songs to *ishi* (my husband) and *baali* (my master). In turn, the children's names are redeemed in this idealized vision.

There simply is no coherent order to Hosea's book, so that it can be admired only in its repeated paradox of a humanized Yahweh who nevertheless goes on insisting he is not human. There is an extraordinary rhetorical effect in 11:1–11:

1 When Israel *was* a child, then I loved him, and called my son out of Egypt.

2 *As* they called them, so they went from them: they sacrificed unto Baalim, and burned incense to graven images.

3 I taught Ephraim also to go, taking them by their arms; but they knew not that I healed them.

4 I drew them with cords of a man, with bands of love: and I was to them as they that take off the yoke on their jaws, and I laid meat unto them.

5 ¶ He shall not return into the land of Egypt, but

the Assyrian shall be his king, because they refused to return.

6 And the sword shall abide on his cities, and shall consume his branches, and devour *them,* because of their own counsels.

7 And my people are bent to backsliding from me: though they called them to the most High, none at all would exalt *him.*

8 How shall I give thee up, Ephraim? *how* shall I deliver thee, Israel? how shall I make thee as Admah? *how* shall I set thee as Zeboim? mine heart is turned within me, my repentings are kindled together.

9 I will not execute the fierceness of mine anger, I will not return to destroy Ephraim: for I *am* God, and not man; the Holy One in the midst of thee: and I will not enter into the city.

10 They shall walk after the LORD: he shall roar like a lion: when he shall roar, then the children shall tremble from the west.

11 They shall tremble as a bird out of Egypt, and as a dove out of the land of Assyria: and I will place them in their houses, saith the LORD.

Though he is God, not man, he yields to a father's anguished love. Biblical scholars call this a theology; it seems more useful to regard an unresolved tension as a psychology, however obscure. I think the central difficulty ensues from the prophetic daring of literalizing the trope of whoring after strange gods. The marriage of Gomer and Hosea simply cannot serve clearly as a representation of the Covenant between Israel and Yahweh. We are not told anything inward about Hosea, and have to be baffled by the inward travail of Yahweh.

Hosea's text is frequently dubious, and the Geneva Bible and the KJB reflect this difficulty by a surprising lack of eloquence. No one easily forgets Hosea's situation, but as a poet he cannot challenge Amos and Isaiah, or the Jeremiah that he renders possible.

Amos

Some of the great prophets make me uneasy—Jeremiah and Ezekiel in particular. Some are uncanny—Elijah and Elisha—while Isaiah of Jerusalem is almost too lofty to be approached. Amos is my favorite: the inaugural left-wing champion of the poor and exploited, and the herald to this day of the call for social justice. His brief, nine-chapter book may be the most memorable poetic achievement in the Hebrew Bible, and is rendered magnificently by the KJB, following after Geneva.

The first of the writing prophets, Amos established the modes of discourse for Isaiah and Micah. His *tone* is the text's crucial attribute: whether we hear the prophet's own rhetoric or that of a devoted disciple-editor cannot be known, yet the singularity of the voice endures, however diverse the tenor of its messages.

This could be called the motto of Amos:

The lion hath roared, who will not fear? the Lord God hath spoken, who can but prophesy?

[3:8]

And yet Amos refuses the traditional role of the seer; he is a herdsman and not a prophet of a professional kind. In chapter 7 he has a memorable spat with Amaziah, high priest of the royal sanctuary of Bethel and overlord of the guild prophets who pontificate there:

10 ¶ Then Amaziah the priest of Bethel sent to Jeroboam king of Israel, saying, Amos hath conspired against thee

in the midst of the house of Israel: the land is not able to bear all his words.

11 For thus Amos saith, Jeroboam shall die by the sword, and Israel shall surely be led away captive out of their own land.

12 Also Amaziah said unto Amos, O thou seer, go, flee thee away into the land of Judah, and there eat bread, and prophesy there:

13 But prophesy not again any more at Beth-el: for it *is* the king's chapel, and it *is* the king's court.

14 ¶ Then answered Amos, and said to Amaziah, I *was* no prophet, neither *was* I a prophet's son; but I *was* an herdman, and a gatherer of sycomore fruit:

15 And the LORD took me as I followed the flock, and the LORD said unto me, Go, prophesy unto my people Israel.

16 Now therefore hear thou the word of the LORD: Thou sayest, Prophesy not against Israel, and drop not *thy word* against the house of Isaac.

17 Therefore thus saith the LORD; Thy wife shall be an harlot in the city, and thy sons and thy daughters shall fall by the sword, and thy land shall be divided by line; and thou shalt die in a polluted land: and Israel shall surely go into captivity forth of his land.

The KJB mistranslates the tense in 7:14, where the Hebrew says, "I am not a prophet nor the son of a prophet," a categorical denial on the part of Amos. Then what is he? A landowner from a rural village to Jerusalem's south, he leaves a comfortable existence in Judah to cry out against the oppression of the poor in Israel before turning against his own country's iniquities. As the initial writing prophet, Amos is one of the strongest poets in what has become a Western tradition. His voicing is extraordinary: who else shares his Yahweh's zeal for social justice?

21 ¶ I hate, I despise your feast days, and I will not smell in your solemn assemblies.

22 Though ye offer me burnt offerings and your meat offerings, I will not accept *them:* neither will I regard the peace offerings of your fat beasts.

23 Take thou away from me the noise of thy songs; for I will not hear the melody of thy viols.

24 But let judgment run down as waters, and righteousness as a mighty stream.

[5:21–24]

The "viols" are English for "lyres" in the Hebrew, and "judgment" mistranslates "justice." Verse 24, the epitome of KJB Amos, improves its Geneva original by two touches, "But" for "And," "stream" for "river":

And let judgment run down as waters, and righteousness as a mighty river.

[Geneva]

But let judgment run down as waters, and righteousness as a mighty stream.

[KJB]

I wince at the Anchor Yale Bible (1989) version:

But let justice roll on like the ocean,
    and equity like a perennial stream.

A particular poetic triumph comes in 8:1–7:

1 Thus hath the Lord God shewed unto me: and behold a basket of summer fruit.

2 And he said, Amos, what seest thou? And I said, A basket of summer fruit. Then said the Lord unto me, The end is come upon my people of Israel; I will not again pass by them any more.

3 And the songs of the temple shall be howlings in that day, saith the Lord God: *there shall be* many dead bodies in every place; they shall cast *them* forth with silence.

4 ¶ Hear this, O ye that swallow up the needy, even to make the poor of the land to fail,

5 Saying, When will the new moon be gone, that we may sell corn? and the sabbath, that we may set forth wheat, making the ephah small, and the shekel great, and falsifying the balances by deceit?

6 That we may buy the poor for silver, and the needy for a pair of shoes; *yea,* and sell the refuse of the wheat?

7 The Lord hath sworn by the excellency of Jacob, Surely I will never forget any of their works.

"Excellency" is "arrogance" in the Hebrew text, yet has a resonance to it that "pride" does not. Here the KJB scarcely alters Geneva. The poor are purchased as debtor-servants, pragmatically not far from slavery. Reading Amos in the United States in May 2010 (when I write) is disconcerting. What could be more unwelcome than an Amos who came to us now?

I cannot better the summary of Herbert Marks: "The torrent of language, initially provoked by the spectacle of injustice, overflows until the 'mighty stream' of righteousness itself becomes catastrophic. . . . The message is intolerable but the language is sublime."

A creation-by-catastrophe is the mode of Amos as strong poet: "Woe to them *that are* at ease in Zion" (6:1). Jews, throughout history, never have been at ease in Zion, or anywhere else. You can say in regard to Amos that he can seem redundant to fellow Jews, but that is to neglect his superb command of language. Every society always will need him, though none gives him welcome.

Jonah

It may seem frivolous to speak of a favorite book in the Bible but mine is Jonah, by far. A sly masterpiece of four brief chapters, Jonah reverberates in Herman Melville's *Moby-Dick,* where it is the text for Father Mapple's grand sermon. Tucked away in the Book of the Twelve, with such fierce prophets as Amos and Micah, Jonah is out of place. It should be with the Writings—Song of Songs, Job, Koheleth—because it too is a literary sublimity, almost the archetypal parable masking as short story. The irony of the J Writer is renewed by the author of Jonah, who may well be composing a parody of the prophet Joel's solemnities. Joel's vision is of nature's devastation: "the day of the locust." Jonah's counter-vision is of survival, dependent upon divine caprice.

I first was charmed by Jonah as a little boy in synagogue on the afternoon of the Day of Atonement, when it is read aloud in full. It seemed to me so much at variance, in tone and implication, from the rest of the service as to be almost Kafkan in effect.

The author of Jonah probably composed it very late in prophetic tradition, sometime during the third century B.C.E. There is a prophetic Jonah in 2 Kings 14:25 who has nothing in common with the feckless Jonah sent against Nineveh. The earlier Jonah is a war prophet, while our Jonah sensibly runs away from his mission.

Nobody comes out looking very impressive from the book of Jonah, whether God, Jonah, the ship captain and his men, or the king of Nineveh and his people. Even the gourd sheltering Jonah from the sun comes to a bad end. There is of course the giant fish (not, alas, a whale) who swallows up Jonah for three days but then disgorges him at God's command. No Moby-Dick, he inspires neither fear nor awe.

William Tyndale translated Jonah, providing the KJB with its base text but not the humor that shines through its revisions. In a rather negative Prologue to his version (a powerful piece of narrative) Tyndale nastily compared the Jews who rejected Jesus to the people of Nineveh who believed Jonah and repented. The comparison is lame but reminds me that Tyndale, a great writer, also was a bigot.

Jonah's book is magnificent literature because it is so funny. Irony, even in Jonathan Swift, could not be more brilliant. Jonah himself is a sulking, unwilling prophet, cowardly and petulant. There is no reason why an authentic prophet should be likable: Elijah and Elisha are savage, Jeremiah is a bipolar depressive, Ezekiel a madman. Paranoia and prophecy seem to go together, and the author of Jonah satirizes both his protagonist and Yahweh in a return to the large irony of the J Writer.

The prophet Jonah, awash with the examples and texts of Isaiah, Jeremiah, and Joel, rightly resents his absurd status as a latecomer sufferer of the anxiety of prophetic influence. Either Nineveh will ignore him and be destroyed, making his mission needless, or, if it takes him to heart, he will prove to be a false prophet. Either way his sufferings are useless, nor does Yahweh show the slightest regard for him. Praying from the fish's belly, he satirizes the situation of all psalmists whosoever.

As for poor Nineveh, where even the beasts are bedecked in sackcloth and ashes, Yahweh merely postpones its destruction. That leaves the Cainlike gourd, whose life is so brief and whose destruction prompts poor Jonah's death-drive. What remains is Yahweh's playfully rhetorical question:

Prophets: Jonah

And should not I spare Nineveh, that great city, wherein are more than sixscore thousand persons that cannot discern between their right hand and their left hand; and *also* much cattle?

Presumably the cattle ("beasts" in the Hebrew) are able to tell one direction from another, unlike the citizens of Nineveh, Jerusalem, or New York City. Tucking Jonah away as another minor prophet was a literary error by the makers of the canon. Or perhaps they judged the little book aptly, and were anxious to conceal this Swiftian coda to prophets and prophecy.

Micah

No reader of the KJB ever can forget Micah 6:6–8:

6 ¶ Wherewith shall I come before the LORD, *and* bow myself before the high God? shall I come before him with burnt offerings, with calves of a year old?

7 Will the LORD be pleased with thousands of rams, *or* with ten thousands of rivers of oil? shall I give my firstborn *for* my transgression, the fruit of my body *for* the sin of my soul?

8 He hath shewed thee, O man, what *is* good; and what doth the LORD require of thee, but to do justly, and to love mercy, and to walk humbly with thy God?

The perfect dignity of 6:8 cannot be surpassed and is the epitome of Micah the prophet, who emerged from a tiny village west of Jerusalem and whose heart remained with the agrarian poor, though he himself was not one of them. He resembles the much fiercer Amos in being a landowner who prophesies against the establishment.

Amos demanded justice and righteousness. Micah, not softer

but gentler, emphasizes also fellow-feeling, not quite what we call compassion but an identification with the wronged. Admonishing Jerusalem, Micah is very close to his contemporary the first Isaiah, and shares the apprehension of Assyrian invasion and destruction. Herbert Marks notes that Isaiah dreads the desecration of Yahweh's temple, and Micah foresees its utter destruction.

Ancient editors so worked over Micah that his book is difficult to hold together. Traces of a personal voice abide, particularly in the first three chapters, but the seventh and final chapter has little individuality. And yet bursting through its conventionality is the terrible warning of 7:5–6, which reverberates in the Talmud:

> 5 ¶ Trust ye not in a friend, put ye not confidence in a guide: keep the doors of thy mouth from her that lieth in thy bosom.
>
> 6 For the son dishonoureth the father, the daughter riseth up against her mother, the daughter in law against her mother in law; a man's enemies *are* the men of his own house.

When matters are this bad, the sages reasoned, then the days of the messiah may be upon us. Micah might have cried this forth; it would find a place in the more personal chapters 1–3. Yet to me he does not seem that harsh insofar as my ear can isolate his individual strain. Though Amos is the roaring lion of denunciatory prophecy, the demand for social justice is even more urgent in Micah:

> 1 Woe to them that devise iniquity, and work evil upon their beds! when the morning is light, they practise it, because it is in the power of their hand.
>
> 2 And they covet fields, and take *them* by violence; and houses, and take *them* away: so they oppress a man and his house, even a man and his heritage.
>
> 3 Therefore thus saith the LORD; Behold, against this

family do I devise an evil, from which ye shall not remove your necks; neither shall ye go haughtily: for this time *is* evil.

[2:1–3]

The triumph of KJB Micah, as noted earlier, comes in 6:6–8, ending with:

He hath shewed thee, O man, what *is* good; and what doth the LORD require of thee, but to do justly, and to love mercy, and to walk humbly with thy God?

"Mercy" translates *hesed,* which is untranslatable. Micah's Yahweh has bruised feelings but is otherwise not one of the angriest Yahwehs. I think that is why Micah's tiny, seven-chapter book goes on holding us and is not obliterated by the shadows of Isaiah, Jeremiah, Ezekiel, and the differing intensities of Amos and Hosea.

Psalms 1

THE LONGEST BOOK IN THE HEBREW BIBLE, Psalms, also is the most
influential throughout the ages, alike upon Jews and Christians.
Aside from its liturgical employments, it has been an immense
stimulus to lyric poetry, both secular and devotional. There are
150 psalms, composed across six centuries, from 996 to 457 B.C.E.
Perhaps a few were written by King David, though some others
may also go back to the Davidic period. Here I intend to appreciate two groups of psalms, chosen for their aesthetic splendor: in
this chapter 18, 19, 22, 23, 24, 46, 68, 69, and in the next 100, 102,
104, 114, 121, 126, 127, 137. That these 16 are representative of
the whole book of Psalms, I would not wish to argue. They mean
most to me.

Psalm 116:17 has long troubled me:

> I will offer to thee the sacrifice of thanksgiving, and will
> call upon the name of the LORD.

Surely it is better to offer thanksgiving rather than a lamb or heifer,
but what does it mean to regard thanksgiving as a sacrifice to God?

Psalm, as an English word, derives from the Greek translation of the Hebrew *mizmor,* a song set to music. Throughout Jewish tradition, the Psalms were called *Tehillim* (Praises), and all of them praise Yahweh under various names. Even the most desperate outcries for God's help adopt a rhetoric of gratitude. A perpetual hail of praise rains down in the book of Psalms. The sorrows of history, both universal and Jewish, harden me against these repetitive givings of thanks. Can a world after Hitler and the Holocaust, and the horrors enacted by Stalin and Mao, allow such profuse praise of what no longer can be praised?

When I read through the Psalms, I struggle to discover whether ancient Hebrew thinking is at all available to us anymore. The Psalms, like much else in Tanakh, work at making praise, gratitude, supplication, and even despair modes of cognition. The God of the Psalms has comforted multitudes, whether in the valley of decision, or in the valley of the shadow of death. He does not comfort me because I do not know how to think in a realm of gratitude.

And yet the Psalms have comforted myriads and go on in that good labor. They pray for a God both more effectual and compassionate than reality can bestow. In the twenty-first Western century they continue to voice a solitary cry of the human. Nothing has taken their place, and perhaps nothing ever will. Herbert Marks wisely remarks that the Psalms are "untouched by irony." They do not say one thing while meaning another. Most literary language does; the Psalms dispute Schlegel's "permanent parabasis of meaning." Any valid account of the Bible's literary achievement needs to confront the greatness of poems such as Psalms 102, 104, 114, and 137. They stand with the strongest lyrics of Western tradition: Greek, Hebrew, Latin, European vernacular. As with Pindar, Isaiah, Horace, Dante, Petrarch, you cannot come to the end of them.

Marks, with his customary acumen, asserts of the Psalter: "There is no other body of literature, ancient or modern, in which the poetic 'I' shows so little reticence in exposing its own vulnerability." One might challenge that with Shakespeare's Sonnets, where the speaker seems naked to every humiliation, except that the poet's self-removal from pathos makes us re-imagine his suffering for ourselves.

The God of the Psalms at moments is an absent father, though he also can be too much of an angry presence. Since Christianity emphasizes reconcilement with God the Father, the Psalter has been read as a large-scale enactment of the life of Jesus Christ, whose sacrifice appeases Yahweh, at least if you have faith. William Tyndale, whose faith was intense, was martyred before he could translate the prophets (except for the book of Jonah) and the Psalms, except for 18, a thanksgiving of David's that is embedded in 2 Samuel 22. Here is the opening of Tyndale's version:

> And he said: The Lord is my rock, my castle and my deliverer. God is my strength, and in him will I trust: my shield and the horn that defendeth me: mine high hold and refuge: O my Saviour, save me from wrong.
>
> I will praise and call on the Lord, and so shall be saved from mine enemies. For the waves of death have closed me about, and the floods of Belial have feared me. The cords of hell have compassed me about, and the snares of death have overtaken me. In my tribulation I called to the Lord, and cried to my God. And he heard my voice out of his temple, and my cry entered into his ears. And the earth trembled and quoke, and the foundations of heaven moved and shook, because he was angry.
>
> Smoke went up out of his nostrils, and consuming fire out of his mouth, that coals were kindled of him.

Psalms 1

And he bowed heaven and came down, and darkness underneath his feet. And he rode upon Cherub and flew: and appeared upon the wings of the wind. And he made darkness a tabernacle round about him, with water gathered together in thick clouds. Of the brightness, that was before him, coals were set on fire.

The Lord thundered from heaven, and the Most High put out his voice. And he shot arrows and scattered them, and hurled lightning and turmoiled them. And the bottom of the sea appeared, and the foundations of the world were seen, by the reason of the rebuking of the Lord, and through the blasting of the breath of his nostrils. He sent from on high and fetched me, and plucked me out of mighty waters.

Writing like a possessed man, overcome by Jehovah's power (*Jehovah* was Tyndale's own coinage, founded upon a spelling error), the martyr-translator's burning Calvinism is fiercely memorable. The KJB softens him:

2 The LORD *is* my rock, and my fortress, and my deliverer; my God, my strength, in whom I will trust; my buckler, and the horn of my salvation, *and* my high tower.

3 I will call upon the LORD, *who is worthy* to be praised: so shall I be saved from mine enemies.

4 The sorrows of death compassed me, and the floods of ungodly men made me afraid.

5 The sorrows of hell compassed me about: the snares of death prevented me.

6 In my distress I called upon the LORD, and cried unto my God: he heard my voice out of his temple, and my cry came before him, *even* into his ears.

7 Then the earth shook and trembled; the foundations

also of the hills moved and were shaken, because he was wroth.

8 There went up a smoke out of his nostrils, and fire out of his mouth devoured: coals were kindled by it.

9 He bowed the heavens also, and came down: and darkness *was* under his feet.

10 And he rode upon a cherub, and did fly: yea, he did fly upon the wings of the wind.

11 He made darkness his secret place; his pavilion round about him *were* dark waters *and* thick clouds of the skies.

12 At the brightness *that was* before him his thick clouds passed, hail *stones* and coals of fire.

13 The LORD also thundered in the heavens, and the Highest gave his voice; hail *stones* and coals of fire.

14 Yea, he sent out his arrows, and scattered them; and he shot out lightnings, and discomfited them.

15 Then the channels of waters were seen, and the foundations of the world were discovered at thy rebuke, O LORD, at the blast of the breath of thy nostrils.

16 He sent from above, he took me, he drew me out of many waters.

[Psalm 18:2–16]

Royal thanksgiving for victory has a limited range, however intense. Psalm 19:1–6 has been far more influential in poetic history:

1 The heavens declare the glory of God; and the firmament sheweth his handywork.

2 Day unto day uttereth speech, and night unto night sheweth knowledge.

3 *There is* no speech nor language, *where* their voice is not heard.

4 Their line is gone out through all the earth, and their words to the end of the world. In them hath he set a tabernacle for the sun,

5 Which *is* as a bridegroom coming out of his chamber, *and* rejoiceth as a strong man to run a race.

6 His going forth *is* from the end of the heaven, and his circuit unto the ends of it: and there is nothing hid from the heat thereof.

Verse 5 is extraordinary: the rising sun, both bridegroom and agonist, is Miltonic before John Milton.

Psalm 22 is uttered (in Aramaic) from the cross by Jesus (Mark 15:34), while with 23 we come to the most famous psalm in the English tradition:

1 The LORD *is* my shepherd; I shall not want.

2 He maketh me to lie down in green pastures: he leadeth me beside the still waters.

3 He restoreth my soul: he leadeth me in the paths of righteousness for his name's sake.

4 Yea, though I walk through the valley of the shadow of death, I will fear no evil: for thou *art* with me; thy rod and thy staff they comfort me.

5 Thou preparest a table before me in the presence of mine enemies: thou anointest my head with oil; my cup runneth over.

6 Surely goodness and mercy shall follow me all the days of my life: and I will dwell in the house of the LORD for ever.

"Still waters" in verse 2 superbly mistranslates the Hebrew for "waters of rest," while in verse 4 the "total darkness" of the Hebrew is transmuted to the "shadow of death." In verse 6 "mercy" should be "loving-kindness" and "for ever" more literally is the ambiguous "for length of days." The dying Sir John Falstaff, as reported by Mistress Quickly in *Henry V*, evidently sang the Twenty-third Psalm, though she garbles the text when she gives it as "a table of green fields," fusing together "green pastures" and "Thou preparest a table before me."

Psalm 24, which Marks thinks could have been sung during processions of the Ark, is one of the KJB's triumphs:

> 1 The earth *is* the Lord's, and the fullness thereof; the world, and they that dwell therein.
>
> 2 For he hath founded it upon the seas, and established it upon the floods.
>
> 3 Who shall ascend into the hill of the Lord? or who shall stand in his holy place?
>
> 4 He that hath clean hands, and a pure heart; who hath not lifted up his soul unto vanity, nor sworn deceitfully.
>
> 5 He shall receive the blessing from the Lord, and righteousness from the God of his salvation.
>
> 6 This *is* the generation of them that seek him, that seek thy face, O Jacob. Selah.
>
> 7 Lift up your heads, O ye gates; and be ye lift up, ye everlasting doors; and the King of glory shall come in.
>
> 8 Who *is* this King of glory? The Lord strong and mighty, the Lord mighty in battle.
>
> 9 Lift up your heads, O ye gates; even lift *them* up, ye everlasting doors; and the King of glory shall come in.
>
> 10 Who is this King of glory? The Lord of hosts, he *is* the King of glory. Selah.

No one knows what *selah* meant. Christians have shown a preference for this psalm, perhaps because Paul quotes from it in 1 Corinthians. As a victory hymn this sublime poem reminds us that Yahweh is a man of war, and celebrates him with stunning power in verse 7, effectively repeated as verse 9.

Isaiah of Jerusalem celebrated the defense of Jerusalem by Yahweh (Isaiah 33, 36–37) and the famous Psalm 46 might have been written for that intervention (though it was not). Again, the KJB men somewhat surpass both Coverdale and Geneva:

> 1 God *is* our refuge and strength, a very present help in trouble.
>
> 2 Therefore will not we fear, though the earth be removed, and though the mountains be carried into the midst of the sea;
>
> 3 *Though* the waters thereof roar *and* be troubled, *though* the mountains shake with the swelling thereof. Selah.
>
> 4 *There is* a river, the streams whereof shall make glad the city of God, the holy *place* of the tabernacles of the most High.
>
> 5 God *is* in the midst of her; she shall not be moved: God shall help her, *and that* right early.
>
> 6 The heathen raged, the kingdoms were moved: he uttered his voice, the earth melted.
>
> 7 The LORD of hosts *is* with us; the God of Jacob *is* our refuge. Selah.
>
> 8 Come, behold the works of the LORD, what desolations he hath made in the earth.
>
> 9 He maketh wars to cease unto the end of the earth; he breaketh the bow, and cutteth the spear in sunder; he burneth the chariot in the fire.
>
> 10 Be still, and know that I *am* God: I will be exalted among the heathen, I will be exalted in the earth.
>
> 11 The LORD of hosts *is* with us; the God of Jacob *is* our refuge. Selah.

There is a strain of rugged ecstasy in this strong hymn that carries over from Isaiah to Luther and beyond. The river of verse 4 appears in Ezekiel and in Revelation as the pure river of the water of life. The outcry of Yahweh is caught sublimely in:

> I will be exalted among the heathen, I will be exalted in
> the earth.

That splendor, though, is directly from Geneva, where the Psalms probably were the work of Anthony Gilby, the best Hebraist. In general the KJB follows Gilby in the Psalms, revising mostly for euphony. Here are the opening thirteen verses of the marvelous— though hard to hold together—Psalm 68:

1   God will arise, and his enemies shall be scattered: they also that hate him, shall flee before him.
2   As the smoke vanisheth, *so* shalt ye drive *them* away: and as wax melteth before the fire, *so* shall ye wicked perish at the presence of God.
3   But the righteous shall be glad, and rejoice before God: yea, they shall leap for joy.
4   Sing unto God, and sing praises unto his Name: exalt him, that rideth upon the heavens, in his Name Jah, and rejoice before him.
5   *He is* a Father of the fatherless, and a Judge of the widows, *even* God in his holy habitation.
6   God maketh the solitary to dwell in families, and delivereth them that were prisoners in stocks: but the rebellious shall dwell in a dry land.
7   O God, when thou wentest forth before thy people: when thou wentest through the wilderness, (Selah)
8   The earth shook, and the heavens dropped at the

presence of this God: *even* Sinai *was moved* at the presence of God, *even* the God of Israel.

9   Thou, o God, sendeth a gracious rain *upon* thine inheritance, and thou didest refresh it when it was weary.

10   Thy Congregation dwelled therein: *for* thou, o God, hast of thy goodness prepared it for the poor.

11   The Lord gave matter to the women to tell of the great army.

12   Kings of the armies did flee: they did flee and she that remained in the house, divided the spoil.

13   Though ye have lien among pots, *yet shall ye be as* the wings of a dove that is covered with silver, and whose feathers *are like* yellow gold.

[Geneva]

1 Let God arise, let his enemies be scattered: let them also that hate him flee before him.

2 As smoke is driven away, *so* drive *them* away: as wax melteth before the fire, *so* let the wicked perish at the presence of God.

3 But let the righteous be glad; let them rejoice before God: yea, let them exceedingly rejoice.

4 Sing unto God, sing praises to his name: extol him that rideth upon the heavens by his name JAH, and rejoice before him.

5 A father of the fatherless, and a judge of the widows, *is* God in his holy habitation.

6 God setteth the solitary in families: he bringeth out those which are bound with chains: but the rebellious dwell in a dry *land*.

7 O God, when thou wentest forth before thy people, when thou didst march through the wilderness; Selah:

8 The earth shook, the heavens also dropped at the presence of God: *even* Sinai itself *was moved* at the presence of God, the God of Israel.

9 Thou, O God, didst send a plentiful rain, whereby thou didst confirm thine inheritance, when it was weary.

10 Thy congregation hath dwelt therein: thou, O God, hast prepared of thy goodness for the poor.

11 The Lord gave the word: great *was* the company of those that published *it*.

12 Kings of armies did flee apace: and she that tarried at home divided the spoil.

13 Though ye have lien among the pots, *yet shall ye be as* the wings of a dove covered with silver, and her feathers with yellow gold.

[KJB]

In verse 5 "judge" should read "defender" while "in families" in 6 might be "in a dwelling-place." Verse 13 haunted one of my critical heroes, Walter Pater, whose passion for it transmuted into the title of a permanent novel by Henry James:

> Though ye have lien among the pots, *yet shall ye be as* the wings of a dove covered with silver, and her feathers with yellow gold.

Addressed to the people, this speaks to me as it did to Pater and James, secularists of the spirit who believed in the resurrectionist powers of the high arts. All of us have lain among broken vessels, and yearned to rise up again in the silver and gold of the ascending dove. I tend to read this in sequence with Psalm 69 (frequently alluded to in the New Testament), where the prophecy of an ascension does not take place, and we are come into the deep waters of affliction and the floods overflow us.

Psalms 2

IN ENGLAND, PSALM 100 IS KNOWN affectionately as "the old Hundredth" and more formally as the "Jubilate." It is sung in the morning at services where *The Book of Common Prayer* (1559) is employed, in the version of Miles Coverdale:

> O be joyful in the Lord all ye lands: serve the Lord with gladness, and come before his presence with a song.
>
> Be ye sure that the Lord he is God: it is he that hath made us, and not we ourselves, we are his people, and the sheep of his pasture.
>
> O go your way into his gates with thanksgiving, and into his courts with praise: be thankful unto him, and speak good of his name.
>
> For the Lord is gracious, his mercy is everlasting: and his truth endureth from generation to generation.

This must have been a hymn sung while entering the Jerusalem Temple. The KJB, mostly following Geneva, receives the aesthetic palm over both it and Coverdale:

1 Make a joyful noise unto the LORD, all ye lands.

2 Serve the LORD with gladness: come before his presence with singing.

3 Know ye that the LORD he *is* God: *it is* he *that* hath made us, and not we ourselves; *we are* his people, and the sheep of his pasture.

4 Enter into his gates with thanksgiving, *and* into his courts with praise: be thankful unto him, *and* bless his name.

5 For the LORD *is* good; his mercy *is* everlasting; and his truth *endureth* to all generations.

The splendor of this is its simplicity, in contrast to the darkly complex and prophetic Psalm 102, where, again following Geneva, the KJB demonstrates its skill at closure, when you compare the two versions:

22 When the people shall be gathered together, and the kingdoms to serve the Lord.

23 He abated my strength in the way, and shortened my days.

24 *And* I said, O my God, take me not away in the midst of my days: thy years *endure* from generation to generation.

25 Thou hast aforetime laid the foundation of the earth, and the heavens are the work of thine hands.

26 They shall perish, but thou shalt endure: even they all shall wax old as doth a garment: as a vesture shalt thou change them, and they shall be changed.

27 But thou art the same, and thy years shall not fail.

28 The children of thy servants shall continue, and their seed shall stand fast in thy flight.

[Geneva]

Psalms 2

22 When the people are gathered together, and the kingdoms, to serve the LORD.

23 He weakened my strength in the way; he shortened my days.

24 I said, O my God, take me not away in the midst of my days: thy years *are* throughout all generations.

25 Of old hast thou laid the foundation of the earth: and the heavens *are* the work of thy hands.

26 They shall perish, but thou shalt endure: yea, all of them shall wax old like a garment; as a vesture shalt thou change them, and they shall be changed:

27 But thou *art* the same, and thy years shall have no end.

28 The children of thy servants shall continue, and their seed shall be established before thee.

[KJB]

The God of Milton's *Paradise Lost* is that great epic's major blemish: he is pompous, self-righteous, and morally dubious. As poet Milton redeems this vindictive tyrant only through the agile energies of book 7, a vision of the Creation far surpassing the Priestly Writer of Genesis 1. Psalm 104, perhaps echoing the ancient Egyptian Hymn to Aten, is the most remarkable celebration of Yahweh's creative power in the Hebrew Bible. Its initial seven verses constitute another of the KJB's glories:

1 Bless the LORD, O my soul. O LORD my God, thou art very great; thou art clothed with honour and majesty.

2 Who coverest *thyself* with light as *with* a garment: who stretchest out the heavens like a curtain:

3 Who layeth the beams of his chambers in the waters: who maketh the clouds his chariot: who walketh upon the wings of the wind:

4 Who maketh his angels spirits; his ministers a flaming fire:

5 *Who* laid the foundations of the earth, *that* it should not be removed for ever.

6 Thou coveredst it with the deep as *with* a garment: the waters stood above the mountains.

7 At thy rebuke they fled; at the voice of thy thunder they hasted away.

In Dante's *Commedia* those who are to be redeemed sing Psalm 114 as they depart this world on their journey to Purgatory:

1 When Israel went out of Egypt, the house of Jacob from a people of strange language;

2 Judah was his sanctuary, *and* Israel his dominion.

3 The sea saw *it,* and fled: Jordan was driven back.

4 The mountains skipped like rams, *and* the little hills like lambs.

5 What *ailed* thee, O thou sea, that thou fleddest? thou Jordan, *that* thou wast driven back?

6 Ye mountains, *that* ye skipped like rams; *and* ye little hills, like lambs?

7 Tremble, thou earth, at the presence of the Lord, at the presence of the God of Jacob;

8 Which turned the rock *into* a standing water, the flint into a fountain of waters.

I remember singing this as a child at Passover, and am impressed now by its economy and its charming humor, particularly in verses 4–6. A fine economy also holds together the famous Psalm 121, a universal favorite:

1 I will lift up mine eyes unto the hills, from whence cometh my help.

2 My help *cometh* from the Lord, which made heaven and earth.

3 He will not suffer thy foot to be moved: he that keepeth thee will not slumber.

4 Behold, he that keepeth Israel shall neither slumber nor sleep.

5 The Lord *is* thy keeper: the Lord *is* thy shade upon thy right hand.

6 The sun shall not smite thee by day, nor the moon by night.

7 The Lord shall preserve thee from all evil: he shall preserve thy soul.

8 The Lord shall preserve thy going out and thy coming in from this time forth, and even for evermore.

I love this without believing it, a purely aesthetic apprehension since I do not trust in the Covenant. Almost the entire history of the Jewish people demonstrates that Yahweh has repeatedly violated his contractual obligations. Earlier, I mentioned the denunciations by T. S. Eliot and C. S. Lewis of all those who would read the KJB as literature, the way we read Shakespeare and Walt Whitman. What is the value of reading Psalm 121 for its beauty even if one does not have an iota of confidence in it? In Psalm 122 we are urged to "pray for the peace of Jerusalem." I am a disciple of Ralph Waldo Emerson, who wrote in his essay *Self-Reliance*: "As men's prayers are a disease of the will, so are their creeds a disease of the intellect."

Against those who decry an aesthetic secularization of the Bible, I myself advocate reading Shakespeare and Whitman as Scripture. Whitman overtly welcomes that enterprise. No one can surmise Shakespeare's precise relation to the Geneva Bible, which evidently he knew in depth and remembered where and when he needed, for purposes that have come to define the aesthetic. I suggest that Shakespeare regarded the Geneva Bible as an alternate Ovid, no less, no more. I read the Psalms as I read Pindar, Milton, and Shelley: in search of the sublime.

I take a particular delight in Psalm 126:

> 1 When the LORD turned again the captivity of Zion, we were like them that dream.
>
> 2 Then was our mouth filled with laughter, and our tongue with singing: then said they among the heathen, The LORD hath done great things for them.
>
> 3 The LORD hath done great things for us; *whereof* we are glad.
>
> 4 Turn again our captivity, O LORD, as the streams in the south.
>
> 5 They that sow in tears shall reap in joy.
>
> 6 He that goeth forth and weepeth, bearing precious seed, shall doubtless come again with rejoicing, bringing his sheaves *with him.*

This turns upon the charmed contrast between verses 2 and 3: the heathen say, "The Lord hath done great things for them," followed by, "the Lord hath done great things for us." A lovely twist, this reflects "Then was our mouth filled with laughter." Redeemed from Babylonian exile, the rejoicing people manifest an aura of restoration that is wonderfully poignant in Psalm 127, where "house" may be taken as the Jerusalem Temple:

> 1 Except the LORD build the house, they labour in vain that build it: except the LORD keep the city, the watchman waketh *but* in vain.
>
> 2 *It is* vain for you to rise up early, to sit up late, to eat the bread of sorrows: *for* so he giveth his beloved sleep.

3 Lo, children *are* an heritage of the LORD: *and* the fruit of the womb *is his* reward.

4 As arrows *are* in the hand of a mighty man; so *are* children of the youth.

5 Happy *is* the man that hath his quiver full of them: they shall not be ashamed, but they shall speak with the enemies in the gate.

A bad sleeper throughout my long life, I am now hopelessly insomniac, a few weeks past my eightieth birthday. That makes me brood intensely on verse 2:

It is vain for you to rise up early, to sit up late, to eat the bread of sorrows: for so he giveth his beloved sleep.

The Hebrew for that last expression is rendered "he provides for his beloved during sleep" by Herbert Marks, but for once I depart from that learned exegete. I read the Hebrew here (it is weirdly difficult) as being more consonant with the earlier part of the verse. If you are sleepless, then Yahweh does not love you.

I conclude with Psalm 137, which since my childhood has moved me most of the entire Psalter:

1 By the rivers of Babylon, there we sat down, yea, we wept, when we remembered Zion.

2 We hanged our harps upon the willows in the midst thereof.

3 For there they that carried us away captive required of us a song; and they that wasted us *required of us* mirth, *saying,* Sing us *one* of the songs of Zion.

4 How shall we sing the LORD's song in a strange land?

5 If I forget thee, O Jerusalem, let my right hand forget *her cunning.*

6 If I do not remember thee, let my tongue cleave to the

roof of my mouth; if I prefer not Jerusalem above my chief joy.

7 Remember, O LORD, the children of Edom in the day of Jerusalem; who said, Rase *it,* rase *it, even* to the foundation thereof.

8 O daughter of Babylon, who art to be destroyed; happy *shall he be,* that rewardeth thee as thou hast served us.

9 Happy *shall he be,* that taketh and dasheth thy little ones against the stones.

[KJB]

On the ninth of Av, memorial day of the Temple's destruction, it is traditional to say this psalm. The KJB adds only minor touches to Geneva:

1 By the rivers of Babel we sat, and there we wept, when we remembered Zion.

2 We hanged our harps upon the willows in the midst thereof.

3 Then they that led us captives, required of us songs and mirth, when we had hanged up *our harps saying,* Sing us *one* of the songs of Zion.

4 How shall we sing, *said we,* a song of the Lord in a strange land?

5 If I forget thee, o Jerusalem, let my right hand forget *to play.*

6 If I do not remember thee, let my tongue cleave to the roof of my mouth: *yea,* if I prefer not Jerusalem to my chief joy.

7 Remember the children of Edom, o Lord, in the day of Jerusalem, which said, Rase it, rase it to the foundation thereof.

8 O daughter of Babel, worthy to be destroyed, blessed

shall he be that rewardeth thee, as thou hast served us.

9 Blessed *shall he be* that taketh and dasheth thy children against the stones.

[Geneva]

And yet how effective those slight revisions are! The first verse acquires a remarkable rhythm of plangency, as does the fourth, and who would prefer: "let my right hand forget to play" to "let my right hand forget her cunning"? Neither "to play" nor "her cunning" is in the Hebrew, where the idea of forgetting is economically total.

The poetry of the Tanakh, and of the KJB in its wake, is more powerful in Job, the Song of Songs, and Isaiah than in the Psalms. And yet the Psalter is (and has been) loved and employed far more extensively by those in grief, travail, and desperation. An endless litany of praise has to be highly acceptable to Yahweh, if he is still listening. Secular poetry of praise achieved an early height in Pindar's celebration of victorious heroes of wealthy households, who could pay the poet his high fees to immortalize agonists in the Greek games. Praise of Yahweh is an immensely different enterprise. It seems fair to observe that few turn to the Psalms now in order to absorb ongoing praise of a God both omnipotent and omniscient. We turn to the Psalms for its sufferers, whose human cry perpetually reverberates.

Proverbs

NO PRECISE ENGLISH TITLE FOR THE book of Proverbs will work; the literary materials involved are too diverse. In Hebrew the title is *Mishlei Shlomo,* more or less "Proverbs of Solomon." None whatsoever are by Solomon. *Mishlei* is the plural of *mashal,* a word whose scope embraces aphorisms, parables, proverbs, and oracles, many of them ironic.

The opening nine of the book of Proverbs' thirty-one chapters are later in composition than those that follow, and of greater literary interest. They are peculiarly zestful in warning foolish males against madly attractive "strange" women:

> 3 ¶For the lips of a strange woman drop *as* an honeycomb, and her mouth *is* smoother than oil:
>
> 4 But her end is bitter as wormwood, sharp as a two-edged sword.
>
> 5 Her feet go down to death; her steps take hold on hell.
>
> 6 Lest thou shouldest ponder the path of life, her ways are moveable, *that* thou canst not know *them.*

7 Hear me now therefore, O ye children, and depart not from the words of my mouth.

8 Remove thy way far from her, and come not nigh the door of her house:

9 Lest thou give thine honour unto others, and thy years unto the cruel:

10 Lest strangers be filled with thy wealth; and thy labours *be* in the house of a stranger;

11 And thou mourn at the last, when thy flesh and thy body are consumed.

[Proverbs 5:3–11]

Though rabbis and scholiasts want to interpret this as "whoring after strange gods," why take away such universal fun? It would be a literary blunder to read Shakespeare's Dark Lady sonnets as allegories of religious infidelity. Think of the great sonnet 129 ("the expense of spirit in a waste of shame"): who desires an exegesis that rends it and gives us a devotional poem?

Over-spiritualizing the Proverbs is deadly, and calls for the magnificent counter-voice of the poet-prophet William Blake in his Proverbs of Hell, one of the wonders of *The Marriage of Heaven and Hell* (1790). What could the compilers of the book of Proverbs have made of Blake's antithetical wisdom?

The tygers of wrath are wiser than the horses of instruction.

Can wisdom be instructed? Blake's rhetoric is antinomian but his argument is not. The book of Proverbs suffers—in my literary judgment—from rather too much agreement between its rhetoric and its argument. The effect can be banal: I wish more of the biblical Proverbs were porcupines (Schlegel's figure for a strong aphorism), but alas few are. A sprinkling of riddles would help, but I cannot find them as readily as Herbert Marks does. There is a great deal of Prudential wisdom, all of it vulnerable to the most brilliant of William Blake's Proverbs of Hell:

Prudence is a rich ugly old maid courted by Incapacity.

Far preferable to Miss Prudence is the brazen hussy of Proverbs 7:6–18:

6 ¶ For at the window of my house I looked through my casement,

7 And beheld among the simple ones, I discerned among the youths, a young man void of understanding,

8 Passing through the street near her corner; and he went the way to her house,

9 In the twilight, in the evening, in the black and dark night:

10 And behold, there met him a woman *with* the attire of an harlot, and subtil of heart.

11 (She *is* loud and stubborn; her feet abide not in her house:

12 Now *is she* without, now in the streets, and lieth in wait at every corner.)

13 So she caught him, and kissed him, *and* with an impudent face said unto him,

14 *I have* peace offerings with me; this day have I payed my vows.

15 Therefore came I forth to meet thee, diligently to seek thy face, and I have found thee.

16 I have decked my bed with coverings of tapestry, with carved *works,* with fine linen of Egypt.

17 I have perfumed my bed with myrrh, aloes, and cinnamon.

18 Come, let us take our fill of love until the morning: let us solace ourselves with loves.

At eighty I forgive myself for being charmed by a "strange woman" who perfumes her bed with myrrh, aloes, and cinnamon.

Contrasted to the female stranger throughout Proverbs is the spectacular woman named Wisdom. Prudential and pragmatic, nevertheless she is a divine figure who troubles the imagination:

20 ¶ Wisdom crieth without; she uttereth her voice in the streets:

21 She crieth in the chief place of concourse, in the openings of the gates: in the city she uttereth her words, *saying,*

22 How long, ye simple ones, will ye love simplicity? and the scorners delight in their scorning, and fools hate knowledge?

23 Turn you at my reproof: behold, I will pour out my spirit unto you, I will make known my words unto you.

24 ¶ Because I have called, and ye refused; I have stretched out my hand, and no man regarded;

25 But ye have set at nought all my counsel, and would none of my reproof:

26 I also will laugh at your calamity; I will mock when your fear cometh;

27 When your fear cometh as desolation, and your destruction cometh as a whirlwind; when distress and anguish cometh upon you.

28 Then shall they call upon me, but I will not answer; they shall seek me early, but they shall not find me:

29 For that they hated knowledge, and did not choose the fear of the LORD:

30 They would none of my counsel: they despised all my reproof.

31 Therefore shall they eat of the fruit of their own way, and be filled with their own devices.

32 For the turning away of the simple shall slay them, and the prosperity of fools shall destroy them.

33 But whoso hearkeneth unto me shall dwell safely, and shall be quiet from fear of evil.

[1:20–33]

This is great writing, the KJB at nearly its most stirring, a trumpet cry of the awakened spirit. The Hebrew goddess Wisdom will become the Shekhinah, or female presence in Yahweh, both in the old rabbinic doctrine of God and in the esoteric Kabbalah. Here in Proverbs 8, she returns triumphantly:

1 Doth not wisdom cry? and understanding put forth her voice?

2 She standeth in the top of high places, by the way in the places of the paths.

3 She crieth at the gates, at the entry of the city, at the coming in at the doors.

4 Unto you, O men, I call; and my voice *is* to the sons of man.

5 O ye simple, understand wisdom: and, ye fools, be ye of an understanding heart.

6 Hear; for I will speak of excellent things; and the opening of my lips *shall be* right things.

7 For my mouth shall speak truth; and wickedness *is* an abomination to my lips.

8 All the words of my mouth *are* in righteousness; *there is* nothing froward or perverse in them.

9 They *are* all plain to him that understandeth, and right to them that find knowledge.

10 Receive my instruction, and not silver; and knowledge rather than choice gold.

11 For wisdom *is* better than rubies; and all the things that may be desired are not to be compared to it.

12 I wisdom dwell with prudence, and find out knowledge of witty inventions.

13 The fear of the LORD *is* to hate evil: pride, and arrogancy, and the evil way, and the froward mouth, do I hate.

14 Counsel *is* mine, and sound wisdom: I *am* understanding; I have strength.

15 By me kings reign, and princes decree justice.

16 By me princes rule, and nobles, *even* all the judges of the earth.

17 I love them that love me; and those that seek me early shall find me.

18 Riches and honour *are* with me; *yea,* durable riches and righteousness.

19 My fruit *is* better than gold, yea, than fine gold; and my revenue than choice silver.

20 I lead in the way of righteousness, in the midst of the paths of judgment:

21 That I may cause those that love me to inherit substance; and I will fill their treasures.

22 The LORD possessed me in the beginning of his way, before his works of old.

23 I was set up from everlasting, from the beginning, or ever the earth was.

24 When *there were* no depths, I was brought forth; when *there were* no fountains abounding with water.

25 Before the mountains were settled, before the hills was I brought forth:

26 While as yet he had not made the earth, nor the fields, nor the highest part of the dust of the world.

27 When he prepared the heavens, I *was* there: when he set a compass upon the face of the depth:

28 When he established the clouds above: when he strengthened the fountains of the deep:

29 When he gave to the sea his decree, that the waters should not pass his commandment: when he appointed the foundations of the earth:

30 Then I was by him, *as* one brought up *with him:* and I was daily *his* delight, rejoicing always before him;

31 Rejoicing in the habitable part of his earth; and my delights *were* with the sons of men.

32 Now therefore hearken unto me, O ye children: for blessed *are they that* keep my ways.

33 Hear instruction, and be wise, and refuse it not.

34 Blessed *is* the man that heareth me, watching daily at my gates, waiting at the posts of my doors.

35 For whoso findeth me findeth life, and shall obtain favour of the LORD.

36 But he that sinneth against me wrongeth his own soul: all they that hate me love death.

Again the KJB, refining Geneva, ascends the heights of sublimity. From 22 to 30, this is both profound and ambiguous. Much turns on "the LORD *possessed* me" in verse 22, and "I was by him, *as* one brought up *with him*" in verse 30. In the Anchor Bible Proverbs (1965), R. B. Y. Scott explores the ambiguity of *qanah* (possess what has been acquired) and *amon* (either "ward, small child" or the wildly different "master workman"), a demiurge. Yet *qanah* also can mean "create" or "engender," and a child ward is a universe away from a cosmic craftsman.

So much of literary and spiritual tradition depends upon a spelling error or a blatant misreading. Boccaccio, in his *Genealogy of the Gentile Gods,* created a new and dread god, Demigorgon, utilizing a mistake by a more-or-less scholarly monk who was misreading Plato's Demiurge in *Timaeus.* Scott severely remarks that the theory of Wisdom as a Shekhinah figure or independent Hebrew goddess is "only a dubious interpretation of an obscure term." So be it: origin scarcely matters and the Wisdom of Proverbs continues her grand career, particularly on its ongoing esoteric side.

Chapter 9 opens with another magnificence:

1 Wisdom hath builded her house, she hath hewn out her seven pillars:

2 She hath killed her beasts; she hath mingled her wine; she hath also furnished her table.

3 She hath sent forth her maidens: she crieth upon the highest places of the city,

4 Whoso *is* simple, let him turn in hither: *as for* him that wanteth understanding, she saith to him,

5 Come, eat of my bread, and drink of the wine *which* I have mingled.

6 Forsake the foolish, and live; and go in the way of understanding.

7 He that reproveth a scorner getteth to himself shame: and he that rebuketh a wicked *man getteth* himself a blot.

8 Reprove not a scorner, lest he hate thee: rebuke a wise man, and he will love thee.

9 Give *instruction* to a wise *man,* and he will be yet wiser: teach a just *man,* and he will increase in learning.

10 The fear of the LORD *is* the beginning of wisdom: and the knowledge of the holy *is* understanding.

11 For by me thy days shall be multiplied, and the years of thy life shall be increased.

12 If thou be wise, thou shalt be wise for thyself: but if thou scornest, thou alone shalt bear it.

After that splendor, Proverbs mostly falls into the mundane, with a poignant recovery in the famous vision of an ideal wife in 31:10–31:

10 ¶ Who can find a virtuous woman? for her price *is* far above rubies.

11 The heart of her husband doth safely trust in her, so that he shall have no need of spoil.

12 She will do him good and not evil all the days of her life.

13 She seeketh wool, and flax, and worketh willingly with her hands.

14 She is like the merchants' ships; she bringeth her food from afar.

15 She riseth also while it is yet night, and giveth meat to her household, and a portion to her maidens.

16 She considereth a field, and buyeth it: with the fruit of her hands she planteth a vineyard.

17 She girdeth her loins with strength, and strengtheneth her arms.

18 She perceiveth that her merchandise *is* good: her candle goeth not out by night.

19 She layeth her hands to the spindle, and her hands hold the distaff.

20 She stretcheth out her hand to the poor; yea, she reacheth forth her hands to the needy.

21 She is not afraid of the snow for her household: for all her household *are* clothed with scarlet.

22 She maketh herself coverings of tapestry; her clothing *is* silk and purple.

23 Her husband is known in the gates, when he sitteth among the elders of the land.

24 She maketh fine linen, and selleth *it;* and delivereth girdles unto the merchant.

25 Strength and honour *are* her clothing; and she shall rejoice in time to come.

26 She openeth her mouth with wisdom; and in her tongue *is* the law of kindness.

27 She looketh well to the ways of her household, and eateth not the bread of idleness.

28 Her children arise up, and call her blessed; her husband *also,* and he praiseth her.

29 Many daughters have done virtuously, but thou excellest them all.

30 Favour *is* deceitful, and beauty *is* vain: *but* a woman *that* feareth the LORD, she shall be praised.

31 Give her of the fruit of her hands; and let her own works praise her in the gates.

This homely tribute lacks the ecstatic rhythms of the goddess Wisdom, yet its quietude proves to be just as memorable, in plain style rather than the KJB's ornate intensity.

Job

BY COMMON AESTHETIC JUDGMENT, the book of Job is the crown of the Bible's poetry even as the Yahwist's strand is the sublime of biblical narrative. Paradoxes crowd about this received truth: the Hebrew text of Job is difficult and sometimes obscure, and perhaps in a few places incoherent. Even when linguistic problems are overcome, the poem defeats the subtlest and best interpreters. Its premises are contradictory. Is it rightly a justification of the ways of God to man? John Calvin thought so, William Blake did not. Søren Kierkegaard changed the question to one of whether Job's spirit had been heroic enough to overcome the world. Herman Melville created an alternative hero (some would say hero-villain) in Captain Ahab of the *Pequod,* who identified Moby-Dick, the White Whale who had maimed him, with Job's Leviathan.

Theodicy is a mug's game: no humane individual could bear to justify God's ways to man. Nazi death camps, schizophrenia, cancer do not yield to ideologues who assert they speak for God. In old age I rebel against moral idiocy. Job, rejecting his horrible comforters, speaks to and for me until the Voice out of the Whirl-wind ("storm" in the Hebrew) silences him in shocked awe at the audacity of the Creation; after that I go back to his superbly laconic wife: "Curse God and die."

In the accents of Job I hear his precursor, the prophet Jeremiah, though Jeremiah (like Ezekiel) is a borderline madman and Job recalcitrantly holds on to his balance until God's rhetorical questions appear to overwhelm him. Job's God, like Jeremiah's, is a return to the Yahwist's uncanny being, although the poem avoids the name YHWH (I think Job himself uses it just once).

Names, always crucial in imaginative literature, are central in the book of Job, as acutely demonstrated by Ken Frieden in a 1985 essay, "Job's Encounters with the Adversary." Job's name possibly derives from the Arabic *awab,* a returner to God. Some ancient rabbis played with Job's name, *eyov,* reversing letters to *oyev,* "enemy."

The pragmatic enemy, the accuser or adversary, is *ha-satan,* whose root is *sin-tet-nun,* not so much the Satan of the New Testament as a kind of prosecuting attorney attached to Yahweh's heavenly court. Perhaps "blocking agent" would be the relevant translation.

Yahweh, named as such in the poem's framing prose, starts all the trouble, as William Empson insisted that God did in Milton's *Paradise Lost,* and as William Blake preceding Empson did by identifying Milton's Messiah with the book of Job's ha-satan.

Job, contemplating his murdered children and suffering sore boils all over his body, curses the day in which he was born and, as Samuel Beckett remarked, by a brilliant flashback, the night in which it was said that a man child had been conceived. After that superb opening, this shocking poem behaves very oddly. Job's friends, his "comforters," rally to him by insisting that he must be wickedly deserving of his losses and torments, which is rather like assuring the victims of death camps that they are culpable. This moral insanity is rejected by Job, who until God drowns him in a storm of rhetorical questions, remains admirably sane and accurate in maintaining his own innocence. If, as Herbert Marks suggests in his Norton Critical Edition of the English Bible, Job's final words are ironic, then Job argues his case even then.

There is nothing stronger in Hebrew poetry than the stormy voice of God in Job 38–41, and the KJB rises to the challenge by sensibly following the Geneva Bible's magnificent rendering, with only a sprinkling of revisions, one of them marvelous:

> When the stars of the morning praised *me* together, and all the children of God rejoiced
>
> [Geneva 38:7]

> When the morning stars sang together, and all the sons of God shouted for joy
>
> [KJB 38:7]

God's ironically mocking voice mounts to a crescendo in his boasting of his two grand mythological monsters, Behemoth, in chapter 40, verses 15–24, and Leviathan, throughout chapter 41. The Hebrew's terse power is transmuted into a threatening rhapsody in KJB:

> 1 Canst thou draw out leviathan with an hook? or his tongue with a cord *which* thou lettest down?
> 2 Canst thou put an hook into his nose? or bore his jaw through with a thorn?
> 3 Will he make many supplications unto thee? will he speak soft *words* unto thee?
> 4 Will he make a covenant with thee? wilt thou take him for a servant for ever?
> 5 Wilt thou play with him as *with* a bird? or wilt thou bind him for thy maidens?

6 Shall the companions make a banquet of him? shall they part him among the merchants?

7 Canst thou fill his skin with barbed irons? or his head with fish spears?

8 Lay thine hand upon him, remember the battle, do no more.

9 Behold, the hope of him is in vain: shall not *one* be cast down even at the sight of him?

10 None *is so* fierce that dare stir him up: who then is able to stand before me?

11 Who hath prevented me, that I should repay *him? whatsoever is* under the whole heaven is mine.

12 I will not conceal his parts, nor his power, nor his comely proportion.

13 Who can discover the face of his garment? *or* who can come *to him* with his double bridle?

14 Who can open the doors of his face? his teeth *are* terrible round about.

15 His scales *are his* pride, shut up together *as with* a close seal.

16 One is so near to another, that no air can come between them.

17 They are joined one to another, they stick together, that they cannot be sundered.

18 By his neesings a light doth shine, and his eyes *are* like the eyelids of the morning.

19 Out of his mouth go burning lamps, *and* sparks of fire leap out.

20 Out of his nostrils goeth smoke, as *out* of a seething pot or caldron.

21 His breath kindleth coals, and a flame goeth out of his mouth.

22 In his neck remaineth strength, and sorrow is turned into joy before him.

23 The flakes of his flesh are joined together: they are firm in themselves; they cannot be moved.

24 His heart is as firm as a stone; yea, as hard as a piece of the nether *millstone*.

25 When he raiseth up himself, the mighty are afraid: by reason of breakings they purify themselves.

26 The sword of him that layeth at him cannot hold: the spear, the dart, nor the habergeon.

27 He esteemeth iron as straw, *and* brass as rotten wood.

28 The arrow cannot make him flee: slingstones are turned with him into stubble.

29 Darts are counted as stubble: he laugheth at the shaking of a spear.

30 Sharp stones *are* under him: he spreadeth sharp pointed things upon the mire.

31 He maketh the deep to boil like a pot: he maketh the sea like a pot of ointment.

32 He maketh a path to shine after him; *one* would think the deep *to be* hoary.

33 Upon earth there is not his like, who is made without fear.

34 He beholdeth all high *things:* he *is* a king over all the children of pride.

[Job 41]

Sometimes I attempt to read this as Captain Ahab would have, who answered No in thunder and yet once more vainly harpooned Moby-Dick. God's sadistic sarcasm merits a Melvillean response, particularly to the plain nastiness of "Will he make a covenant with thee?" In Kabbalah, the companions do make a banquet of the Leviathan when the messiah comes. The poet of Job is as formidable an ironist as the God he depicts. How should we read Job as the great sufferer concludes?

> 1 Then Job answered the LORD, and said,
> 2 I know that thou canst do every *thing,* and *that* no thought can be withholden from thee.
> 3 Who *is* he that hideth counsel without knowledge? therefore have I uttered that I understood not; things too wonderful for me, which I knew not.
> 4 Hear, I beseech thee, and I will speak: I will demand of thee, and declare thou unto me.
> 5 I have heard of thee by the hearing of the ear: but now mine eye seeth thee.
> 6 Wherefore I abhor *myself,* and repent in dust and ashes.
>
> [42:1–6]

Marvin Pope in his Anchor Yale Bible Job addresses the evident contradiction of Yahweh's subsequent anger against Job's comforters:

> And it was *so,* that after the LORD had spoken these words unto Job, the LORD said to Eliphaz the Temanite, My wrath is kindled against thee, and against thy two friends: for ye have not spoken of me *the thing that is* right, as my servant Job *hath.*
>
> [42:7]

Pope is delightfully cheerful as to Yahweh's zeal:

> Job had indeed accused his miserable comforters of lying to defend and flatter God; and he suggested that an honest God would certainly reject and punish the pious sycophants, xiii 4, 7–11. If this verse refers to the argu-

ments of the Dialogue, it is as magnificent a vindication as Job could have hoped for, proving that God values the integrity of the impatient protester and abhors pious hypocrites who would heap accusations on a tormented soul to uphold their theological position.

That is a touch idealizing. Perhaps all that can be concluded there is Yahweh's customary bad temper. Though Job is *not* a Jew, and comes out of wisdom much farther east in Edom (1:2), his poem stems from the fifth century B.C.E. and is post-Exilic Judahite in ambiance. Its author is of course unknown. Was he an Israelite? Scholars argue about this, and perhaps what we have is a translated, edited version of an Arab poem. No matter: the renderer into Hebrew created a great poem. And yet there is a fury against divine injustice throughout that even now cannot subside.

I return to the subtle analysis of Herbert Marks:

42:6 *Wherefore . . . repent in dust and ashes:* much hinges on the translation of this verse, which bristles with difficulties. The most obvious is that the verb *abhor* (despise) lacks an object in Hebrew (KJB adds "myself"). Accordingly, some scholars translate, "I recant" or "I retract," leaving the object undefined (my questions? my whole complaint? my call for God to appear? my belief in a moral universe?); or more literally, "I reject" (conceivably, God's defense or countersuit, in which case the entire speech should be read as ironical; . . .); or even, "I am fed up." . . . The second verb ("repent") is also difficult; possible meanings range from "pity" or "feel sorry" (for my own acts? for all humanity?) to "feel comforted." Finally, the preposition translated "in" ordinarily means "of" or "concerning," while the phrase *dust and ashes* is elsewhere a self-deprecating (or sarcastic) description of human nature at its most elemental (cf. Gen 18:27, where Abraham also contends with God, though to better effect, and Job 30:19, where in his closing soliloquy Job charges God with deliberate cruelty). These alternatives leave the ending doubly ambiguous; read one way, Job is abjectly penitent; read another way, he is holding his ground and either decrying his own humility or pitying wretched mortals ("dust and ashes") for being subject to such a God.

I go with and by the second way. Job holds his dark ground. What else should he do? In the accents of Jeremiah, Job accepts his own self-election of resistance to an adversity outrageously unmerited. William Blake interpreted Behemoth and Leviathan as the War Everlasting by Land and Sea, an anticipation of Judge Holden's Iago-like vision in Cormac McCarthy's *Blood Meridian*. I prefer Blake to John Calvin's blistering reproof in his *Second Sermon on Job*:

> For Job could not better prove his patience than by resolving to be entirely naked, inasmuch as the good pleasure of God was such. Surely, men resist in vain; they may grit their teeth, but they must return entirely naked to the grave. Even the pagans have said that death alone shows the littleness of men. Why? For we have a gulf of covetousness, that we would wish to gobble up all the earth; if a man has many riches, vines, meadows, and possessions, it is not enough; God would have to create new worlds, if He wished to satisfy us.

I give the last word on Job to Kierkegaard in his *Edifying Discourses*:

> And yet there is no hiding place in the wide world where troubles may not find you, and there has never lived a

man who was able to say more than you can say, that you do not know when sorrow will visit your house. So be sincere with yourself, fix your eyes upon Job; even though he terrifies you, it is not this he wishes, if you yourself do not wish it.

Ecclesiastes

Koheleth is Job who failed in the test.
—*Elias Bickerman*

HEBREW TRADITION ASCRIBED TO the eighty-year-old Solomon, nearing the end of his half-century reign, this strikingly heretical meditation upon wisdom. I find it equally magnificent in the original and in the KJB, which transcends Geneva here and achieves astonishing literary power.

The speaker is given the Hebrew name Koheleth, the "assembler" of these aphorisms, which is more suitable than Ecclesiastes, Greco-Latin for the Preacher to a congregation. Of this most searingly eloquent of speakers, we can begin by observing that his skepticism exceeds Montaigne's and that of Montaigne's disciple Hamlet. So radical is this skeptic that we cannot know the limits of his ironies. And yet pragmatically he seems to assume some limit, since his book remains within the Covenant.

Who was he? We cannot even know the date of his life and his aphorisms. Does he live five hundred or seven hundred years after Solomon? If the text emanates from the third century before the Common Era, are we listening to a Hebrew Epicurus? Such a person outrageously would be a living oxymoron, but the sense of reality colliding with an embattled ethos seems central to this book from its opening:

1 The words of the Preacher, the son of David, king in Jerusalem.

2 Vanity of vanities, saith the Preacher, vanity of vanities; all *is* vanity.

3 What profit hath a man of all his labour which he taketh under the sun?

4 *One* generation passeth away, and *another* generation cometh: but the earth abideth for ever.

5 The sun also ariseth, and the sun goeth down, and hasteth to his place where he arose.

6 The wind goeth toward the south, and turneth about unto the north; it whirleth about continually, and the wind returneth again according to his circuits.

7 All the rivers run into the sea; yet the sea *is* not full; unto the place from whence the rivers come, thither they return again.

8 All things *are* full of labour; man cannot utter *it:* the eye is not satisfied with seeing, nor the ear filled with hearing.

9 The thing that hath been, it *is that* which shall be; and that which is done *is* that which shall be done: and *there is* no new *thing* under the sun.

10 Is there *any* thing whereof it may be said, See, this *is* new? it hath been already of old time, which was before us.

11 *There is* no remembrance of former *things;* neither shall there be *any* remembrance of *things* that are to come with *those* that shall come after.

12 I the Preacher was king over Israel in Jerusalem.

Ecclesiastes
209

13 And I gave my heart to seek and search out by wisdom concerning all *things* that are done under heaven: this sore travail hath God given to the sons of man to be exercised therewith.

14 I have seen all the works that are done under the sun; and, behold, all *is* vanity and vexation of spirit.

15 *That which is* crooked cannot be made straight: and that which is wanting cannot be numbered.

16 I communed with mine own heart, saying, Lo, I am come to great estate, and have gotten more wisdom than all *they* that have been before me in Jerusalem: yea, my heart had great experience of wisdom and knowledge.

17 And I gave my heart to know wisdom, and to know madness and folly: I perceived that this also is vexation of spirit.

18 For in much wisdom *is* much grief: and he that increaseth knowledge increaseth sorrow.

"Vanity" brilliantly mistranslates the Hebrew *hevel,* a mere breath, vapor of vapors, the thing itself, or nothing at all. "Vexation of spirit" renders something like "herding the mind" in the Hebrew, an unforgettable trope for futility. A genius for metaphor belies the dark burden of this meditation. Can it be that the irony of irony here is so incisive that a mode of gaiety rises out of this festival of negation? Herbert Marks sees this as a Wallace Stevens–like "gaiety of language"; I myself think of it as the timbre of a unique voice, both in and out of the game and watching and wondering at it, as Walt Whitman might phrase such a stance. Koheleth the aphorist stands back from the malady of the quotidian while reflecting nevertheless on its reward:

4 ¶ For to him that is joined to all the living there is hope: for a living dog is better than a dead lion.

5 For the living know that they shall die: but the dead know not any thing, neither have they any more a reward; for the memory of them is forgotten.

6 Also their love, and their hatred, and their envy is now perished; neither have they any more a portion for ever in any *thing* that is done under the sun.

7 Go thy way, eat thy bread with joy, and drink thy wine with a merry heart; for God now accepteth thy works.

8 Let thy garments be always white; and let thy head lack no ointment.

9 Live joyfully with the wife whom thou lovest all the days of thy life of thy vanity, which he hath given thee under the sun, all the days of thy vanity: for that *is* thy portion in *this* life, and in thy labour which thou takest under the sun.

10 Whatsoever thy hand findeth to do, do *it* with thy might; for *there is* no work, nor device, nor knowledge, nor wisdom, in the grave, whither thou goest.

11 ¶ I returned, and saw under the sun, that the race *is* not to the swift, nor the battle to the strong, neither yet bread to the wise, nor yet riches to men of understanding, nor yet favour to men of skill; but time and chance happeneth to them all.

[9:4–11]

Are we being implored to seize the day? Marks acutely crystallizes the ultimate irony of the book, that it is finally life's "vanity that makes it precious." Shakespeare's Falstaff, often and angrily accused of "vanity" by that grand Christian gentleman Prince Hal/Henry V, truly shows us the glory of Koheleth's "vanity," a hevel that merely constitutes the breath of life.

Let us, with the immortal Falstaff, seize vanity:

1 Remember now thy Creator in the days of thy youth, while the evil days come not, nor the years draw nigh, when thou shalt say, I have no pleasure in them;

2 While the sun, or the light, or the moon, or the stars, be not darkened, nor the clouds return after the rain:

3 In the day when the keepers of the house shall tremble, and the strong men shall bow themselves, and the grinders cease because they are few, and those that look out of the windows be darkened,

4 And the doors shall be shut in the streets, when the sound of the grinding is low, and he shall rise up at the voice of the bird, and all the daughters of musick shall be brought low;

5 Also *when* they shall be afraid of *that which is* high, and fears *shall be* in the way, and the almond tree shall flourish, and the grasshopper shall be a burden, and desire shall fail: because man goeth to his long home, and the mourners go about the streets:

6 Or ever the silver cord be loosed, or the golden bowl be broken, or the pitcher be broken at the fountain, or the wheel broken at the cistern.

7 Then shall the dust return to the earth as it was: and the spirit shall return unto God who gave it.

8 ¶ Vanity of vanities, saith the preacher; all *is* vanity.

[12:1–8]

This is one of the KJB's miracles. I brood, at eighty and counting, daily on these verses, as my fingers tremble, my legs bow themselves, my teeth cease, my eyes darken, my ears shut, bird-song grows fainter, heights increase my fear of falling, and even walking finds fears in the way. Spring will begin again (in Jerusalem) with the flowering of the almond tree, but the burgeoning grass will bring no seasonal renewal to desire, because the *"long* home" (a KJB trope for the *eternal* grave) is prefigured by my generation's mourners.

The Hebrew in verse 6 is "smashed" and not the KJB's "loosed," and there may be a Hebrew pun on "grave" in the cistern. When the dust returns to the earth in 12:7, there is an allusion to Genesis 2:7.

Northrop Frye, in his *The Great Code* (1982), a work whose massive typology I tend to resist, nonetheless wrote brilliantly about Koheleth. For Frye the book transforms wisdom into "a program of continuous mental energy," and its author is "a vigorous realist," whose deepest insight is that "all things are full of emptiness." Whether, as Frye suggests, this is akin to the "void," *shunyata,* of Buddhist thought, I am uncertain, but for Koheleth "fullness" and "emptiness" are cognate.

In his classic study *Koheleth: The Man and His World* (1955), Robert Gordis compared the Preacher to another Jewish heretic, Baruch Spinoza, remarking that both emphasized conventional terms while transfiguring them from within. Religious vocabulary in Ecclesiastes therefore is deceptive, and the ironies of the text range far. But then the book's presence in Tanakh is itself an irony, reminding us that the Hebrew Bible anthologizes a people as well as a Covenant.

Elias Bickerman wrote brilliantly on Koheleth in his *Four Strange Books of the Bible: Jonah, Daniel, Koheleth, Esther* (1967). Superbly, Bickerman reminds us that "the Synagogue wisely understood this despairing book as an appeal to happiness," and yet "the despair of Koheleth is that he cannot be a hedonist." Best of all, Bickerman writes, "There is something of a Fallen Angel in the author of Ecclesiastes." I would suggest that the book's universal appeal depends upon the Fallen Angel in every reader. The wisest of Shakespeare's characters are Falstaff, Hamlet, Iago, and Cleopatra. Except for Falstaff, these are all Fallen Angels. Only the Cherub Falstaff cannot fall because he loves laughter above all people, including Prince Hal and himself.

Koheleth is an Invoker who evades Yahweh and prefers the divine name Elohim, plural and less numinous than the Tetragrammaton. More important, the Elohim are impersonal compared to Yahweh, and Koheleth sensibly desires to keep God at a distance. God's justice is for Ecclesiastes a nonstarter, even as the concept of righteousness is empty as vapor.

A work of wisdom literature that rejects wisdom, Ecclesiastes vies with Job as the negative crown of the Hebrew Bible. And yet it challenges Job also for the palm of eloquence.

The Song of Songs

THE FINAL DAYS OF PASSOVER IN Jewish circles throughout the ages are the context for reading the Song of Songs. Yahweh at Sinai appeared as an older man, but at the parting of the Red Sea as a young man of war. Solomon's Song, to certain early exegetes, celebrated Yahweh in love. In Kabbalah the object of Yahweh's love is within him, the Shekhinah, what Walt Whitman called his Fancy, the Real Me or Me Myself, and Wallace Stevens celebrated as the Interior Paramour.

Saul Lieberman, in an appendix he contributed to Gershom Scholem's *Jewish Gnosticism, Merkabah Mysticism and Talmudic Tradition* (1960), cited a midrash to Song of Songs 5:9–16:

> 9 ¶ What *is* thy beloved more than *another* beloved, O thou fairest among women? what *is* thy beloved more than *another* beloved, that thou dost so charge us?
>
> 10 My beloved is white and ruddy, the chiefest among ten thousand.
>
> 11 His head *is as* the most fine gold, his locks *are* bushy, *and* black as a raven.

12 His eyes *are* as *the eyes* of doves by the rivers of waters, washed with milk, *and* fitly set.

13 His cheeks *are* as a bed of spices, *as* sweet flowers: his lips *like* lilies, dropping sweet smelling myrrh.

14 His hands *are as* gold rings set with the beryl: his belly *is as* bright ivory overlaid *with* sapphires.

15 His legs *are as* pillars of marble, set upon sockets of fine gold: his countenance *is* as Lebanon, excellent as the cedars.

16 His mouth *is* most sweet: yea, he *is* altogether lovely. This *is* my beloved, and this *is* my friend, O daughters of Jerusalem.

This alludes to the tradition of the *shi'ur komah shel yotzer bereshit,* the measurements of the divine body of the Creator. Arthur Green, in an illuminating essay on the Song of Songs in early Kabbalah, splendidly juxtaposes Maimonides with one of the first Kabbalists, Rabbi Abraham ben David. Maimonides announces that "one who says that God has a body or a depictable form is a heretic," which the Kabbalist glossed: "Greater and better persons than he believed it."

I prefer a Kabbalistic reading of the Song of Solomon because I weary of most scholarly interpretations, for whom this grandest of erotic poems is reduced to a royal wedding celebration or a cultic ceremony or a suite of folk songs. The great Rabbi Akiba ben Joseph, founder of normative Judaism, kept the Song of Songs in the canon, presumably because he saw it as an esoteric component in the Oral Torah given by Yahweh at Sinai. Kabbalah always insists it is identical with Oral Torah.

Whether you read the Song of Songs as a dramatic lyric celebrating (and contrasting) the erotic ecstasy of a woman and a man or as a visionary canticle of Yahweh's own sexual fulfillment you encounter a unique instance of ancient Hebrew poetry: intensely metaphoric and having rather more in common with its literary descendants than with other biblical poetry. When I read the Song of Songs, whether in Hebrew or in the Geneva Bible or in the KJB, I think of the poetic tradition it fostered, which flows from the Kabbalah of Isaac Luria through Renaissance erotic lyricists on to Walt Whitman, Coventry Patmore, and Hart Crane. Saint John of the Cross, Luis de León, Edmund Spenser, and Shakespeare's "Venus and Adonis" all manifest the Song's influence. In the nineteenth century, atheistic poets—Shelley, Swinburne, Dante Gabriel Rossetti—carried this tradition on. W. B. Yeats, Theodore Roethke, and Dylan Thomas a century later seem to have closed out this current, perhaps forever.

The mode fostered by Solomon's Song is curiously elegiac, particularly when you consider its bridal aspects. But then the darkness is there already:

> Set me as a seal upon thine heart, as a seal upon thine arm: for love *is* strong as death; jealousy *is* cruel as the grave: the coals thereof *are* coals of fire, *which hath* a most vehement flame.

The Hebrew calls love as intensely fierce as dying, and chants that "passion is as strong as Sheol." "Coals of fire" in the Hebrew are "darts of fire." Whether in the original or in the KJB we are brought close to Freud's dialectical relationship between eros and the death drive. In a Dark Lady sonnet, Shakespeare sighs that "desire is death." His only peer among Western poets, Dante in his "stony sestina," proclaims that he would sleep away his life in stone, or feed like beasts upon the grass, only to see his lady Pietra's garments cast a shade.

The remorseless intensity of the Song must cause some tremors in the afterlife, if Akiba was accurate in proclaiming that the blessed would read it there incessantly. To read allegorically is also to read ironically, and ironic eros is scarcely manifested in this great sequence, and would wound its fused immediacy. Anyone steeped in the art of reading poetry ought to see rapidly that this is a unified poem, a single work, not an anthology.

The KJB takes the Song from the Geneva version, improving its style of rapture in many places, and making some corrections, but essentially not altering the Geneva eloquence. Whoever was the prime Geneva hand at rendering the song (I would guess Anthony Gilby), he performed awesomely. Robert Alter aptly calls the Song a "garden of metaphor," and it is extraordinary in the original. Marvelous as the KJB Job is, that is not always worthy of the Hebrew. But if ever the KJB goes beyond its original in beauty and splendor, it is in the Song of Songs.

I try to defend against my own judgment here by reflecting upon the rich tradition in Western poetry informed by Solomon's Song. There are the tragic *conversos,* the Jewish Catholics, who emulated the poem: Saint Teresa of Avila, Saint John of the Cross, and Fray Luis de León. In English the great poem is Edmund Spenser's "Epithalamium," composed for his own wedding, but I hear the Song of Songs also in Shakespeare's "Venus and Adonis." Both Spenser and Shakespeare read the Geneva Bible. This tradition came alive again in the odes of the Victorian Catholic Coventry Patmore and even more resplendently in the New World's greatest poet and poem, Walt Whitman's "Lilacs" elegy for Lincoln. Hart Crane's "Voyages" carries Whitman into the twentieth century.

The most helpful reading of the Song is by Herbert Marks in his Norton Critical Edition of the English Bible, which I will build upon here. Marks traces the intricate counterpoint between the male and female lovers, with the young woman's voice dominant. Accurately and charmingly, Marks observes: "Ardent but unreliable, his desire, when aroused, is fully displayed and marvelously directed. Hers, by contrast, is more inward and complex, and she often seems less focused on him than on the love that consumes his to the exclusion of all else." This enclosed ecstasy, which becomes a dangerous psychic self-intoxication in Tennyson's disturbing "Mariana," is an exultant ecstasy in the Song:

1 I *am* the rose of Sharon, *and* the lily of the valleys.

2 As the lily among thorns, so *is* my love among the daughters.

3 As the apple tree among the trees of the wood, so *is* my beloved among the sons. I sat down under his shadow with great delight, and his fruit *was* sweet to my taste.

4 He brought me to the banqueting house, and his banner over me *was* love.

5 Stay me with flagons, comfort me with apples: for I *am* sick of love.

6 His left hand *is* under my head, and his right hand doth embrace me.

7 I charge you, O ye daughters of Jerusalem, by the roes, and by the hinds of the field, that ye stir not up, nor awake *my* love, till he please.

8 ¶ The voice of my beloved! behold, he cometh leaping upon mountains, skipping among the hills.

9 My beloved is like a roe or a young hart: behold, he standeth behind our wall, he looketh forth at the windows, shewing himself through the lattice.

10 My beloved spake, and said unto me, Rise up, my love, my fair one, and come away.

11 For, lo, the winter is past, the rain is over *and* gone;

12 The flowers appear on the earth; the time of the singing *of birds* is come, and the voice of the turtle is heard in our land;

13 The fig tree putteth forth her green figs, and the vines *with* the tender grape give a *good* smell. Arise, my love, my fair one, and come away.

14 ¶ O my dove, *that art* in the clefts of the rock, in the secret *places* of the stairs, let me see thy countenance, let me hear thy voice; for sweet *is* thy voice, and thy countenance *is* comely.

15 Take us the foxes, the little foxes, that spoil the vines: for our vines *have* tender grapes.

16 ¶ My beloved *is* mine, and I *am* his: he feedeth among the lilies.

17 Until the day break, and the shadows flee away, turn, my beloved, and be thou like a roe or a young hart upon the mountains of Bether.

[2:1–17]

As with much in Shakespeare, this is now so familiar to us that it might be worn out with repetition, yet the perfection of its diction, the inevitability of its cadences, maintains freshness. All the particulars and tropes of this passage are there in the Hebrew, and erotic power certainly is florabundant, yet this is one of the miraculous epiphanies of the KJB.

And yet, are these truly the accents of fulfillment? An odd ambiguity hovers in the Hebrew, evaded by the KJB's ecstatic tone. The Hebrew poet knows more about eros than do his exegetes and translators, and ambivalence may be the essence of eros. Secret encounters and group disapproval are necessary to raise what Sigmund Freud wryly named "the incitement premium." William Blake warned against "dark secret love" but the Song of Songs exalts it.

Chapter 3, verses 1–5, exquisitely modulates from ambivalence into erotic ambiguity:

1 By night on my bed I sought him whom my soul loveth: I sought him, but I found him not.

2 I will rise now, and go about the city in the streets, and in the broad ways I will seek him whom my soul loveth: I sought him, but I found him not.

3 The watchmen that go about the city found me: *to whom I said,* Saw ye him whom my soul loveth?

4 *It was* but a little that I passed from them, but I found him whom my soul loveth: I held him, and would not let him go, until I had brought him into my mother's house, and into the chamber of her that conceived me.

5 I charge you, O ye daughters of Jerusalem, by the roes, and by the hinds of the field, that ye stir not up, not awake *my* love, till he please.

Is her lover reluctant or less ardent than this marvelous singer? Marvin H. Pope, in his massive commentary on the Song of Songs (Anchor Yale Bible, 1995), catalogues the allegorical readings, which here miss not less than everything. Far better interpretation can be found in the poems of Saint John of the Cross and Walt Whitman, authentic heirs of Solomon's Song.

My late friend John Frederick Nims, an admirable American poet, caught the tonalities of the Song of Songs in his translation of "The Dark Night" of Saint John of the Cross:

> Once in the dark of night
> when love burned bright with yearning, I arose
> (O windfall of delight!)
> and how I left none knows—
> dead to the world my house in deep repose;
>
> in the dark, where all goes right,
> thanks to a secret ladder, other clothes,

(O windfall of delight!)
in the dark, enwrapped in those—
dead to the world my house in deep repose.

There in the lucky dark,
none to observe me, darkness far and wide;
no sign for me to mark,
no other light, no guide
except for my heart—the fire, the fire inside!

That led me on
true as the very noon is—truer too!—
to where there waited one
I knew—how well I knew!—
in a place where no one was in view.

John of the Cross catches the secretive quality of the Song of Songs. There is a sense in which the Song's eros is concealed and even negative. A love that is strong as death indeed is as terrible as an army with banners. The deepest significance of the Song of Songs is that it knowingly celebrates a love so dangerously intense that it can cost not less than everything.

The Apocrypha

The Hidden Books

THE SIXTEENTH-CENTURY PROTESTANT leader Andreas Bodenheim von Karlstadt first called the varied works gathered together in the margins of the canonical the Apocrypha (hidden). This naming is hard to dislodge even though the books involved are not secretive. The KJB followed the Geneva Bible in retaining the Apocrypha but printing it separately, in defiance of strict Calvinist practice, which excluded it. Geneva and the KJB were thus in accord with the Lutherans.

The book of Judith I have discussed earlier, and I will make some comments on 2 Esdras and on the charmingly comic Tobit and the delightful History of Susanna. But the works I care deeply about in the Apocrypha are Ecclesiasticus (the Wisdom of Ben Sira) and the Wisdom of Solomon. Each is immensely eloquent in certain passages that are among the glories of the KJB. Though it is a scholarly cliché to affirm that the Geneva Job influenced *King Lear,* I find more of the Wisdom of Solomon in Shakespeare's most shattering play.

Esdras

RATHER ODDLY COMBINED, AND WRITTEN two and a half centuries apart, 1 and 2 Esdras (Ezra) form a complete contrast as visions of ancient Jewish history and destiny. The first Esdras, a source book for the Judaic quisling and historian Flavius Josephus, evidently was composed in Aramaic about 150 B.C.E., essentially as a chronicle of the destruction of the First Temple and its restoration by Nehemiah and Ezra. I find it of no particular literary appeal.

Far different is 2 Esdras, an apocalyptic work, particularly in chapters 3–14. It is more or less Jewish Christian, written after the fall of Jerusalem to the Romans in 70 C.E. Theodicy clearly is its design, as in the book of Job or Milton's *Paradise Lost,* but the wildness of 2 Esdras is of another order, a kind of prelude to the Revelation of Saint John the Divine, which concludes the New Testament. As such it has considerable aesthetic interest.

Ezra, regarded as a prophet rather than a scribe, experiences seven visions in chapters 3–14. The most vivid are the last three: 11:1–12:51, 13:1–58, 14:1–48. In chapters 11–12, Ezra confronts an eagle with twelve wings and three heads. A man emerges out of the sea in chapter 13 and has to overcome a host of assaults. Ezra himself centers chapter 14, in which he cries out in an ecstatic flow of language for forty days and nights to five scribes. Ninety-four books ensue, twenty-four for proclamation but seventy for esoteric perusal by carefully chosen sages.

Two passages of 2 Esdras stay with me. The angel Uriel (with whom Emerson was to identify) appears to Ezra, and the scribe-turned-prophet ascends to the challenge:

> 1 And the angel that was sent unto me, whose name was Uriel, gave me an answer,
> 2 And said, Thy heart hath gone too far in this world, and thinkest thou to comprehend the way of the most High?
> 3 Then said I, Yea, my lord.
>
> [4:1–3]

There is a note of a latecomer prophet's audacity there, worthy of Blake and Shelley. That audacity energizes the eagle (Roman Empire) vision of chapters 11–12, where the three heads are Vespasian and his son Titus, who destroyed Jerusalem, and his other son Domitian, who came after them as emperor. A lion, reserved until the end of days, is the Davidic messiah who will destroy Rome.

The man who comes up out of the sea in chapter 13 has to battle all the nations of the world. Another representation of the messiah, he obliterates his enemies by fire. Both apocalyptic images, lion and sea-hero, have origins in the book of Daniel. What is more original and impressive is the final vision, of Ezra as a second Moses, in chapter 14. Both a lawgiver and a companion of God's messianic son, Ezra becomes the seer of esoteric knowledge by dictating a hidden library of seventy books of unrevealed wisdom.

The most memorable image in 2 Esdras comes in 14:25, when God speaks to Ezra:

And come hither, and I shall light a candle of understanding in thine heart, which shall not be put out.

Protestant martyrs from Hugh Latimer and Nicholas Ridley in 1555 to Milton's friend Sir Henry Vane, victimized by the Stuart Restoration, held fast to that image of the heart's candle of understanding, illuminated by the Inner Light by which each Protestant read the English Bible for himself or herself (among the Quakers).

Tobit

ABOUT 300 B.C.E. A JEWISH WRITER composed the book of Tobit, a somewhat zany romance novella that continues to entertain lively readers. Its most distinguished admirer was Søren Kierkegaard, who exalted its hapless heroine, Sara. Seven husbands, each in turn, are murdered by the demon Asmodeus just before they can embrace the beautiful Sara in her marriage bed. This delightfully outrageous story centers upon Tobit, a Joblike exemplary sufferer who has been exiled to sinful Nineveh in the realm of the Assyrians.

Blinded in the course of virtue, Tobit prays for death, as does his kinswoman Sara in Media. Tobias, son of the sufferer, journeys with the disguised angel Raphael to Media in search of a bride and a fortune. Inevitably, he and Sara fall in love, but how is he to avoid becoming the eighth unconsummated victim of Asmodeus?

Bathing in the Tigris River, Tobias is attacked by a large fish that wishes to devour the young man. At Raphael's direction, Tobias catches the fish and sets aside its heart, liver, and gall. After the fish has been roasted and eaten, the angel instructs him in the use of its organs: smoked, the heart and liver will chase off Asmodeus, and the gall will heal Tobit's blindness.

All ends happily, with the final touch that Tobit is assured that Jonah's prophecy against Nineveh will finally be fulfilled. Virtue, wisdom, and the godly triumph. This madcap tale is told with no apparent irony, and with appropriate narrative zest.

The KJB is content to repeat the Geneva text, which could have been improved by some ornate touches, but that might have marred its folktale simplicity.

The Wisdom of Solomon

SHAKESPEARE MUST HAVE HAD HIS OWN copy of the Geneva Bible because his allusions to it are incessant. Though his ultimate achievement, *King Lear,* shatters the limits of art, you can trace much of its origin to biblical promptings. Since *King Lear* is "a pagan play for a Christian audience" (William Elton) this can become an imagistic puzzle. The most tragic of all tragedies, the play cannot sustain a Christian interpretation. Shakespeare borrows the plain style of Tyndale in certain crucial passages, and also echoes Geneva's Job and Jeremiah.

The models for Lear are Solomon in advanced old age, Koheleth (Ecclesiastes), and the Apocrypha's Wisdom of Solomon, which the KJB men reprinted from Geneva with very few changes. David Winston, in his Anchor Yale Bible edition of the Wisdom of Solomon (1979), dates this Alexandrian Jewish discourse to 37–41 C.E., the reign of the insane Roman emperor Caligula. Rome had captured Alexandria in 30 B.C.E, and with it a highly sophisticated, Greek-speaking Jewry.

Much of the Wisdom of Solomon is Neoplatonist philosophy assimilated to Judaic thought in the mode of Philo of Alexandria.

I myself am moved only by 6:22–10:21, as Shakespeare must have been. Solomon speaks most powerfully in 7:1–6, which I juxtapose with *King Lear* 4.6.176–83:

> 1 I myself also am a mortal man, like to all, and the off-spring of him that was first made of the earth,
>
> 2 And in my mother's womb was fashioned to be flesh in the time of ten months, being compacted in blood, of the seed of man, and the pleasure that came with sleep.
>
> 3 And when I was born, I drew in the common air, and fell upon the earth, which is of like nature, and the first voice which I uttered was crying, as all others do.
>
> 4 I was nursed in swaddling clothes, and that with cares.
>
> 5 For there is no king that had any other beginning of birth.
>
> 6 For all men have one entrance into life, and the like going out.
>
> [Wisdom of Solomon 7:1–6]

> LEAR. If thou wilt weep my fortunes, take my eyes.
>   I know thee well enough, thy name is Gloucester.
>   Thou must be patient; we came crying hither.
>   Thou know'st, the first time that we smell the air
>   We wawl and cry. I will preach to thee. Mark.
>   [*Lear takes off his crown of weeds and flowers.*]
> GLOU. Alack, alack the day!
> LEAR. When we are born, we cry that we are come
>   To this great stage of fools.
>
> [*King Lear* 4.6.176–83]

Why does Shakespeare so clearly echo the Wisdom of Solomon? We are at the imaginative center of the play in act 4, scene 6, lines 80–185. Frank Kermode admirably observed that these hundred lines, the meeting of the mad Lear and the blinded Gloucester, do not advance the plot and yet are the height of Shakespeare's tragic art.

Shakespeare wants us to associate Lear's realization of the human mortality that great kings share with Solomon's prior understanding. The great stage of fools at once is Solomon's kingdom and Lear's and our own, since "fools" means "victims" as well as those we love.

Ecclesiasticus
The Wisdom of Ben Sira

IN THE ANCHOR YALE BIBLE Wisdom of Ben Sira (1995), the learned Franciscan Alexander Di Lella speculates upon the original Hebrew title of the book, since neither the title nor the first chapter has been recovered. The author, Yeshua the son of Eleazer Ben Sira, a scribe by profession, uniquely signed his own name as author to his massive book. Under correction, I would venture that this is the first assertion of pride as a writer under one's own name in Jewish tradition. The Greek translation of the book was done by Ben Sira's grandson, a proper tribute for a work that memorializes the Wisdom of the Fathers.

The most renowned (and moving) part of Ben Sira is chapters 44:1–50:21, starting with a wonderful KJB chant:

> 1 Let us now praise famous men, and our fathers that begat us.
>
> 2 The Lord hath wrought great glory by them through his great power from the beginning.
>
> 3 Such as did bear rule in their kingdoms, men renowned

for their power, giving counsel by their understanding, and declaring prophecies:

4 Leaders of the people by their counsels, and by their knowledge of learning meet for the people, wise and eloquent in their instructions:

5 Such as found out musical tunes, and recited verses in writing:

6 Rich men furnished with ability, living peaceably in their habitations:

7 All these were honoured in their generations, and were the glory of their times.

8 There be of them, that have left a name behind them, that their praises might be reported.

9 And some there be, which have no memorial; who are perished, as though they had never been; and are become as though they had never been born; and their children after them.

10 But these were merciful men, whose righteousness hath not been forgotten.

11 With their seed shall continually remain a good inheritance, and their children are within the covenant.

[44:1–11]

"Let us now praise famous men" was appropriated by the poet-novelist James Agee as the title of his poignant study of Alabama sharecroppers with photographs by Walker Evans (1941). The KJB relies heavily on Geneva in the Apocrypha, but as always the ear for prose rhythm is better in the later work:

Let us now commend the famous men, and our fathers, of whom we are begotten.

[Geneva 44:1]

Ben Sira begins with Enoch, who took walks with Yahweh and was taken up by him, ascending into heaven without the necessity of dying. The sequence that follows is traditional: Noah, Abraham, Isaac, Israel (Jacob), on to Moses; Aaron and his grandson Phinehas. The strong emphasis upon Aaron and his descendants rather than Moses shows Ben Sira's devotion to the hereditary priesthood, which reaches apotheosis in 45:25–26, a poem celebrating Simeon, the high priest of the temple. Between Aaron and Simeon the usual exemplars are rounded up: Joshua, Caleb, Samuel, Nathan the prophet, David, Solomon, Elijah, Elisha, King Hezekiah, Isaiah, King Josiah. What carries this off in the KJB is the marvelous rhythmic continuity, which prompts me to a digression on such mastery.

George Saintsbury, in his *History of English Prose Rhythm* (1911), found in the KJB an origin for "the triumph of the ornate style" in Robert Burton's *The Anatomy of Melancholy* (1621), Milton's prose polemics, and the reveries of Sir Thomas Browne. Taking as text the magnificent opening of KJB Isaiah 60, Saintsbury employs it as a touchstone for English baroque prose rhythm:

1 Arise, shine; for thy light is come, and the glory of the Lord is risen upon thee.

2 For, behold, the darkness shall cover the earth, and gross darkness the people: but the Lord shall arise upon thee, and his glory shall be seen upon thee.

3 And the Gentiles shall come to thy light, and kings to the brightness of thy rising.

4 Lift up thine eyes round about, and see: all they gather themselves together, they come to thee: thy sons shall come from far, and thy daughters shall be nursed at *thy* side.

5 Then thou shalt see, and flow together, and thine heart shall fear, and be enlarged; because the abundance of

the sea shall be converted unto thee, the forces of the Gentiles shall come unto thee.

[Isaiah 60:1–5]

That is overwhelming, even for the KJB at its strongest. Ben Sira is not the Second Isaiah, and such propulsive power is beyond his range or his desire. He wrote early in the second century B.C.E., before the Hellenization of the Temple enforced by the Syrian-Macedonian tyrant Antiochus Epiphanes. Ben Sira's Jewish world was not yet in crisis when he died in 175 B.C.E. or so. The Maccabean rebellion against Antiochus Epiphanes began in 166 B.C.E., and the Jewish world was radically altered.

Ecclesiasticus is best seen as its author's subtle polemic against the more gradual Hellenization of the Jews that had begun with Alexander the Great's conquest of Palestine. Wisdom from the Greeks is accepted by Ben Sira in chapter 7 of his book, but it is secondary to the wisdom of his own tradition.

Ecclesiasticus concludes with an autobiographical poem by Ben Sira, who had taught wisdom for a lifetime even as he worked at being a scribe. At eighty, fifty-five years into a teaching career, I identify with much of this:

> 13 When I was yet young, or ever I went abroad, I desired wisdom openly in my prayer.
>
> 14 I prayed for her before the temple, and will seek her out even to the end.
>
> 15 Even from the flower till the grape was ripe hath my heart delighted in her: my foot went the right way, from my youth up sought I after her.
>
> 16 I bowed down mine ear a little, and received her, and gat much learning.
>
> 17 I profited therein, *therefore* will I ascribe the glory unto him that giveth me wisdom.

Ecclesiasticus

18 For I purposed to do after her, and earnestly I followed that which is good; so shall I not be confounded.

19 My soul hath wrestled with her, and in my doings I was exact: I stretched forth my hands to the heaven above, and bewailed my ignorances of her.

20 I directed my soul unto her, and I found her in pureness: I have had my heart joined with her from the beginning, therefore shall I not be forsaken.

21 My heart was troubled in seeking her: therefore have I gotten a good possession.

22 The Lord hath given me a tongue for my reward, and I will praise him therewith.

23 Draw near unto me, ye unlearned, and dwell in the house of learning.

24 Wherefore are ye slow, and what say ye of these things, seeing your souls are very thirsty?

25 I opened my mouth, and said, Buy her for yourselves without money.

26 Put your neck under the yoke, and let your soul receive instruction: she is hard at hand to find.

27 Behold with your eyes, how that I have had but little labour, and have gotten unto me much rest.

28 Get learning with a great sum of money, and get much gold by her.

29 Let your soul rejoice in his mercy, and be not ashamed of his praise.

30 Work your work betimes, and in his time he will give you your reward.

[51:13–30]

Verse 23 troubles me, for how many now dwell in the house of learning? Ben Sira's serene meditations can be read as an extended commentary on the book of Proverbs, which he cites repeatedly, more than any other text in Tanakh. This Wisdom figure is certainly Platonized by him, yet she always remains the Hebrew goddess of Proverbs 9:13:

> The fear of the Lord is the beginning of wisdom: and the knowledge of the holy is understanding.

The History of Susanna

SHAKESPEARE, WITH WHAT I HAVE to regard as viciously cruel irony, has Shylock hail Portia, disguised as a male, Balthasar, as "a Daniel come to judgment" (4.1.220). This first allusion is to the moment in the book of Daniel when the prophet arrives under the name of Balthasar at the court of Babylon's king in order to defend the Jews. The monstrous anti-Semite Gratiano, who would have graced Himmler's S.S., gleefully repeats "a Daniel come to judgment" after Portia defeats Shylock. Gratiano's allusion is to the Daniel who saves Susanna from the lustful elders in one of the Apocrypha's additions to the book of Daniel.

My appreciative concern here is with the winsome tale of Susanna and the elders, but as a loyal Bardolator severely tried by *The Merchant of Venice,* I am aware that the play is hugely complex. No two critics, readers, playgoers ever will agree about it. I set it aside for now only to observe that pragmatically it is a very harmful anti-Semitic work of genius, which is not to judge that Shakespeare personally suffered from any hatred for whatever Jews he may have met.

Much more happily, I observe that the story of Susanna is

the jewel of the Apocrypha. We have no Hebrew or Aramaic text of Susanna, but the Greek version has repeated Semitic idioms and frequently a Hebraic sentence construction. Nor do we know when or where the tale was written. Probably we can assume it to be Judea in the second century B.C.E.

The History of Susanna is a masterly very short story, of just one chapter in sixty-four verses. A wealthy Jew of the Babylonian Exile, Joakim, marries the beautiful and virtuous Susanna. Two elderly respected judges (never named) fall fiercely in lust with Susanna, and resolve upon a joint rape of the lady.

Susanna goes to bathe in her garden fountain and declines to be violated, though the pious judges warn her they will testify that they caught her with a young man. She is duly condemned to death by stoning and is rescued by the young Daniel, who separately questions the judges as to under what tree they saw her embracing the nonexistent partner in her supposed adultery. One votes for a mastick (clove) tree and the other for a holm (yew) tree. The false judges duly are stoned to death.

This all goes off with a lilt, though without any memorable phrasing on the KJB's part, again closely following Geneva. The story's intrinsic verve carries it through, and one sees why it has been so fecund in fostering later paintings and poems. There is no hesitation in awarding the palms for each to Rembrandt (his piquant Susanna hangs in Berlin) and Wallace Stevens for the beautiful "Peter Quince at the Clavier" in *Harmonium:*

> Susanna's music touched the bawdy strings
> Of those white elders; but, escaping,
> Left only Death's ironic scraping.
> Now, in its immortality, it plays
> On the clear viol of her memory,
> And makes a constant sacrament of praise.

The Greek New Testament

The Literary Merit of the
Greek New Testament

I REMIND MY READER THAT THIS BOOK is a literary appreciation only, and neither a polemic nor a defense of the Jewish people. No one who has read the Hebrew Bible and the Greek New Testament closely and has any skill or experience as a literary critic will find much affinity between the two works. The Greek New Testament is mostly composed by people thinking in Aramaic or Hebrew but writing in demotic Greek. David Norton, in *A History of the Bible as Literature* (1993), tells us that the three great scholarly saints—Ambrose, Augustine, and Jerome—all of them good classicists, were so repelled by the text's ugliness as language and style that they insisted that the Holy Spirit disdained aesthetic quality in the truth of their faith.

More than four-fifths of the KJB is translated Tanakh, where it has been appropriate for me to judge the English against the Hebrew Bible in their aesthetic agon. In the remainder of this book, that would be an absurd procedure: for the most part (with only a few exceptions, as I will note), the translation is an immense improvement. William Tyndale should be considered one of the greatest writers in English, standing only after Shakespeare,

Chaucer, and Milton. The KJB New Testament is 85 percent Tyndale, and what is not Tyndale essentially is a transmutation of his superb plain style into the aureate, orotund baroque splendor that misleadingly renders the New Testament into the idiom of the English Bible's characteristic rhetoric.

It is now more than sixty years since I spent an undergraduate semester at Cornell studying the Greek New Testament in the seminar of Friedrich Solmsen, a German-Jewish exile professor of classics. I recall that we worked our way rigorously through the entire New Testament, checking the Greek against various translations, including the KJB and Luther's German. At the close of the term, relieved that we would be going back to studying Aeschylus and Pindar, I asked Solmsen whether he found any aesthetic value in the original New Testament text. The author of a distinguished book on Plato's theology, Solmsen softly replied, "No." Robert Carroll and Stephen Prickett, in their edition of the KJB, half-heartedly allow for "flashes of literary merit and fascinating passages of writing in the parables of Jesus, some of Paul's writing, the Epistle to the Hebrews, Second Peter, and the Apocalypse." Except for the parables, that seems to me special pleading.

I suggested earlier that an implicit aestheticism was an undercurrent in the canonization of the Hebrew Bible. The inclusion of the Song of Songs, Ecclesiastes, Job, and other writings in the canon is strong evidence. Palpably, there could be no aesthetic motivations in the formation of the New Testament canon. Usurpation is the stance of the Greek New Testament toward the Hebrew Bible. Fulfillment is the asserted attitude, but that is a mask for leading the Jewish Scriptures as a captive prize in the wake of the triumphant chariot of the church.

The Greek New Testament, except for Paul and James the brother of Jesus, is a viciously anti-Jewish work. Paul is anti-Judaic but not a hater of the Jews. He states his pride at having sat at the feet of the great Rabbi Gamaliel. Otherwise what I call the Belated Testament has hatred at its core despite its doctrine of love. This is particularly virulent in the totally belated Gospel of John.

I will be highly selective in my choices for aesthetic apprehension in the KJB: the Gospels of Mark and of John, Paul's epistles to the Corinthians and the Romans, the epistle to the Hebrews, the general epistle of James, and the Revelation of Saint John the Divine. Of these, Hebrews and James come closest to possessing aesthetic dignity in the original. But since all are fundamentally Tyndale filtered through Geneva and touched up by the KJB, they have held their readers and always will do so.

Mark

LIKE THE J WRITER'S YAHWEH, Mark's Jesus is both a person and a personality. You cannot apprehend either J's Yahweh or the Marcan Jesus by employing theology: it would not work. Both J and whoever wrote Mark are *uncanny* writers, but J is sublime and Mark is weird. I intend no deprecation of Mark by that distinction. J is a great writer, comparable to Homer and Tolstoy, while Mark reminds me of Edgar Allan Poe, a bad stylist who yet fascinates. Both dream universal nightmares.

The Gospels in their present form were written from thirty years to more than fifty after the Crucifixion. Mark, Matthew, and Luke deal with the three final years of the life of Jesus, while the Gospel of John concerns his last ten weeks. Despite the arrangement of the New Testament, Paul's work long precedes the Gospels. His earliest epistle (that we have) is to the Galatians in 49 C.E., perhaps seventeen years after the death of Jesus. The Corinthian letters are 53–55, and Romans is 56. Paul was martyred in Rome in about 64, and Mark's gospel may date to 65–67. Jerusalem fell to the Romans in 70. Hebrews may date to about 95, and the Gospel of John could be as late as 115. Revelation could have been composed in 93–96, during Domitian's reign of terror against Roman Christians.

The Gospel of Mark is utterly unlike anyone's expectations, a surprise beautifully analyzed by Frank Kermode in *The Genesis of Secrecy* (1979) as a dark, riddling, severe narrative. I sense what the other Gospel authors want me to believe, but not Mark. What or who does he regard Jesus as being? His Jesus, as Paula Fredriksen notes in *From Jesus to Christ* (1988), is always in a hurry. Standing still is not possible because the end time is near. I find it puzzling that the Marcan Jesus is simultaneously both rushed and secretive. Weirdly, he seems persuaded of his own return from death in the lifetime of his disciples, who are portrayed as slow-witted when confronted by the radical newness of their master.

Only the demons in Mark know and understand Jesus. To apprehend him you must interpret his silences. I received a number of abusive letters five years back in reaction to what I still regard as the most profound observation I made in *Jesus and Yahweh: The Names Divine* (2005): "Almost all New Testament scholars, and other believing Christians, think they are delighted and grateful insiders. Are they? Does their sainthood transcend that of the disciples? I hardly think we as yet have absorbed the discomfort that only what is demonic *in us* can accurately perceive the identity of Christ Jesus." As a principle of interpretation that seems to me essential for reading Mark, but what extraordinary effects it would produce if we applied it to other texts, whether scriptural or secular! William Blake said that John Milton was a true poet and so a member of the Devil's party without knowing it. Something in Mark preludes that shock of recognition. Only the devils can get things right, and poor Peter is identified by Jesus with Satan after blundering into a truth the rocklike disciple cannot understand. Mark's Jesus dies in horrible despair, and readers need to be warned that the original text ends at verse 8 of chapter 16:

Mark

249

1 And when the sabbath was past, Mary Magdalene, and Mary the *mother* of James, and Salome, had bought sweet spices, that they might come and anoint him.

2 And very early in the morning the first *day* of the week, they came unto the sepulcher at the rising of the sun.

3 And they said among themselves, Who shall roll us away the stone from the door of the sepulcher?

4 And when they looked, they saw that the stone was rolled away: for it was very great.

5 And entering into the sepulcher, they saw a young man sitting on the right side, clothed in a long white garment; and they were affrighted.

6 And he saith unto them, Be not affrighted: Ye seek Jesus of Nazareth, which was crucified: he is risen; he is not here: behold the place where they laid him.

7 But go your way, tell his disciples and Peter that he goeth before you into Galilee: there shall ye see him, as he said unto you.

8 And they went out quickly, and fled from the sepulcher; for they trembled and were amazed: neither said they any thing to any *man;* for they were afraid.

[16:1–8]

The remaining verses, 9–20, are a pious editorial afterthought, and betray the Marcan vision. And yet how is that strange apprehension to be described? I wonder why the Gospel of Mark was canonized. It refreshes me that it was, yet that may have been an irony of the process of canonization. The burden of this strange work is misunderstanding, and its Jesus is not interested in saving everyone—only the discerning.

Salvation is hardly the dominant theme in Mark; demonic

possession is. Morton Smith wrote a study of Jesus the magician (1978, 1998), and that does seems to be his role in this earliest of the gospels. Obsession with demons and with magic to restrain them may be why there seems to be no narrator in this gospel.

Demoniacs and unclean spirits recognize Jesus (as did John the Baptist), perhaps because he *does not want to be recognized*. His own family cannot, and his own disciples seem equally imperceptive. The Gospel of Mark is a very strange text, and I am not persuaded that most theological exegetes have understood it. Something in its recalcitrance cries out for a *literary* response if its difficult Jesus is to emerge into focus at all.

Kermode seems to me unsurpassable as a literary critic of Mark, and his keenest insight is that Mark's Jesus is unknowable. Since this Jesus is totally misunderstood by his own disciples and his own family, why should we believe that Christian interpreters and churches have a more accurate view of him?

Kermode doubtless would not embrace my wilder surmise that only the devil in each of us has a hope of finding the true Jesus. I hold to it nevertheless and turn now to a closer reading of Mark in search of what a literary appreciation must perform if indeed it is to be literary.

Weirdness in Mark commences in Capernaum:

> 23 And there was in their synagogue a man with an unclean spirit; and he cried out,
>
> 24 Saying, Let *us* alone; what have we to do with thee, thou Jesus of Nazareth? art thou come to destroy us? I know thee who thou art, the Holy One of God.
>
> 25 And Jesus rebuked him, saying, Hold thy peace, and come out of him.

26 And when the unclean spirit had torn him, and cried with a loud voice, he came out of him.

27 And they were all amazed, insomuch that they questioned among themselves, saying, What thing is this? what new doctrine *is* this? for with authority commandeth he even the unclean spirits, and they do obey him.

28 And immediately his fame spread abroad throughout all the region round about Galilee.

[1:23–28]

Healing as he goes, Jesus "suffered not the devils to speak, because they knew him" (1:34). Therapeutic in the tradition of Elijah and Elisha, Jesus stays out in desert places and treats all who come to him. His disciples are gifted by him with "power to heal sickness and to cast out devils" yet not to know him. Even the transparent Parable of the Sower is too hard for them:

1 And he began again to teach by the sea side: and there was gathered unto him a great multitude, so that he entered into a ship, and sat in the sea; and the whole multitude was by the sea on the land.

2 And he taught them many things by parables, and said unto them in his doctrine,

3 Hearken; Behold, there went out a sower to sow:

4 And it came to pass, as he sowed, some fell by the way side, and the fowls of the air came and devoured it up.

5 And some fell on stony ground, where it had not much earth; and immediately it sprang up, because it had no depth of earth:

6 But when the sun was up, it was scorched; and because it had no root, it withered away.

7 And some fell among thorns, and the thorns grew up, and choked it, and it yielded no fruit.

8 And other fell on good ground, and did yield fruit that sprang up and increased; and brought forth, some thirty, and some sixty, and some an hundred.

9 And he said unto them, He that hath ears to hear, let him hear.

10 And when he was alone, they that were about him with the twelve asked of him the parable.

11 And he said unto them, Unto you it is given to know the mystery of the kingdom of God: but unto them that are without, all *these* things are done in parables:

12 That seeing they may see, and not perceive; and hearing they may hear, and not understand; lest at any time they should be converted, and *their* sins should be forgiven them.

[4:1–12]

Isaiah 6:8–10 is the starting point for Mark's Jesus here. Prophet and healer share a frightening irony:

8 Also I heard the voice of the Lord, saying, Whom shall I send, and who will go for us? Then said I, Here *am* I; send me.

9 ¶ And he said, Go, and tell this people, Hear ye indeed, but understand not; and see ye indeed, but perceive not.

10 Make the heart of this people fat, and make their ears heavy, and shut their eyes; lest they see with their eyes, and hear with their ears, and understand with their heart, and convert, and be healed.

[Isaiah 6:8–10]

Yahweh's irony becomes more extreme in Mark's Jesus, whose outsiders (all of humankind except a dozen!) are not to understand the parables "lest at any time they should be converted, and their sins should be forgiven them." Since the disciples also do not understand, who is left? The ideal or idealized reader might be an answer, but irony here is so powerfully pervasive that meaning itself is in some danger of wandering off. Does Mark understand the ironies of Jesus? What is the good news if nobody is there to receive it? And is the bitterness of Mark's Jesus his own or a redacted version of Isaiah's? Whose story is it anyway?

The Parable of the Sower, 4:14–20, is lost on the disciples, and perhaps on Mark also. The Apostles, who, like the birds, devour Christ's seeds, are satanic. Mark presumably understands, unlike most Christian authors after him down to the present day. They join the disciple in seeing, hearing, misunderstanding, and denying. "He is beside himself" (3:21) is the response of those who cannot respond.

The rhetorical immediacy of Mark's stance is shocking and echoes the rapidity and ambivalence of his Jesus. Jesus is too new for his auditors, and Mark's gospel seems to me still beyond absorption. That is its perpetual aesthetic power, in Tyndale's abruptness and in the barely modified KJB.

Kermode accurately speaks of the "gloomy ferocity" of Mark's Jesus, which prompts me to a question that may seem outrageous yet is merely pragmatic. Granted that the disciples, except for Judas (Judah), are a thick lot, why did so original a spiritual consciousness as Jesus take so little care in assembling them? There is an impatient and despairing gesture in his throwaway procedure. He must have *desired* their imperceptiveness. If he is to be regarded as human, this is perverse; if divine, is it another mystery?

The Gospel of Mark cultivates an ambiguity so rich that I have to seek its equivalents in *Hamlet* and Kafka. Rather than continue to labor its paradoxes I want to conclude by examining my favorite passage in it, which is not at all ambiguous:

17 ¶ And when he was gone forth into the way, there came one running, and kneeled to him, and asked him, Good Master, what shall I do that I may inherit eternal life?

18 And Jesus said unto him, Why callest thou me good? *there is* none good but one, *that is,* God.

19 Thou knowest the commandments, Do not commit adultery, Do not kill, Do not steal, Do not bear false witness, Defraud not, Honour thy father and mother.

20 And he answered and said unto him, Master, all these have I observed from my youth.

21 Then Jesus beholding him loved him, and said unto him, One thing thou lackest: go thy way, sell whatsoever thou hast, and give to the poor, and thou shalt have treasure in heaven: and come, take up the cross, and follow me.

22 And he was sad at that saying, and went away grieved: for he had great possessions.

23 ¶ And Jesus looked round about, and saith unto his disciples, How hardly shall they that have riches enter into the kingdom of God!

24 And the disciples were astonished at his words. But Jesus answereth again, and saith unto them, Children, how hard is it for them that trust in riches to enter into the kingdom of God!

25 It is easier for a camel to go through the eye of a needle, than for a rich man to enter into the kingdom of God.

26 And they were astonished out of measure, saying among themselves, Who then can be saved?

Mark

27 And Jesus looking upon them saith, With men *it is* impossible, but not with God: for with God all things are possible.

[10:17–27]

Almost straight Tyndale, should this not be read aloud at all political occasions whatsoever, particularly on the floor of Congress and at our national conventions?

John

~~

EACH TIME I REREAD THE GOSPEL OF John, I am detoured by its anti-Semitism. I agree with Robert Carroll in his *Wolf in the Sheepfold* (1997) when he writes, "I know many good Christian scholars have found it possible to exonerate the New Testament writings from all blame in this matter of Christian anti-Semitism. I do not find it easy to separate biblical rhetoric from the consequences of people taking such rhetoric seriously." A literary appreciation of the KJB Gospel of John should not set that aside and yet needs to place emphasis elsewhere. *The Merchant of Venice* is a Shakespearean masterpiece, however morally flawed, and the Fourth Gospel, at least in Tyndale and his revisionists, merits the same aesthetic judgment.

Frank Kermode, whose brilliant treatment of Mark has proved unmatchable, also has ventured a reading of John, which somewhat disappoints me because I find it rather too circumspect. Still, it is useful, and I am indebted to it here. Kermode emphasizes how much of John's gospel turns upon *doxa,* "glory," as the ultimate quality of God the Father and his only begotten Son. Paul tells us that faith, hope, and love (*caritas*) abide but that the greatest of these three is the Father's and the Son's love for us, in the Greek sense of *agape,* the love of a superior for an inferior. No Christian theologian would agree with me, but I take Kermode's hint as to what is definitive for John: divine glory.

I myself regard his gospel as a concealed gnosis. There are of course overt Gnostic gospels, like the Gospel of Truth by Valentinus and the equally superb Gospel of Thomas. John is something different. As we have the text now, the Word (Logos) became flesh and dwelt among us as the man Jesus. Was it the original version that the Word became spirit (*pneuma*) and lived with us?

The canonical New Testament worked hard at excluding Gnosticism. Paul denounces its influence among the Corinthians, but there are Gnostic strains in his thought. The essence of Gnosticism is to hold that the Fall and the Creation were one and the same event: a spark or pneuma remains in each of us, and it is no part of the Creation. The creator god is a mere demiurge, and the true God is a stranger, alien to our cosmos.

The most famous passage in the Gospel of John is its opening poem:

1 In the beginning was the Word, and the Word was with God, and the Word was God.

2 The same was in the beginning with God.

3 All things were made by him; and without him was not any thing made that was made.

4 In him was life; and the life was the light of men.

5 And the light shineth in darkness; and the darkness comprehended it not.

6 ¶ There was a man sent from God, whose name *was* John.

7 The same came for a witness, to bear witness of the Light, that all *men* through him might believe.

The Greek New Testament

8 He was not that Light, but *was sent* to bear witness of that Light.

9 *That* was the true Light, which lighteth every man that cometh into the world.

10 He was in the world, and the world was made by him, and the world knew him not.

11 He came unto his own, and his own received him not.

12 But as many as received him, to them gave he power to become the sons of God, *even* to them that believe on his name:

13 Which were born, not of blood, nor of the will of the flesh, nor of the will of man, but of God.

14 And the Word was made flesh, and dwelt among us, (and we beheld his glory, the glory as of the only begotten of the Father,) full of grace and truth.

Kermode admirably says that this is a "threshold" poem. The great critic Angus Fletcher taught me that the "threshold" stands between the labyrinth and the temple, which is where I think this hymn to the logos stations itself. But what is the logos, before its epiphany at the inception of John's gospel?

I center upon *logos* itself, the most celebrated Greek word for "word." Though he writes in koine, or common, Greek, the author of John is thinking in Hebrew (or perhaps in Aramaic). The biblical Hebrew word for "word" is *davar.* "Logos" is a strange translation for *davar,* another instance of the radical incompatibility of Greek and Hebrew. The root meaning of *logos* is to gather or assemble, while the origins of *davar* involve the thrusting forward into the light of something which has been held back in the self.

The poem introducing John probably existed before the gospel appropriated it, and clearly it is a kind of hermetic revision of the opening of Genesis. In this recasting, when God says, "Let there be light," Jesus Christ is begotten, a bold translation or interpretation that is dazzling in its audacity. The ambiance of *logos* is vastly extended as a rhetorical term or metaphor, reminding me of how embattled the word for "word" was in ancient Greek. Very broadly, this hymn quoted or reworked at the inception of John is part of Platonic tradition: Plato opposed his logos to that of the brilliant Sicilian rhetorician, the sophist Gorgias.

I rely here upon a superb book, Mario Untersteiner's *The Sophists* (1954), in which Gorgias is seen as arguing that truth cannot be incarnated in logos. The logoi (there are many) contradict one another and each is ambivalent. Gorgias, unable to reconcile his enthusiasm for both the celebratory Pindar and the tragic dramatists, arrives at a vision of the tragedy of knowledge. Eternal Being precludes any beginning since Being cannot be created. Scorned by Socrates, these realizations were fiercely rejected by Plato and his tradition after him.

What would the Gospel of John be without its opening hymn? However revised, this poem is consonant with the Alexandrian *Hermetica,* the pagan gnosis that achieved a crucial place in the spiritual world of Renaissance Florence, particularly with its visionary humanists Marsilio Ficino, Giovanni Pico della Mirandola, and Giordano Bruno. Renaissance Hermetists, except for Bruno, found no conflict between their ethos and the spirituality of the Fourth Gospel.

Kermode emphasizes rightly that in John the Word is known for its glory (doxa). Opening with the logos poem (in whatever form) more than suggests that the belated gospel is a new Genesis, displacing the original "in the beginning." John triumphs not only over the Jewish Bible but over the three Synoptic Gospels. Any authority that either Tanakh or the Synoptics could assert fades, as the Fourth Gospel affirms its priority and their lateness.

If there is revisionary gain, there is also loss since John's resentment ensues. For all its triumphalism and proclamation of glory, the Fourth Gospel exceeds even Mark in anxious expectations. Its Jesus manifests this by his self-contradictions. He declines to work miracles, then goes on to perform them anyway. These may be his indecision, not John's, who is aware of the pattern and always understands, even when Jesus may not. Kermode shrewdly refers to "John the novelist."

John's Jesus has no doubts about his own glory since he knows his divine identity. In the Synoptics, Mark particularly, Jesus, movingly, is ambivalent and is given to questioning exactly who he is. Impatient with uncertainty, John assumes and maintains omniscience. Not only does he give us a Jesus who affirms that he himself is both the truth and the Father, but it becomes clear that John himself believes that *he,* John, is the truth. His negative stance toward Moses is crucial for understanding his gospel. The Torah *cannot* be the truth for John, and yet he needs to steal his own authority from it.

To call this ambivalence is not sufficient. A battle against the priority and authority of the Mosaic books is incessant throughout John. And yet though it is subtler, an agon is also conducted by John with the Synoptic Gospels, Matthew in particular. Lest I be dismissed as a dismayed opponent of John, I rely directly here upon Benedict Viviano, O.P., a profound scholar of the New Testament. Here is his summary of his essay on the matter:

> The question of the gospel of John's relation to the synoptic gospels is a classic one. This article presupposes direct Johannine knowledge of the Synoptics and some inner-canonical polemic. It explores twelve instances of John's knowledge of Matthew's gospel and his reaction to Matthew: from flat contradiction, to restrained criticism, to

refinement, acceptance and deepening. The cases concern
Emmanuel, the light of the world, Elijah and the Baptist,
the transfiguration, the messianic secret, the Sabbath, the
role of Peter, turning the other cheek, the use of the Old
Testament, Christology, judgment, and discipleship.

[*Matthew and His World* (2007)]

Viviano, a faithful Christian, wistfully seeks to confine polemic
and conflict taking place *within* the New Testament to acceptable
limits. But John knows no limits and implicitly savages Matthew,
as he does the books of Moses.

I rub my eyes a little when I see the admirable Carroll and
Prickett, in their note to the Gospel of John, tell me, "John's gospel is one of the major pieces of world literature." In the original:
no, in thunder. In Tyndale and his legatees, Geneva and the KJB:
alas, yes.

The Writings of Paul

MUCH OF WHATEVER I CAN UNDERSTAND of Paul I have learned from reading Wayne Meeks, who tellingly named the apostle "the Christian Proteus."

Not only are the earliest writings in the New Testament Paul's, but they occupy a third of the text when taken together with the book of Acts, essentially an account of Paul's life and work. He cannot be called the inventor of Hellenistic Christianity, with its substitution of Greek theological philosophy for the teachings of the rabbi Jesus. In fact, he was *converted* to that religion, perhaps seventeen years before he wrote his epistles. Originally Jews of the Diaspora, the first Hellenistic Christians in Antioch and Rome separated themselves from formal Judaism and then conducted missions to the Gentiles. For them, well prior to Paul, Jesus Christ had replaced the man Jesus. Nevertheless, the manic energy and will-to-power of Paul subsumed Hellenistic Christianity and made it forever Pauline.

In his Norton Critical Edition of the writings of Saint Paul (1972), Meeks sensibly says that Paul was not a theologian but a figurative thinker who made the cross, an instrument of Roman torture, into a metaphor for the logos, which I discussed in my chapter on the Gospel of John. And the logos of the cross for Paul is a new cosmos, abolishing the stale worlds of Gentiles and Jews alike.

Paul's power as an imaginer is strong in the Greek texts of his letters, but nothing like what it becomes in William Tyndale's translation and in Geneva and the KJB absorbing Tyndale. Meeks calls Paul a "master of metaphor," but that is not rhetorically exact: the mastery of figurative language is overwhelming in Tyndale and only tentative in Paul.

Nobody else misreads the texts of the Hebrew Bible so outrageously as Paul does, and always by design. More even than the rest of the New Testament (except the Gospel of John) the writings of Paul suffer an anxiety of influence in regard to the Hebrew Bible. Seeking power and freedom, Paul tears to shreds the authority of Tanakh. To call this ambivalence toward Torah and the prophets is not sufficient.

Usurpation is the central resource alike of the strong poet and the spiritual renovator. Not even Isaiah and Jeremiah were enough for Paul to overgo; Moses himself was to be surpassed.

Antipathy to Paul is as old as Paul: it began with the Jewish Christians, led by James the Just of Jerusalem. The case against Paul was most eloquently argued by Friedrich Nietzsche and George Bernard Shaw, but most usefully by the scholar Hans Joachim Schoeps: "Because Paul had lost all understanding of the character of the Hebraic *berith* as a partnership involving mutual obligations, he failed to grasp the inner meaning of the Mosaic law, namely, that it is an instrument by which the covenant is realized. Hence the Pauline theology of law and justification begins with the fateful misunderstanding in consequence of which he tears asunder covenant and law, and then represents Christ as the end of the law" (*Paul,* 1979). I add to Schoeps only that Paul's was a *willed* misunderstanding, what I have learned to call "misprision."

Meeks makes the point: Paul insists "the crucifixion and resurrection of God's Messiah was the ultimate revelation in weakness of God's power." I myself cannot think of anything so foreign to Yahweh as that insistence.

Romans

The Epistle to the Romans is thought to have been written by Paul in Corinth in about 57. He had fulfilled his mission to the East and hoped that his work in Rome would culminate his career. Perhaps it did: he died there in about 64, after two years in prison. The tradition is that he was executed at about the time Nero's persecution of the Christians intensified.

Romans is a tangled text, reflecting the emotional perplexities of Paul at his most pungent. How ought we to react to his advertisement for himself in chapter 15, verses 14–32?

> 14 And I myself also am persuaded of you, my brethren, that ye also are full of goodness, filled with all knowledge, able also to admonish one another.
>
> 15 Nevertheless, brethren, I have written the more boldly unto you in some sort, as putting you in mind, because of the grace that is given to me of God,
>
> 16 That I should be the minister of Jesus Christ to the Gentiles, ministering the gospel of God, that the offering up of the Gentiles might be acceptable, being sanctified by the Holy Ghost.
>
> 17 I have therefore whereof I may glory through Jesus Christ in those things which pertain to God.
>
> 18 For I will not dare to speak of any of those things which Christ hath not wrought by me, to make the Gentiles obedient, by word and deed,

19 Through mighty signs and wonders, by the power of the Spirit of God; so that from Jerusalem, and round about unto Illyricum, I have fully preached the gospel of Christ.

20 Yea, so have I strived to preach the gospel, not where Christ was named, lest I should build upon another man's foundation:

21 But as it is written, To whom he was not spoken of, they shall see: and they that have not heard shall understand.

22 For which cause also I have been much hindered from coming to you.

23 But now having no more place in these parts, and having a great desire these many years to come unto you;

24 Whensoever I take my journey into Spain, I will come to you: for I trust to see you in my journey, and to be brought on my way thitherward by you, if first I be somewhat filled with your *company.*

25 But now I go unto Jerusalem to minister unto the saints.

26 For it hath pleased them of Macedonia and Achaia to make a certain contribution for the poor saints which are at Jerusalem.

27 It hath pleased them verily; and their debtors they are. For if the Gentiles have been made partakers of their spiritual things, their duty is also to minister unto them in carnal things.

28 When therefore I have performed this, and have sealed to them this fruit, I will come by you into Spain.

29 And I am sure that, when I come unto you, I shall come in the fulness of the blessing of the gospel of Christ.

30 Now I beseech you, brethren, for the Lord Jesus

Christ's sake, and for the love of the Spirit, that ye strive together with me in *your* prayers to God for me;

31 That I may be delivered from them that do not believe in Judea; and that my service which *I have* for Jerusalem may be accepted of the saints;

32 That I may come unto you with joy by the will of God, and may with you be refreshed.

Carroll and Prickett are content to call this "obsessive egotism." Since I am so alienated from Paul, I hesitate to judge. Romans 1–11 centers on the dialectic of Gentile and Jew in the scheme of salvation, and Paul boldly sees himself as the secret of that vexed relation. I weary of his overassertions of his Jewishness while granting his role as apostle to the Gentiles.

Meeks notes the Judaic emphasis upon repentance in Romans 2:4, but in its context this element seems to me obliterated:

1 Therefore thou art inexcusable, O man, whosoever thou art that judgest: for wherein thou judgest another, thou condemnest thyself; for thou that judgest doest the same things.

2 But we are sure that the judgment of God is according to truth against them which commit such things.

3 And thinkest thou this, O man, that judgest them which do such things, and doest the same, that thou shalt escape the judgment of God?

4 Or despisest thou the riches of his goodness and forbearance and longsuffering; not knowing that the goodness of God leadeth thee to repentance?

5 But after thy hardness and impenitent heart treasurest up unto thyself wrath against the day of wrath and revelation of the righteous judgment of God;

6 Who will render to every man according to his deeds:

7 To them who by patient continuance in well doing seek for glory and honour and immortality, eternal life:

8 But unto them that are contentious, and do not obey the truth, but obey unrighteousness, indignation and wrath,

9 Tribulation and anguish, upon every soul of man that doeth evil, of the Jew first, and also of the Gentile;

10 But glory, honour, and peace, to every man that worketh good, to the Jew first, and also to the Gentile:

11 For there is no respect of persons with God.

12 For as many as have sinned without law shall also perish without law: and as many as have sinned in the law shall be judged by the law.

[2:1–12]

Paul has a bad conscience in regard to the Teaching (Torah) or "law." This produces the weird assertion that Abraham was justified by faith (*pistis*) and not by works. From Abraham to the present day, Jews are not required to have faith but to trust (*emunah*) in the Covenant. Paul will not cease laboring his dubious point:

> Therefore *it is* of faith, that *it might be* by grace; to the end the promise might be sure to all the seed; not to that only which is of the law, but to that also which is of the faith of Abraham; who is the father of us all.
>
> [4:16]

KJB Romans again essentially is Tyndale's, but this text matters more to theologians than to literary readers, unlike Corinthians or the ferocious Galatians. I rarely reread Romans, but I wickedly enjoy Galatians, where Paul is very much his dreadful self.

1 Corinthians

Ancient Corinth, a prosperous double seaport, always was renowned for its erotic liveliness, to which Aristophanes brazenly alluded. An international city with many Jews, it was the site of a church founded by Paul, possibly in 58. Five years later he wrote to the members, in considerable concern at their antics, both spiritual and sexual.

Charismatics had arisen among the Corinthian Christians, teaching a gnosis that may have had esoteric Jewish origins and that anticipates the Christian Gnosticism of a century later. Speaking in tongues accompanies this secret "knowledge," which possesses the *perfect* ones, who believe that with Christ they already have been resurrected in the body before he died and while they are still alive.

Though Paul seems to regard this as a parody of his doctrine, there inevitably were Gnostic elements in early Christianity. Chapter 15 of 1 Corinthians centers on this conflict:

> 10 But by the grace of God I am what I am: and his grace which *was bestowed* upon me was not in vain; but I laboured more abundantly than they all: yet not I, but the grace of God which was with me.
>
> 11 Therefore whether *it were* I or they, so we preach, and so ye believed.
>
> 12 Now if Christ be preached that he rose from the dead, how say some among you that there is no resurrection of the dead?
>
> 13 But if there be no resurrection of the dead, then is Christ not risen:
>
> 14 And if Christ be not risen, then *is* our preaching vain, and your faith *is* also vain.
>
> 15 Yea, and we are found false witnesses of God; be-

cause we have testified of God that he raised up Christ: whom he raised not up, if so be that the dead rise not.

16 For if the dead rise not, then is not Christ raised:

17 And if Christ be not raised, your faith *is* vain; ye are yet in your sins.

18 Then they also which are fallen asleep in Christ are perished.

19 If in this life only we have hope in Christ, we are of all men most miserable.

20 But now is Christ risen from the dead, *and* become the firstfruits of them that slept.

21 For since by man *came* death, by man *came* also the resurrection of the dead.

22 For as in Adam all die, even so in Christ shall all be made alive.

23 But every man in his own order: Christ the firstfruits; afterward they that are Christ's at his coming.

24 Then *cometh* the end, when he shall have delivered up the kingdom to God, even the Father; when he shall have put down all rule and all authority and power.

25 For he must reign, till he hath put all enemies under his feet.

26 The last enemy *that* shall be destroyed *is* death.

This is all Tyndale, and it is hardly that strong in Paul's original.

Tyndale rises to a particular rhetorical glory in what will become in KJB 1 Corinthians 15:51–55:

Behold I show you a mystery. We shall not all sleep: but we shall all be changed, and that in a moment, and in the twinkling of an eye, at the sound of the last trumpet. For the trumpet shall blow, and the dead shall rise incorruptible, and we shall be changed. For this corruptible must put on incorruptibility: and this mortal must put on immortality.

When this corruptible hath put on incorruptibility, and this mortal hath put on immortality: then shall be brought to pass the saying that is written: Death is consumed into victory. Death where is thy sting? Hell where is thy victory?

[Tyndale]

51 Behold, I shew you a mystery; We shall not all sleep, but we shall all be changed,

52 In a moment, in the twinkling of an eye, at the last trump: for the trumpet shall sound, and the dead shall be raised incorruptible, and we shall be changed.

53 For this corruptible must put on incorruption, and this mortal *must* put on immortality.

54 So when this corruptible shall have put on incorruption, and this mortal shall have put on immortality, then shall be brought to pass the saying that is written, Death is swallowed up in victory.

55 O death, where *is* thy sting? O grave, where *is* thy victory?

[KJB]

The reader must decide whether the KJB changes here enhance or diminish Tyndale, but I vote for the pioneer translator. And even more, I prefer Tyndale in the most famous passage of 1 Corinthians, chapter 13:

Though I spake with the tongues of men and angels, and yet had no love, I were even as sounding brass: or as a tinkling cymbal. And though I could prophesy, and understood all secrets, and all knowledge: yea, if I had all faith so that I could move mountains out of their places, and yet had no love, I were nothing. And though I bestowed all my goods to feed the poor, and though I gave my body even that I burned, and yet had no love, it profiteth me nothing.

Love suffereth long, and is courteous. Love envieth not. Love doth not frowardly, swelleth not, dealeth not dishonestly, seeketh not her own, is not provoked to anger, thinketh not evil, rejoiceth not in iniquity: but rejoiceth in the truth, suffereth all things, believeth all things, hopeth all things, endureth in all things. Though that prophesying fail, or tongues shall cease, or knowledge vanish away, yet love falleth never away.

For our knowledge is imperfect, and our prophesying is imperfect. But when that which is perfect is come, then that which is imperfect shall be done away. When I was a child, I spake as a child, I understood as a child, I imagined as a child. But as soon as I was a man, I put away childishness. Now we see in a glass even in a dark speaking: but then shall we see face to face. Now I know imperfectly: but then shall I know even as I am known. Now abideth faith, hope, and love, even these three: but the chief of these is love.

[Tyndale]

1 Though I speak with the tongues of men and of angels, and have not charity, I am become *as* sounding brass, or a tinkling cymbal.

2 And though I have *the gift of* prophecy, and understand all mysteries, and all knowledge; and though I have all faith, so that I could remove mountains, and have not charity, I am nothing.

The Greek New Testament

3 And though I bestow all my goods to feed *the poor,* and though I give my body to be burned, and have not charity, it profiteth me nothing.

4 Charity suffereth long, *and* is kind; charity envieth not; charity vaunteth not itself, is not puffed up,

5 Doth not behave itself unseemly, seeketh not her own, is not easily provoked, thinketh no evil;

6 Rejoiceth not in iniquity, but rejoiceth in the truth;

7 Beareth all things, believeth all things, hopeth all things, endureth all things.

8 Charity never faileth: but whether *there be* prophecies, they shall fail; whether *there be* tongues, they shall cease; whether *there be* knowledge, it shall vanish away.

9 For we know in part, and we prophesy in part.

10 But when that which is perfect is come, then that which is in part shall be done away.

11 When I was a child, I spake as a child, I understood as a child, I thought as a child: but when I became a man, I put away childish things.

12 For now we see through a glass, darkly; but then face to face: now I know in part; but then shall I know even as also I am known.

13 And now abideth faith, hope, charity, these three; but the greatest of these *is* charity.

[KJB]

Paul uses the Greek *agape, caritas* in Jerome's Vulgate, and so KJB's "charity." For me, Tyndale's "love" works better, and I also prefer his "I imagined as a child" to the KJB "thought." Best of all is Tyndale's "even in a dark speaking" rather than the KJB "darkly." And yet again I must commend Tyndale over the apostle himself, strictly as a literary judgment.

2 Corinthians

Paul's personality—rugged, mercurial, egomaniacal—emerges strongly in 2 Corinthians. His vainglory is near allied to what I think must be called his shamanism, a propensity for out-of-the-body experiences:

Chapter 11

16 I say again, Let no man think me a fool; if otherwise, yet as a fool receive me, that I may boast myself a little.

17 That which I speak, I speak *it* not after the Lord, but as it were foolishly, in this confidence of boasting.

18 Seeing that many glory after the flesh, I will glory also.

19 For ye suffer fools gladly, seeing ye *yourselves* are wise.

20 For ye suffer, if a man bring you into bondage, if a man devour *you,* if a man take *of you,* if a man exalt himself, if a man smite you on the face.

21 I speak as concerning reproach, as though we had been weak. Howbeit whereinsoever any is bold, (I speak foolishly,) I am bold also.

22 Are they Hebrews⸮ so *am* I. Are they Israelites⸮ so *am* I. Are they the seed of Abraham⸮ so *am* I.

23 Are they ministers of Christ⸮ (I speak as a fool) I *am* more; in labours more abundant, in stripes above measure, in prisons more frequent, in deaths oft.

24 Of the Jews five times received I forty *stripes* save one.

25 Thrice was I beaten with rods, once was I stoned, thrice I suffered shipwreck, a night and a day I have been in the deep;

26 *In* journeyings often, *in* perils of waters, *in* perils of robbers, *in* perils by *mine own* countrymen, *in* perils in the wilderness, *in* perils in the sea, *in* perils among false brethren;

27 In weariness and painfulness, in watchings often, in hunger and thirst, in fastings often, in cold and nakedness.

28 Beside those things that are without, that which cometh upon me daily, the care of all the churches.

29 Who is weak, and I am not weak? who is offended, and I burn not?

30 If I must needs glory, I will glory of the things which concern mine infirmities.

31 The God and Father of our Lord Jesus Christ, which is blessed for evermore, knoweth that I lie not.

32 In Damascus the governor under Aretas the king kept the city of the Damascenes with a garrison, desirous to apprehend me:

33 And through a window in a basket was I let down by the wall, and escaped his hands.

Chapter 12

1 It is not expedient for me doubtless to glory. I will come to visions and revelations of the Lord.

2 I knew a man in Christ above fourteen years ago, (whether in the body, I cannot tell; or whether out of the body, I cannot tell: God knoweth;) such an one caught up to the third heaven.

3 And I knew such a man, (whether in the body, or out of the body, I cannot tell: God knoweth;)

4 How that he was caught up into paradise, and heard unspeakable words, which it is not lawful for a man to utter.

5 Of such an one will I glory: yet of myself I will not glory, but in mine infirmities.

6 For though I would desire to glory, I shall not be a fool; for I will say the truth: but *now* I forbear, lest any man should think of me above that which he seeth me *to be,* or *that* he heareth of me.

7 And lest I should be exalted above measure through the abundance of the revelations, there was given to me a thorn in the flesh, the messenger of Satan to buffet me, lest I should be exalted above measure.

8 For this thing I besought the Lord thrice, that it might depart from me.

9 And he said unto me, My grace is sufficient for thee: for my strength is made perfect in weakness. Most gladly therefore will I rather glory in my infirmities, that the power of Christ may rest upon me.

10 Therefore I take pleasure in infirmities, in reproaches, in necessities, in persecutions, in distresses for Christ's sake: for when I am weak, then am I strong.

Jeremiah was self-regarding enough, and became known to his adversaries as "terror-all-around." Compared to Paul (whom he influenced), Jeremiah is a model of stoic decorum. Paul is "a man" (12:3) who was caught up to the third heaven and heard unspeakable things. As for his innumerable sufferings, they need not be doubted, but must they be relished? It may not be expedient for him to glory, but glory he does. Various characters in Charles Dickens come to my mind whenever I read Paul. Created by Dickens, he could consort with the Reverend Chadband in *Bleak House* and Uriah Heep in *David Copperfield*. His "thorn in the flesh" (12:7) is sublimely Dickensian.

I confess that I like Paul least in 2 Corinthians, chapter 3:

1 Do we begin again to commend ourselves? or need we, as some *others,* epistles of commendation to you, or *letters* of commendation from you?

2 Ye are our epistle written in our hearts, known and read of all men:

3 *Forasmuch as ye are* manifestly declared to be the epistle of Christ ministered by us, written not with ink, but with the Spirit of the living God; not in tables of stone, but in fleshy tables of the heart.

4 And such trust have we through Christ to God-ward:

5 Not that we are sufficient of ourselves to think any thing as of ourselves; but our sufficiency *is* of God;

6 Who also hath made us able ministers of the new testament; not of the letter, but of the spirit: for the letter killeth, but the spirit giveth life.

7 But if the ministration of death, written *and* engraven in stones, was glorious, so that the children of Israel could not stedfastly behold the face of Moses for the glory of his countenance; which *glory* was to be done away:

8 How shall not the ministration of the spirit be rather glorious?

9 For if the ministration of condemnation *be* glory, much more doth the ministration of righteousness exceed in glory.

10 For even that which was made glorious had no glory in this respect, by reason of the glory that excelleth.

11 For if that which is done away *was* glorious, much more that which remaineth *is* glorious.

12 Seeing then that we have such hope, we use great plainness of speech:

13 And not as Moses, *which* put a vail over his face, that the children of Israel could not stedfastly look to the end of that which is abolished:

14 But their minds were blinded: for until this day remaineth the same vail untaken away in the reading of the old testament; which *vail* is done away in Christ.

15 But even unto this day, when Moses is read, the vail is upon their heart.

16 Nevertheless when it shall turn to the Lord, the vail shall be taken away.

17 Now the Lord is that Spirit: and where the Sprit of the Lord *is,* there *is* liberty.

18 But we all, with open face beholding as in a glass the glory of the Lord, are changed into the same image from glory to glory, *even* as by the Spirit of the Lord.

Does the spirit give life by an outrageous departure from the text of Exodus 34:33–35? Paul is not creatively misinterpreting here but lying. This is the text:

33 And *till* Moses had done speaking with them, he put a vail on his face.

34 But when Moses went in before the LORD to speak with him, he took the vail off, until he came out. And he came out, and spake unto the children of Israel *that* which he was commanded.

35 And the children of Israel saw the face of Moses, that the skin of Moses' face shone: and Moses put the vail upon his face again, until he went in to speak with him.

As Meeks notes, the glory of Moses' face was identified with the image of God, lost by Adam when he fell but restored at Sinai. By misrepresenting this, Paul suggests that the veil was meant to conceal Moses' loss of glory. The text in Exodus has nothing of this, and Judaic interpretation held that the face of Moses still had this brightness when he died. In Paul's allegory, the glory had to fade and be replaced by the glory of Christ.

Galatians

There's a great text in Galatians,
 Once you trip on it, entails
Twenty-nine distinct damnations,
 One sure, if another fails:
If I trip him just a-dying,
 Sure of heaven as sure can be,
Spin him round and send him flying
 Off to hell, a Manichee?

That is from Robert Browning's zestful "Soliloquy of the Spanish Cloister," published in his *Dramatic Lyrics* (1842). The "great text" cited by the fiercely hating monk is Galatians 5:19–21:

> 19 Now the works of the flesh are manifest, which are *these;* Adultery, fornication, uncleanness, lasciviousness,
> 20 Idolatry, witchcraft, hatred, variance, emulations, wrath, strife, seditions, heresies,
> 21 Envyings, murders, drunkenness, revellings, and such like: of the which I tell you before, as I have also told *you* in time past, that they which do such things shall not inherit the kingdom of God.

Alas, the exuberant monk has increased seventeen "works of the flesh" to twenty-nine, but he is in the hyperbolic spirit of Paul, who cuts loose in Galatians. If ever we hear his true voice of feeling it is in this fury of an epistle, written about 54. The identity of his adversaries has never been clarified. But then Galatians does not have a clear or consistent argument. Paul proclaims that Christianity is the spirit's freedom even as he fulminates against any creed that does not emanate from himself.

I enjoy Galatians because for once no Pauline scholar of his theology can succeed in toning him down: he is sublimely intemperate:

8 But though we, or an angel from heaven, preach any other gospel unto you than that which we have preached unto you, let him be accursed.

9 As we said before, so say I now again, If any *man* preach any other gospel unto you than that ye have received, let him be accursed.

[1:8–9]

Casting curses, can you also affirm?

22 But the fruit of the Spirit is love, joy, peace, longsuffering, gentleness, goodness, faith,

23 Meekness, temperance: against such there is no law.

24 And they that are Christ's have crucified the flesh with the affections and lusts.

25 If we live in the Spirit, let us also walk in the Spirit.

26 Let us not be desirous of vain glory, provoking one another, envying one another.

[5:22–26]

It is difficult for me not to hear a Dickens character in this pious admonition against "vain glory." And yet I am aware that I am an outsider from Paul's perspective: a Jew of Gnostic tendencies who neither trusts in the Covenant nor shares Christian faith in the Resurrection. Paul is not quite all things to all women and all men.

The last word on Paul, Wayne Meeks insists, cannot be rendered. I myself think it was spoken by George Bernard Shaw in 1913, in the preface to his *Androcles and the Lion*. A century later, this has not been bettered:

Paul, however, did not get his great reputation by mere imposition and reaction. It is only in comparison with Jesus (to whom many prefer him) that he appears common and conceited. Though in The Acts he is only a vulgar revivalist, he comes out in his own epistles as a genuine poet,—though by flashes only. He is no more a Christian than Jesus was a Baptist; he is a disciple of Jesus only as Jesus was a disciple of John. He does nothing that Jesus would have done, and says nothing that Jesus would have said, though much, like the famous ode to charity, that he would have admired. He is more Jewish than the Jews, more Roman than the Romans, proud both ways, full of startling confessions and self-revelations that would not surprise us if they were slipped into the pages of Nietzsche, tormented by an intellectual conscience that demanded an argued case even at the cost of sophistry, with all sorts of fine qualities and occasional illumina- tions, but always hopelessly in the toils of Sin, Death, and Logic, which had no power over Jesus. As we have seen, it was by introducing this bondage and terror of his into the Christian doctrine that he adapted it to the Church and State systems which Jesus transcended, and made it practicable by destroying the specifically Jesuist side of it. He would have been quite in his place in any modern Protestant State; and he, not Jesus, is the true head and founder of our Reformed Church, as Peter is of the Roman Church. The followers of Paul and Peter made Christen- dom, whilst the Nazarenes were wiped out.

Hebrews

THE EPISTLE OF PAUL THE APOSTLE to the Hebrews is not an epistle, not by Saint Paul, and perhaps not directed to Hebrew Christians or to any other Jews. Rhetorically it is impressive, better written in the original Greek than anything else in the New Testament. Each time I reread it, I find it ultimately less and less persuasive, but its eloquence, enhanced by Tyndale and then the KJB, renders it of real literary interest.

Whoever wrote Hebrews, he was a dogmatist through and through, and neither perceptive nor loving in his relation to Tanakh. As a misreader of the Jewish Scriptures he was less outrageous than Paul, since he was subtler, but he dries out the text and makes it lifeless. The greatness of Tanakh is in its representation of human beings, who can be almost of Shakespearean capaciousness. That magnificence vanishes utterly in Hebrews.

I suspect that nearly all the believing Christians among my friends would be puzzled if I asked whether they thought of Jesus Christ as a high priest, presiding over a heavenly sanctuary or temple. That is how he is presented in Hebrews:

Wherefore in all things it behoved him to be made like unto *his* brethren, that he might be a merciful and faithful high priest in things *pertaining* to God, to make reconciliation for the sins of the people.

[2:17]

Wherefore, holy brethren, partakers of the heavenly calling, consider the Apostle and High Priest of our profession, Christ Jesus.

[3:1]

This is then expanded:

Chapter 4

14 Seeing then that we have a great high priest, that is passed into the heavens, Jesus the Son of God, let us hold fast *our* profession.

15 For we have not an high priest which cannot be touched with the feeling of our infirmities; but was in all points tempted like as *we are, yet* without sin.

16 Let us therefore come boldly unto the throne of grace, that we may obtain mercy, and find grace to help in time of need.

Chapter 5

1 For every high priest taken from among men is ordained for men in things *pertaining* to God, that he may offer both gifts and sacrifices for sins:

2 Who can have compassion on the ignorant, and on them that are out of the way; for that he himself also is compassed with infirmity.

3 And by reason hereof he ought, as for the people, so also for himself, to offer for sins.

4 And no man taketh this honour unto himself, but he that is called of God, as *was* Aaron.

5 So also Christ glorified not himself to be made an high priest; but he that said unto him, Thou art my Son, to day have I begotten thee.

6 As he saith also in another *place,* Thou *art* a priest for ever after the order of Melchisedec.

7 Who in the days of his flesh, when he had offered up prayers and supplications with strong crying and tears unto him that was able to save him from death, and was heard in that he feared;

8 Though he were a Son, yet learned he obedience by the things which he suffered;

9 And being made perfect, he became the author of eternal salvation unto all them that obey him;

10 Called of God an high priest after the order of Melchisedec.

Most readers will be puzzled by the obsessive recourse to Melchisedec, who then occupies much of chapter 7:

1 For this Melchisedec, king of Salem, priest of the most high God, who met Abraham returning from the slaughter of the kings, and blessed him;

2 To whom also Abraham gave a tenth part of all; first being by interpretation King of righteousness, and after that also King of Salem, which is, King of peace;

3 Without father, without mother, without descent, having neither beginning of days, nor end of life; but made like unto the Son of God; abideth a priest continually.

4 Now consider how great this man *was,* unto whom even the patriarch Abraham gave the tenth of the spoils.

5 And verily they that are of the sons of Levi, who re-

ceive the office of the priesthood, have a commandment to take tithes of the people according to the law, that is, of their brethren, though they come out of the loins of Abraham:

6 But he whose descent is not counted from them received tithes of Abraham, and blessed him that had the promises.

7 And without all contradiction the less is blessed of the better.

8 And here men that die receive tithes; but there he *receiveth them,* of whom it is witnessed that he liveth.

9 And as I may so say, Levi also, who receiveth tithes, payed tithes in Abraham.

10 For he was yet in the loins of his father, when Melchisedec met him.

11 If therefore perfection were by the Levitical priesthood, (for under it the people received the law,) what further need *was there* that another priest should rise after the order of Melchisedec, and not be called after the order of Aaron?

12 For the priesthood being changed, there is made of necessity a change also of the law.

13 For he of whom these things are spoken pertaineth to another tribe, of which no man gave attendance at the altar.

14 For *it is* evident that our Lord sprang out of Juda; of which tribe Moses spake nothing concerning priesthood.

15 And it is yet far more evident: for that after the similitude of Melchisedec there ariseth another priest,

16 Who is made, not after the law of a carnal commandment, but after the power of an endless life.

17 For he testifieth, Thou *art* a priest for ever after the order of Melchisedec.

18 For there is verily a disannulling of the command-

ment going before for the weakness and unprofitableness thereof.

19 For the law made nothing perfect, but the bringing in of a better hope *did;* by which we draw nigh unto God.

20 And inasmuch as not without an oath *he was made priest:*

21 (For those priests were made without an oath; but this with an oath by him that said unto him, The Lord sware and will not repent, Thou *art* a priest for ever after the order of Melchisedec:)

22 By so much was Jesus made a surety of a better testament.

23 And they truly were many priests, because they were not suffered to continue by reason of death:

24 But this *man,* because he continueth ever, hath an unchangeable priesthood.

25 Wherefore he is able also to save them to the uttermost that come unto God by him, seeing he ever liveth to make intercession for them.

26 For such an high priest became us, *who is* holy, harmless, undefiled, separate from sinners, and made higher than the heavens;

27 Who needeth not daily, as those high priests, to offer up sacrifice, first for his own sins, and then for the people's: for this he did once, when he offered up himself.

28 For the law maketh men high priests which have infirmity; but the word of the oath, which was since the law, *maketh* the Son, who is consecrated for evermore.

In the very odd chapter 14 of Genesis, Abram (hardly a warrior!) leads his household retainers in a victorious battle against an alliance of Canaanite "kings." Returning, he is welcomed by Melchizedek:

18 And Melchizedek king of Salem brought forth bread and wine: and he *was* the priest of the most high God.

19 And he blessed him, and said, Blessed *be* Abram of the most high God, possessor of heaven and earth:

20 And blessed be the most high God, which hath delivered thine enemies into thy hand. And he gave him tithes of all.

The priest-king of Salem blesses Abram by fusing Yahweh and the Canaanite chief god El into one divinity. It should be noted that *he* pays a tithe to Abram, rather than the reverse, as in Hebrews. Psalm 110 had returned to Genesis 14:18–20 in verse 4:

The LORD hath sworn, and will not repent, Thou *art* a priest for ever after the order of Melchizedek.

Since Salem was to become Jerusalem, the city of David, early messianic exegesis, well before Christianity, enabled the Christian reading that David thus paid homage to his descendant Jesus in Psalm 110. Hebrews 5–7 vastly expands this into a new myth of Jesus as the culmination of a supernatural order established by the priest-king of Salem:

Without father, without mother, without descent,
having neither beginning of days, nor end of life;
but made like unto the Son of God; abideth a priest
continually.

[7:3]

Midrash is a madly inventive mode, but is this one of its triumphs or one of its outrages? The writer of Hebrews invites us to a picnic in which Genesis 14:18–20 and Psalm 110:4 provide the words and he supplies the meanings. Since we are told nothing of the birth or the death of the priest-king of Salem, he has to be supernatural, like Jesus Christ himself. His divine priesthood triumphs over that of the Levites, descendants of Aaron. Since David was of the tribe of Judah, this means Jesus was also.

And yet the KJB Hebrews abounds in memorable eloquence. "*It is* a fearful thing to fall into the hands of the living God" (10:31) is Tyndale's but the famous opening of Chapter 11 improves upon him:

> Faith is a sure confidence of things which are hoped for, and a certainty of things which are not seen.
>
> [Tyndale]

> Now faith is the substance of things hoped for, the evidence of things not seen.
>
> [KJB]

This leads off a grand litany in chapter 11: Abel, Enoch, Noah, Abraham, Jacob, Joseph, Moses on, culminating in Christ. In the concluding chapter, 13, Hebrews has a splendid opening in the KJB:

> 1 Let brotherly love continue.
> 2 Be not forgetful to entertain strangers; for thereby some have entertained angels unawares.

There is a poignant wistfulness scattered through these final verses:

> 8 Jesus Christ the same yesterday, and to day, and for ever.

> 14 For here have we no continuing city, but we seek one to come.

One could wish that all of Hebrews had that saving pathos.

James

ONLY WITH JAMES AM I AT REST in rereading the Greek New Testament. Martin Luther hated this Jewish Christian sermon and deplored its presence in Scripture, calling it "an epistle of straw." Its Greek, unlike almost all the remainder of the New Testament, is quite good. James the Just, reputed to be the brother of Jesus and the leader of the Ebionites, or "poor men," could not have been the author, though he may well have preached this sermon or its model in Aramaic or Hebrew. Executed sometime between 62 and 67, James the Just was revered not only by the Ebionites but by so many others, ranging from Gnostics to anti-Pauline Gentile Christians, that the actual writer is difficult to isolate. But I think scholars date the book too late, to the close of the first century C.E. A good surmise might be any time in the decade after the fall of Jerusalem and the Roman destruction of the Temple in 70. Another guess is that the writer might have been an Alexandrian Jew who joined the Ebionites in Pella, Jordan, where they fled the ruin of Jerusalem.

The basis of James's sermon is a purely implicit Christ, though

Jesus is alluded to in 2:8. Paul also is not mentioned, but he is the clear adversary against whom this discourse is argued. In Romans 3:28 Paul concludes that "a man is justified by faith without the deeds of the law," to which James 2:24 replies, "Ye see then how that by works a man is justified, and not by faith only."

Returning to Amos 5:21–24, James 5:4 sounds the prophetic cry at its most poignant:

> Behold, the hire of the labourers who have reaped down your fields, which is of you kept back by fraud, crieth: and the cries of them which have reaped are entered into the ears of the Lord of sabaoth.

For eloquence and visionary invention, the author of James achieves a sublime height in chapter 3, with its memorable image of the tongue:

> 1 My brethren, be not many masters, knowing that we shall receive the greater condemnation.
>
> 2 For in many things we offend all. If any man offend not in word, the same *is* a perfect man, *and* able also to bridle the whole body.
>
> 3 Behold, we put bits in the horses' mouths, that they may obey us; and we turn about their whole body.
>
> 4 Behold also the ships, which though *they be* so great, and *are* driven of fierce winds, yet are they turned about with a very small helm, withersoever the governor listeth.
>
> 5 Even so the tongue is a little member, and boasteth great things. Behold, how great a matter a little fire kindleth!
>
> 6 And the tongue *is* a fire, a world of iniquity: so is the

tongue among our members, that it defileth the whole body, and setteth on fire the course of nature; and it is set on fire of hell.

7 For every kind of beasts, and of birds, and of serpents, and of things in the sea, is tamed, and hath been tamed of mankind:

8 But the tongue can no man tame; *it is* an unruly evil, full of deadly poison.

9 Therewith bless we God, even the Father; and therewith curse we men, which are made after the similitude of God.

10 Out of the same mouth proceedeth blessing and cursing. My brethren, these things ought not so to be.

11 Doth a fountain send forth at the same place sweet *water* and bitter?

12 Can the fig tree, my brethren, bear olive berries? either a vine, figs? so *can* no fountain both yield salt water and fresh.

13 Who *is* a wise man and endued with knowledge among you? let him shew out of a good conversation his works with meekness of wisdom.

14 But if ye have bitter envying and strife in your hearts, glory not, and lie not against the truth.

15 The wisdom descendeth not from above, but *is* earthly, sensual, devilish.

16 For where envying and strife *is,* there *is* confusion and every evil work.

17 But the wisdom that is from above is first pure, then peaceable, gentle, *and* easy to be intreated, full of mercy and good fruits, without partiality, and without hypocrisy.

18 And the fruit of righteousness is sown in peace of them that make peace.

In that marvelous warning against slander and backbiting, a universal evil that all of us have suffered, the sermon of James the Just renews Hebrew wisdom and implies a stricture upon the furies of Paul. For me at least, it is the antidote to John's Gospel.

Revelation

WHEN I WAS A YOUNG LITERARY SCHOLAR, I remember being fascinated by the genre of apocalypse. I turned eighty just two days ago and find I now have a certain distaste for apocalyptic literature. I have just reread Revelation in the demotic Greek original, and then its remarkable transmutations by Tyndale, Geneva, and the KJB. Very aware of its influence upon Dante's *Purgatorio* and Blake's brief epics, I cannot dispute its effect upon a tradition of great poetry, but in itself it threatens readers who do not share in its dogma.

Composed probably in Asia Minor as the first Christian century closed, Revelation (Latin for the Greek *apocalypse,* "an unveiling") presumably reacts directly to Rome's persecution of Christians, perhaps under Domitian. Informed scholars wildly disagree about this text, and no single interpretation is dominant among them.

The Roman Empire is called Babylon in Revelation, since the entire book is what Austin Farrer calls "a rebirth of images" in his study of that title (1986). As Farrer and many other scholars have demonstrated, Revelation is an anxious network of allusions to the

Hebrew Bible. For an aesthetic critic, the problem arises that the citations from Isaiah, Ezekiel, Hosea, and even Daniel are much stronger than the text that seeks to appropriate them.

So close are Geneva and the KJB to Tyndale's Apocalypse that they nearly merge into a single work. Much of the English Bible's Revelation is a sublime rant, but there are lovely exceptions:

> 1 And I saw a new heaven and a new earth: for the first heaven and the first earth were passed away; and there was no more sea.
>
> 2 And I John saw the holy city, new Jerusalem, coming down from God out of heaven, prepared as a bride adorned for her husband.
>
> 3 And I heard a great voice out of heaven saying, Behold, the tabernacle of God *is* with men, and he will dwell with them, and they shall be his people, and God himself shall be with them, *and be* their God.
>
> 4 And God shall wipe away all tears from their eyes; and there shall be no more death, neither sorrow, nor crying, neither shall there be any more pain: for the former things are passed away.
>
> 5 And he that sat upon the throne said, Behold, I make all things new. And he said unto me, Write: for these words are true and faithful.
>
> 6 And he said unto me, It is done. I am Alpha and Omega, the beginning and the end. I will give unto him that is athirst of the fountain of the water of life freely.
>
> 7 He that overcometh shall inherit all things; and I will be his God, and he shall be my son.
>
> [21:1–7]

I read this as John Milton did in his magnificent elegy "Lycidas":

There entertain him all the Saints above,
In solemn troops, and sweet Societies
That sing, and singing in their glory move,
And wipe the tears for ever from his eyes.

[ll. 178–81]

Alas, this is followed by a more characteristic gesture:

But the fearful, and unbelieving, and the abominable,
and murderers, and whoremongers, and sorcerers, and
idolaters, and all liars, shall have their part in the lake
which burneth with fire and brimstone: which is the
second death.

[Revelation 21:8]

This book has been a *literary* appreciation of the English Bible.
No reader can change history by the art of reading, and I am totally cognizant that most who will continue to read and study the
Hebrew Bible and the Greek New Testament do not regard them as
imaginative literature but as some kind of truth. I tend frequently
to remark that I myself read Shakespeare as my scripture. We never
really will know the inner Shakespeare because he conceals himself. Dante, his only peer among the poets, enters the *Commedia*
as the Pilgrim, but that too is a sublime fiction.

I feel odd finishing this book because I have been writing it
all my long life, and I am eighty. Perhaps in earlier decades I might
have done it differently, but I too am what I am.

Acknowledgments

I acknowledge throughout the deep influence upon this book of Herbert Marks. Peter Cole generously read the manuscript and saved me from many errors. My editor Jennifer Banks was supportive and incisive throughout, and rightly restrained my sometimes negative exuberance. Susan Laity, best of manuscript editors, has been a grand resource for me these thirty years.

For the past third of a century, my literary agents, Glen Hartley and Lynn Chu, have been family to my own immediate household. They have sustained me in myriad ways far transcending the obligations that they have assumed.

Thayne Stoddard, my research assistant, worked with skill and intelligence in helping me revise this book.

Index

Index

68–71; and Creation story,
28, 29–31; and expulsion
from Eden, 32–33; as ironist,
11, 13, 32–33, 40, 50, 53, 65,
86, 93, 164, 165; and Jonah,
165; and Joseph, 48; and
Judith, 93; and Moses, 53,
55, 65–66, 108; and Noah,
34; and the Tower of Babel,
35; and women, 86